IMAGES
of America

RICHMOND COUNTY *and the* SEABOARD AIR LINE RAILWAY

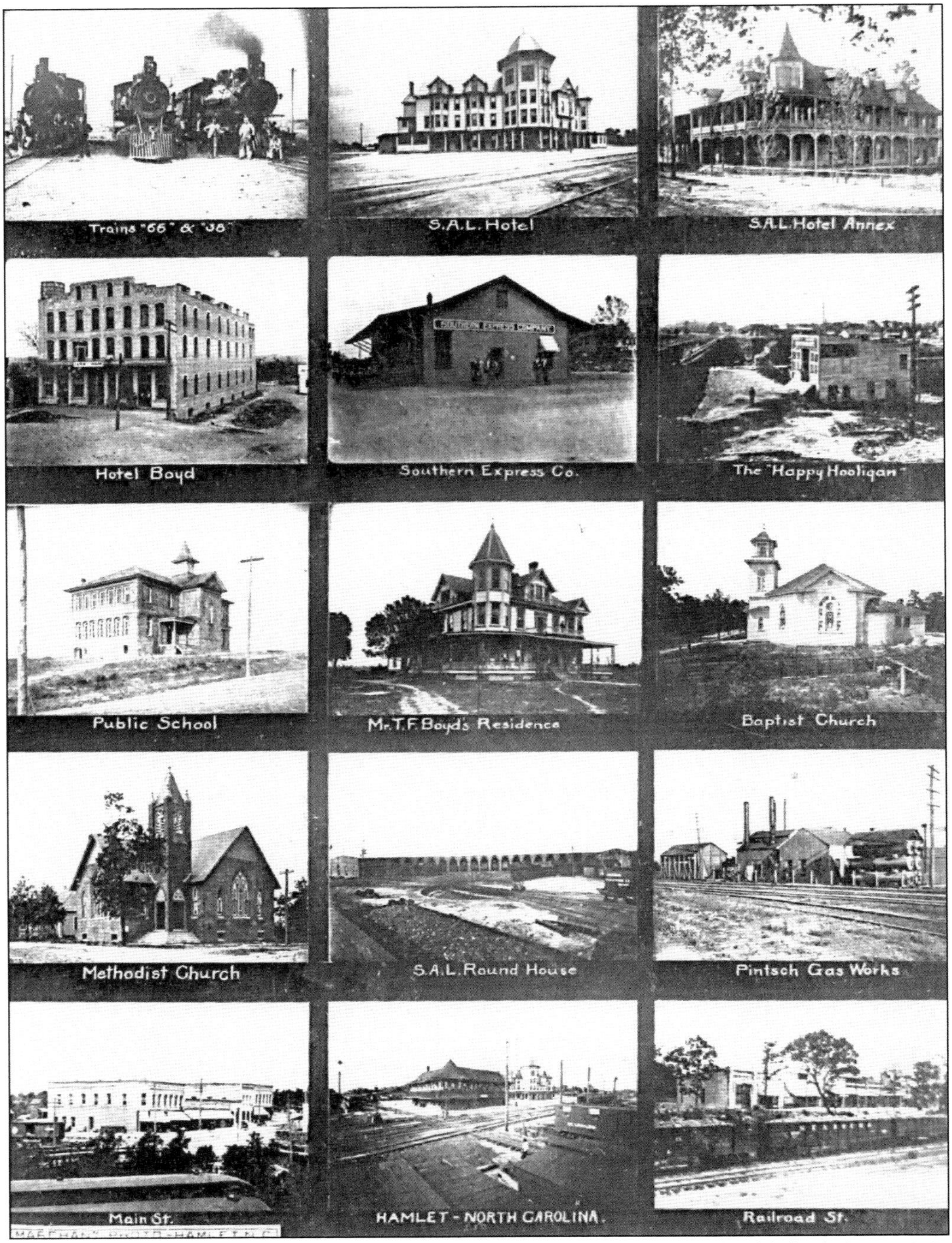

Multiple views of Hamlet are reproduced here from a composite postcard published about 1917. Some of the subjects include the Hotel Boyd, the Southern Express Company office, Thomas F. Boyd's residence, First Baptist Church, and the Pintsch Compressing Company gas plant. (Courtesy C. Vernon Vallance.)

IMAGES
of America

RICHMOND COUNTY *and the* SEABOARD AIR LINE RAILWAY

Stephen E. Massengill
and C. Vernon Vallance

ARCADIA
PUBLISHING

ISBN 978-0-7385-1754-4

Published by Arcadia Publishing
Charleston, South Carolina

Printed in the United States of America

Library of Congress Catalog Card Number: 2004114133

For all general information contact Arcadia Publishing at:
Telephone 843-853-2070
Fax 843-853-0044
E-mail sales@arcadiapublishing.com
For customer service and orders:
Toll-Free 1-888-313-2665

Visit us on the Internet at www.arcadiapublishing.com

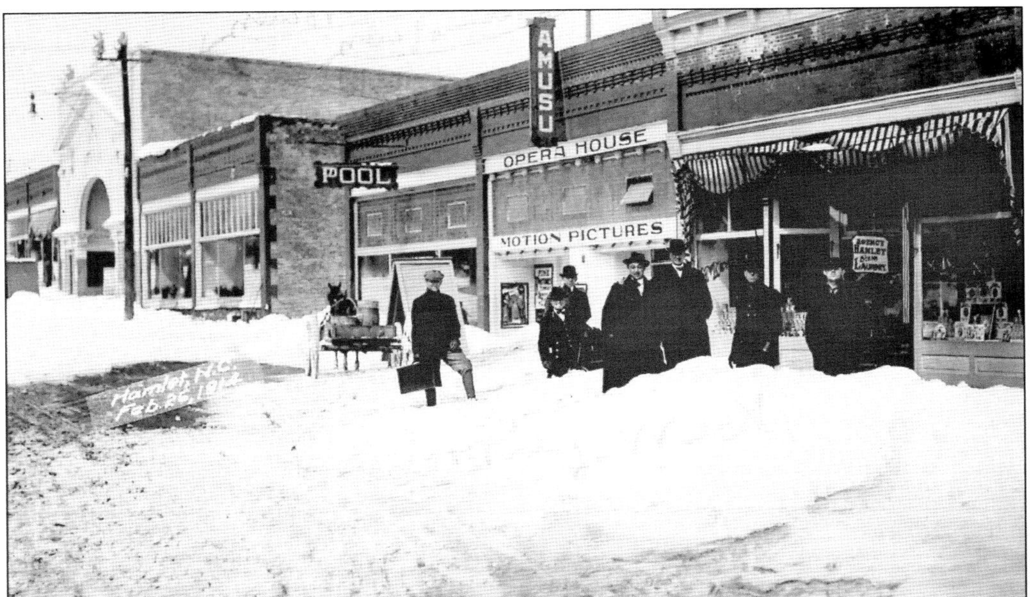

Frederick Marchant photographed this snowy scene on Main Street in Hamlet on February 26, 1914. Businesses shown include a pool hall, the Amusu Opera House Motion Pictures (movie theater), and the store of McKethan and Niemyer. (Courtesy Wayne Chapman.)

CONTENTS

ACKNOWLEDGMENTS

We would like to express our sincere thanks to the following individuals who assisted in the preparation of this publication. Norma McKee, the widow of Charles F. McKee, donated to the State Archives her husband's valuable photograph collection, including railroad-related images taken by Marchant. The compilers used many of these visual records in the chapters entitled "The Seaboard Air Line Railway" and "Wrecks and Derailments." Durwood Barbour, T.T. Beckham, Joe Blalock, J. Neal Cadieu Jr., Wayne Chapman, Jeff Eastland, Aubrey T. Haddock, John Hamer, Dan Hicks, Sadie Jenkins, Edward "Tug" Jones, Phil Perkinson, Sarah M. Pope, and the Hamlet Public Library all provided postcards and other images to help illustrate the book. Alan L.Westmoreland expertly scanned the images for reproduction in the book. Robert M. Topkins provided valuable editorial advice and indexed the book. Other individuals who assisted with the effort are William Allen III, Stephen Fletcher, B.T. Fowler, Charlene Gilmore, Trey Gilmore, Buddy Jones, Irving Long, John Hutchinson, Keith Longiotti, R. Carol McLean, and Amanda Robertson, as well as Adam Latham and Sarah San Angelo of Arcadia Publishing.

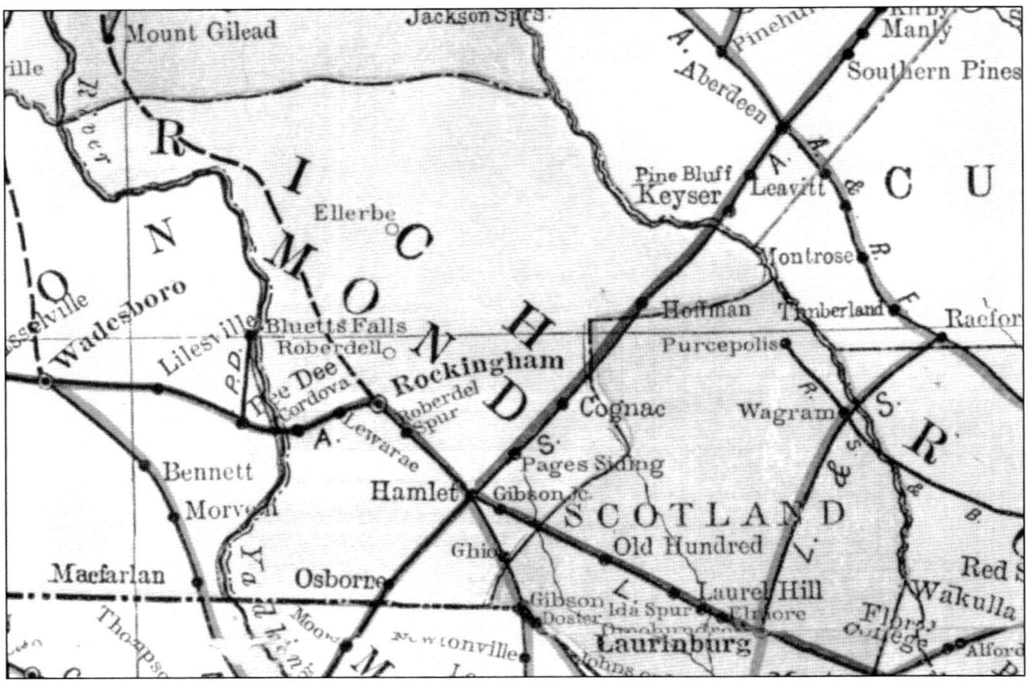

This portion of a 1909 railroad map of North Carolina shows the route of the Seaboard Air Line Railway through Richmond County. (Courtesy North Carolina Office of Archives and History, Raleigh, hereafter cited as A&H.)

INTRODUCTION

At the beginning of the 20th century, the economy of Richmond County was dominated by agriculture and textile manufacturing located principally in and around the city and county seat of Rockingham. After 1900, the small town of Hamlet developed into a railroad center. Soon after the opening of Hamlet's railroad shops, freight terminal, and passenger depot, the town became widely known as the "hub" of the Seaboard Air Line Railway, which by 1901 connected New York City with Tampa, Florida. Five railroad lines extending from Hamlet served most of the major seaports along the Atlantic coast. The railroad industry provided numerous jobs and spawned other related businesses. The population of Hamlet grew from 600 people in 1900 to some 5,000 inhabitants by the early 1920s. The county's textile industry benefited greatly from the convenient rail facilities as well as from the construction of the Blewett Falls Dam on the Pee Dee River and the resulting electrical power the dam generated for the manufacturing enterprises.

Richmond County was fortunate to have in its midst one of the more gifted photographers in the state during the first quarter of the 20th century. Frederick "Frank" Marchant (1872–1942), a native of Philadelphia, settled in Hamlet after 1900. Apparently, the town's emergence as an important railroad junction and the promising economic environment attracted him to the small town. Marchant may have worked in the field of civil engineering as a surveyor for the Seaboard for several years before turning to a career in photography about 1907. He rented space for a studio on the second floor of O.T. Goodwin's wholesale grocery store on Raleigh Street. Marchant's work was so highly regarded that he served for a number of years as the official photographer for the Seaboard Air Line Railroad.

Marchant developed a keen eye for interesting subjects, and some of his work took on an almost photojournalistic quality. Most of his surviving photographs were made on location rather than in a studio. Few studio portraits have emerged, indicating that he preferred outdoor work. Marchant took numerous views in and around Hamlet and Rockingham. Among his favorite subjects were railroad trains, train wrecks and derailments, town scenes, snow scenes, cotton fields, hotels, dam construction, and African Americans. He seemed to have a particular fascination with African-American subjects, former slaves, and wintertime scenes.

The Hamlet photographer sometimes photographed newsworthy and unusual events and offbeat subjects that he believed would appeal to the traveling public. His realm stretched beyond the borders of Richmond County into the nearby counties of Anson, Robeson, Scotland, and Union. He also ventured across the border into South Carolina to take some of his views. Marchant boarded the train to record wrecks and derailments along the Seaboard line in Richmond, Moore, Lee, and Warren Counties, as far west as Rutherford County, and to the railroad's eastern terminus in Wilmington. His camera also documented the construction of the Blewett Falls Dam and powerhouse on the Pee Dee River at the Richmond-Anson County line between 1909 and 1912. Marchant also traveled to Wilson County in 1911 to photograph the infamous trial of Lewis West and his gang of desperados.

Unfortunately, only a small percentage of the thousands of images taken by Marchant have survived. A significant portion of these images is in the form of picture postcards. Marchant published some of his better views as black-and-white "real-photo" postcards and in 1911 submitted a few of them to the Copyright Office in Washington, D.C., to prohibit competitors from reproducing them. Souvenir postcards were in vogue during the years prior to World War I, and Marchant took advantage of that popularity by offering his views for sale in hotels, drugstores, and depots. Thousands of rail travelers passed through Hamlet, and many purchased his penny postcards to mail to relatives and friends throughout the country.

Marchant continued his work as a commercial photographer at Hamlet into the 1920s. The Great Depression and his addiction to alcohol led to a decline in his career in the late 1920s and early 1930s. By the 1930s, the Hamlet resident had almost ceased taking photographs but continued to develop film for a living. He also may have sold some of his old photographs to make ends meet. By 1935, his funds were so limited that he was unable to pay the small license fee that was required by law to practice photography in the state. At the time of his death in 1942, he was living as a pauper in an old tin-roofed shack on Vance Street. Marchant died of kidney disease at Hamlet Hospital and was buried at Mary Love Cemetery. Since he had no wife or next of kin, it was reported that town officials discarded his meager belongings, including his remaining photographs and negatives. Unfortunately, there is no known likeness of the man. Older citizens of Richmond County remember him as a standing about 5 feet, 11 inches tall, weighing 180 pounds, and sporting a white, nicotine-stained beard. Marchant's reclusive ways and his Northern accent led many to label him as a "town curiosity."

Marchant's photographs have gained greater attention in recent years from several groups, including postcard collectors, railroad enthusiasts, and regional and state historians. As more and more examples of his work emerge, there is a greater appreciation for the outstanding visual record that he left of Richmond County and the Seaboard Air Line Railway. Most of his work exhibits excellent composition, and the quality of his exposures ranks with the best operators of that time. The following 200-plus examples of Marchant's photographs were culled from private collections, archival repositories, libraries, and publications. They have been arranged into topical chapters to lend some organization and flow to his work. A few of the images included in this volume have not been positively identified as Marchant's work but are nevertheless almost certainly attributable to him. Together his images reveal a rare glimpse of life in and around Richmond County during the first few decades of the 20th century.

One

Hamlet

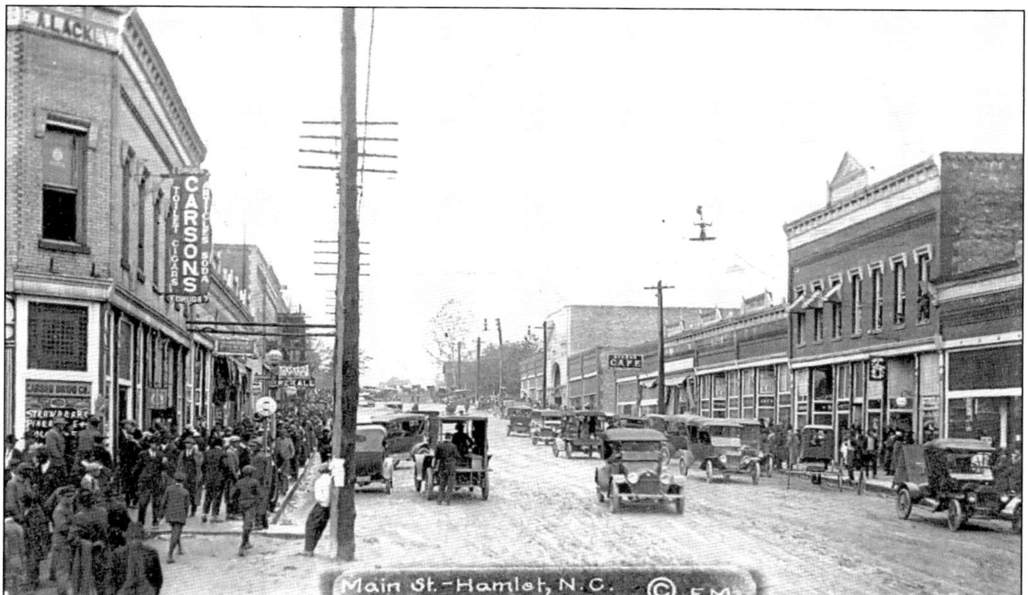

A bustling crowd fills Main Street in Hamlet about 1919 in anticipation of a performance by a traveling circus. In the distance, a circus caravan is moving southward on Lackey Street. (Courtesy A&H.)

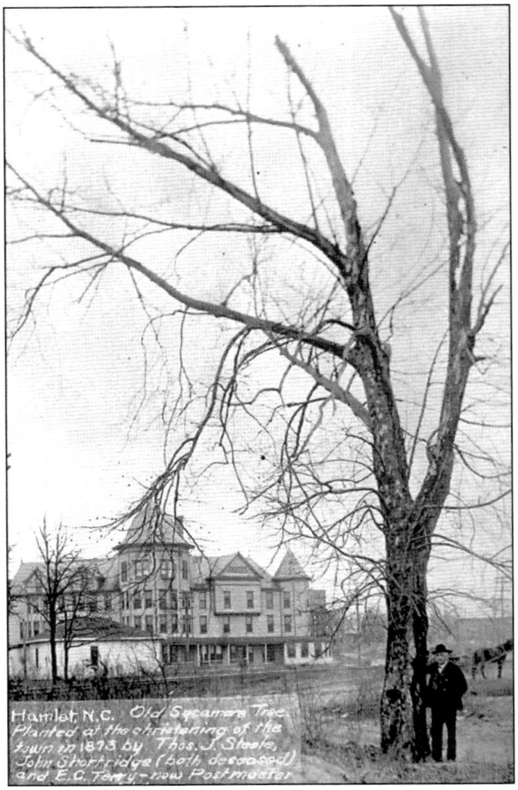

Postmaster Elisha C. Terry stands beneath a historic sycamore tree that was planted on the occasion of the formation of Hamlet about 1873. The Seaboard Hotel is visible in the distance. (Courtesy A&H.)

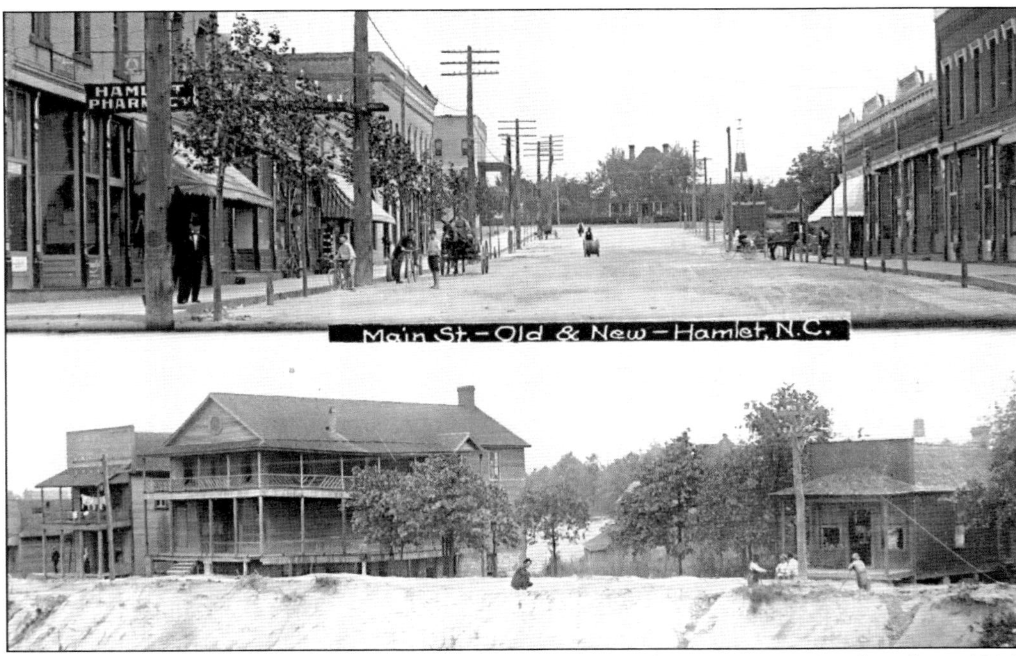

Shown here are contrasting views—the old and the new—of Main Street, Hamlet, about 1911. (Courtesy A&H.)

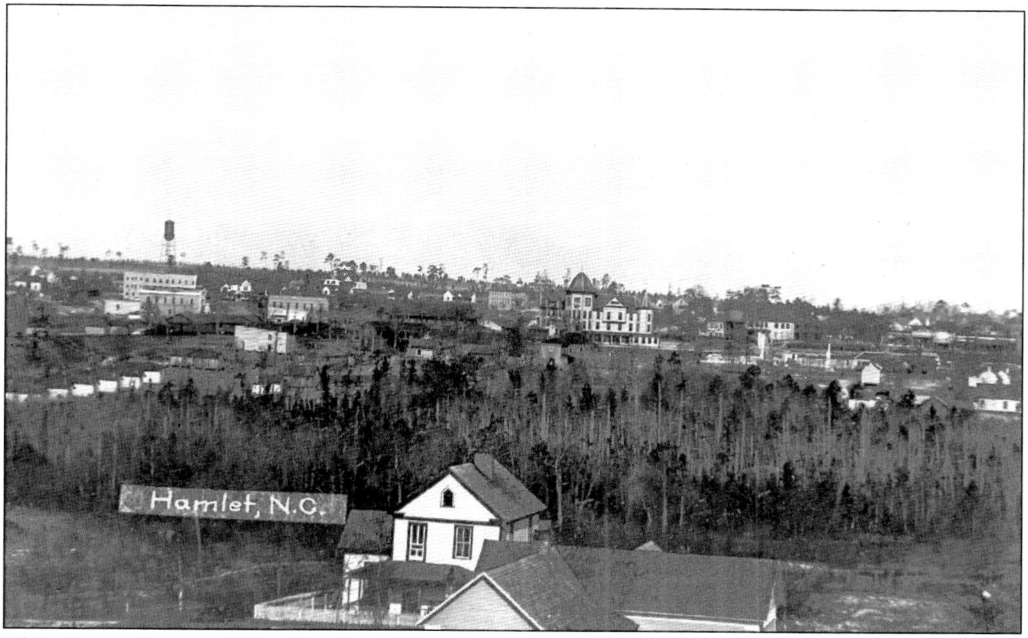

This elevated view of Hamlet about 1909 includes buildings on Main Street (the E.A. Lackey Building, the Central Hotel, and Lackey House) and the Seaboard Hotel in the distance. (Courtesy A&H.)

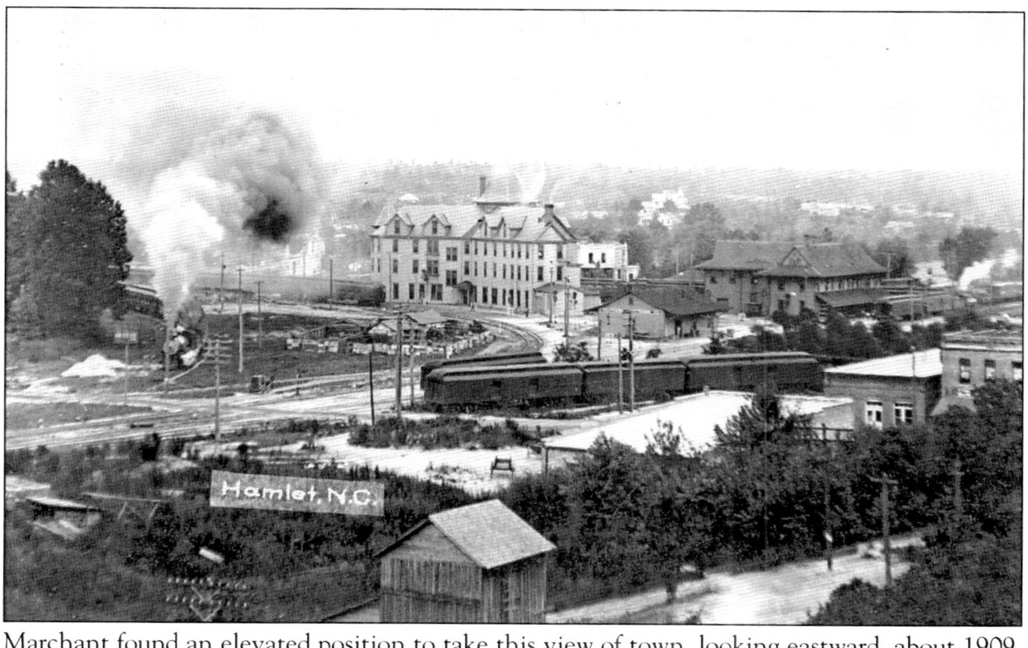

Marchant found an elevated position to take this view of town, looking eastward, about 1909. The three buildings at center are the Seaboard Hotel, the Southern Express Company office, and the Seaboard Air Line Railway Depot. (Courtesy Stephen E. Massengill.)

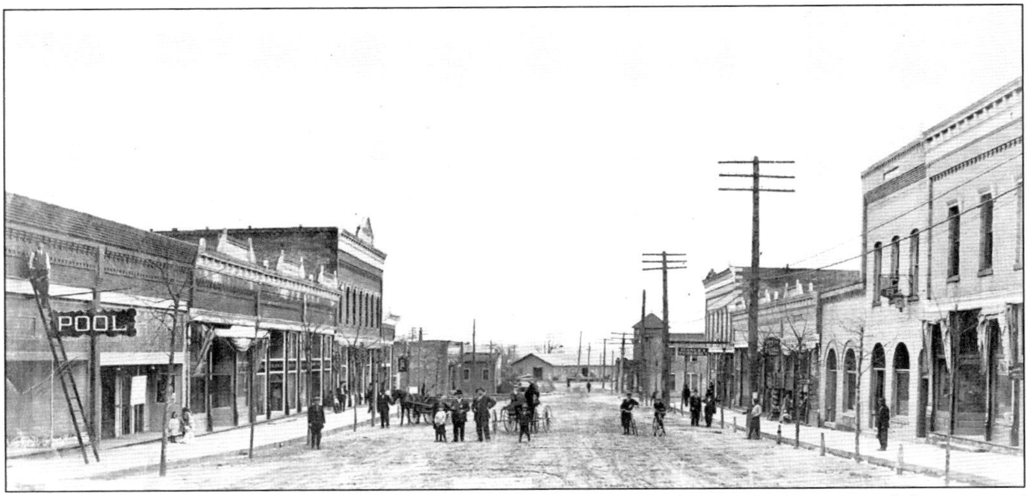

Marchant positioned his camera in the middle of Main Street, facing east, to record this view of the town in 1912. The Terminal Hotel and the E.A. Lackey Building are shown in the distance on the right-hand side of the street. (Courtesy A&H.)

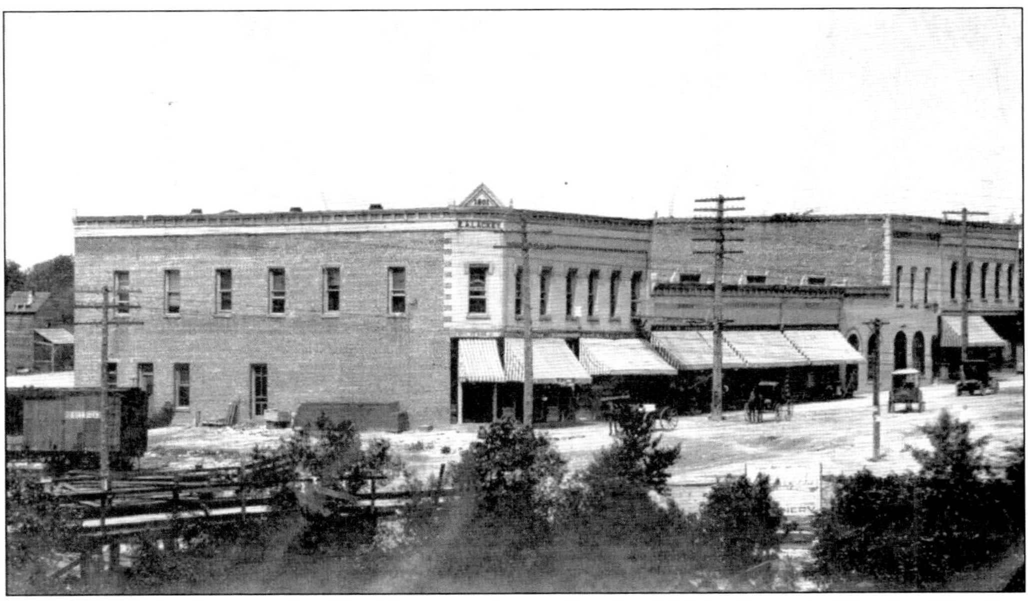

Here is an early photograph of buildings on the south side of Main Street in Hamlet. The first edifice on the left is the E.A. Lackey Building. Marchant took this view from the vicinity of the railroad depot about 1907. (Courtesy Durwood Barbour.)

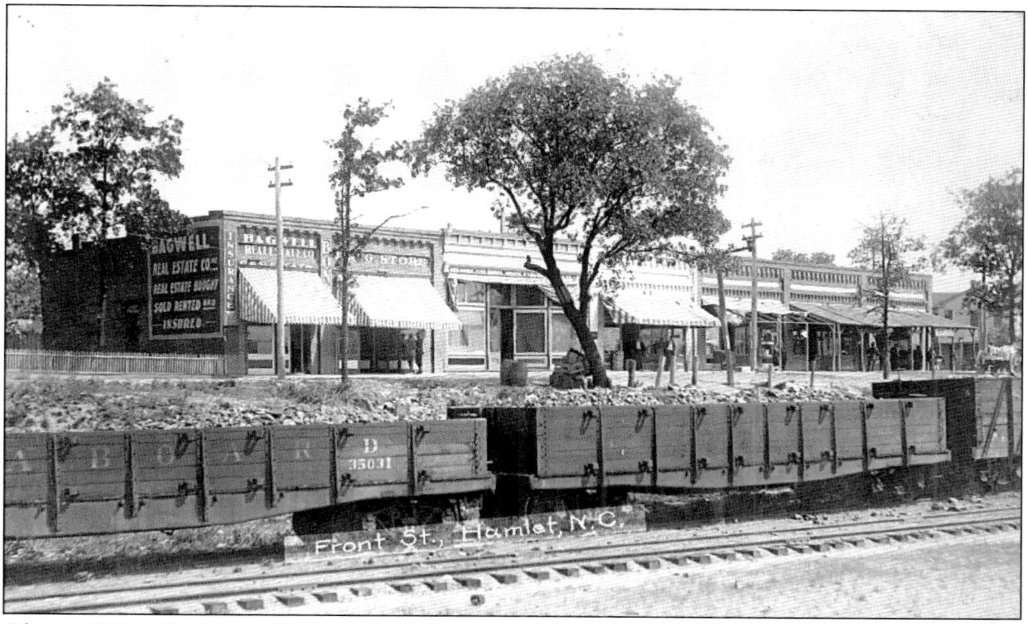

About 1911, Marchant photographed these gondolas in front of the stores along Front Street (formerly Railroad Street). (Courtesy C. Vernon Vallance.)

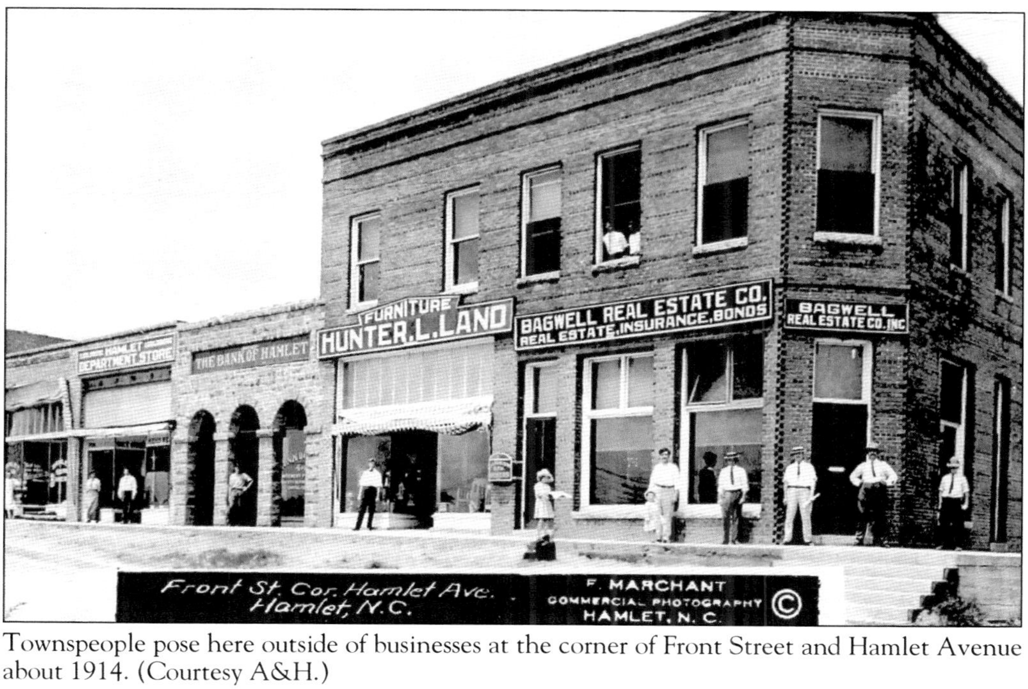

Townspeople pose here outside of businesses at the corner of Front Street and Hamlet Avenue about 1914. (Courtesy A&H.)

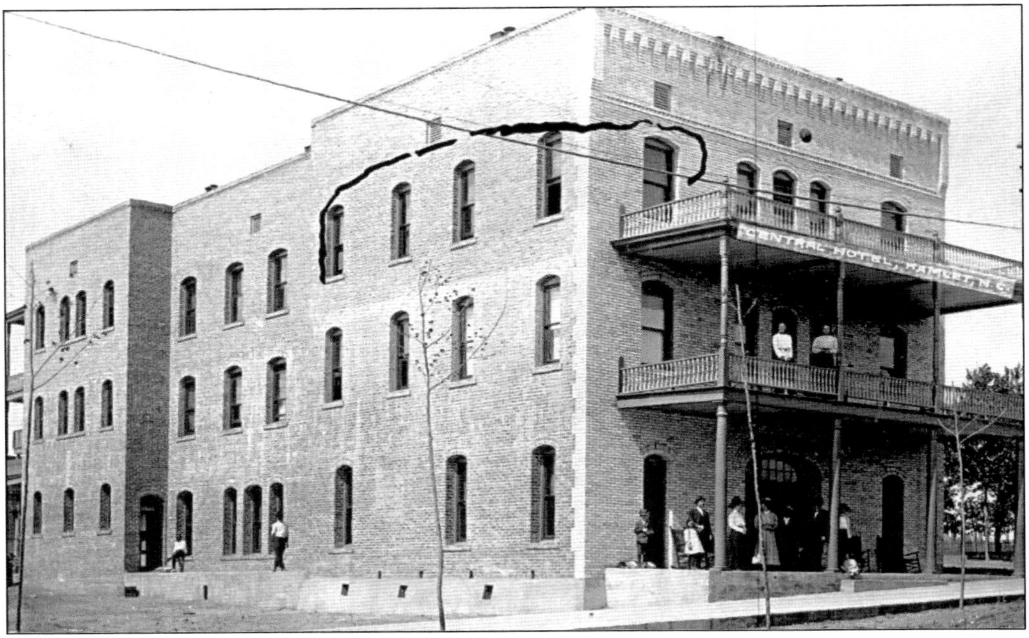

Guests pose for Marchant on the porch of the Central Hotel on Main Street in Hamlet in these two views of the establishment about 1918. The hotel's bus is shown in the bottom image. The Central Hotel opened about a decade after the Seaboard Hotel. The building still stands but is no longer used as a hotel. (Above, courtesy Wayne Chapman; below, courtesy A&H.)

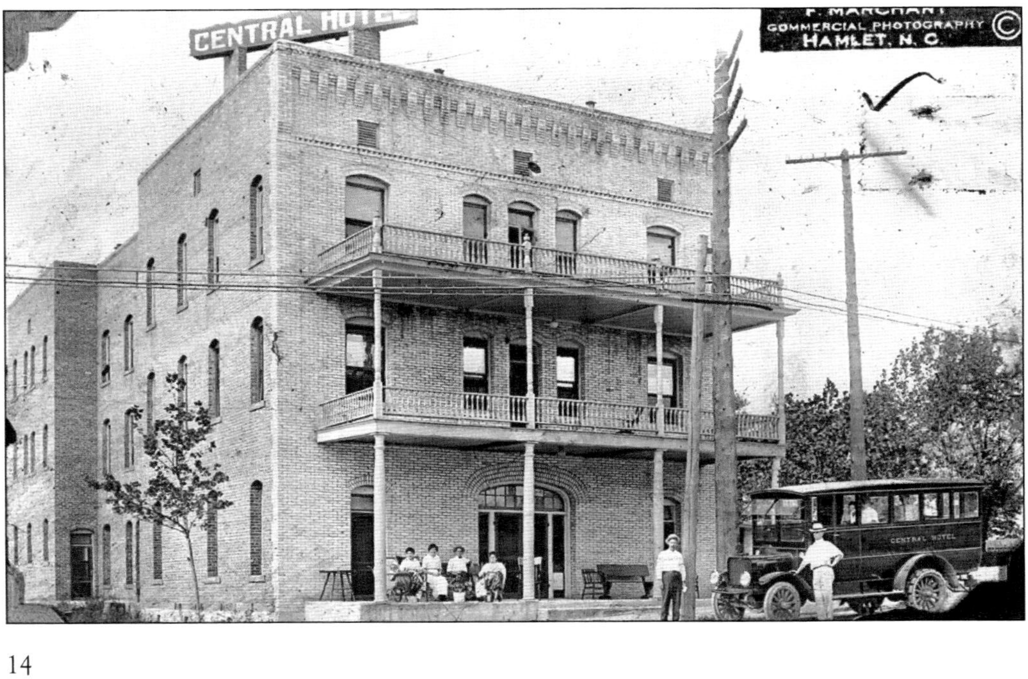

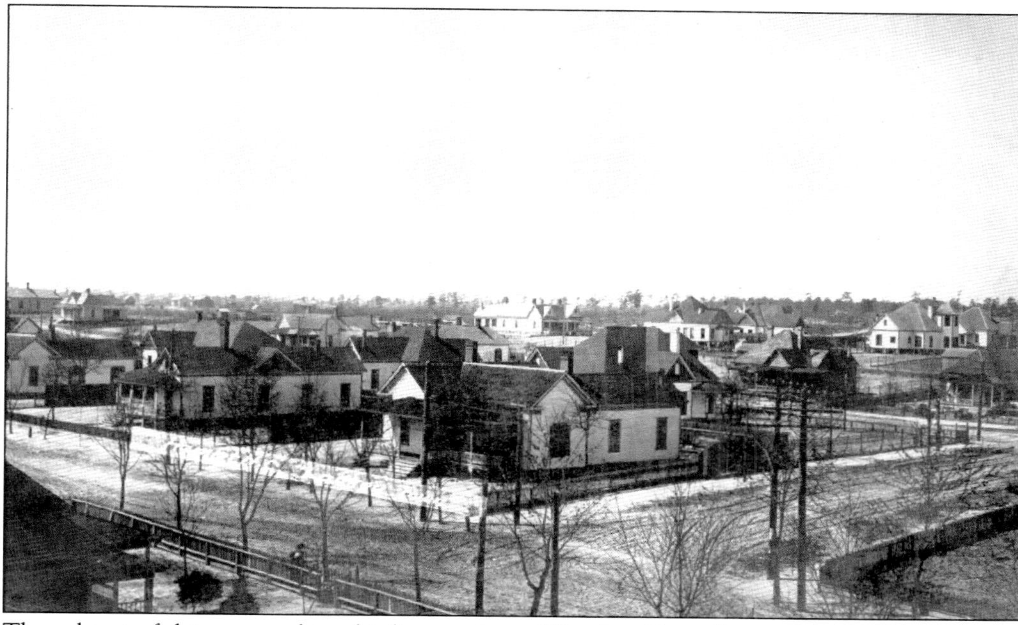

The subject of this postcard is a bird's-eye view of "Lackey Town," a neighborhood in Hamlet about 1909. The section was named for Eli A. Lackey (1861–1918), a leading citizen of the town. (Courtesy C. Vernon Vallance.)

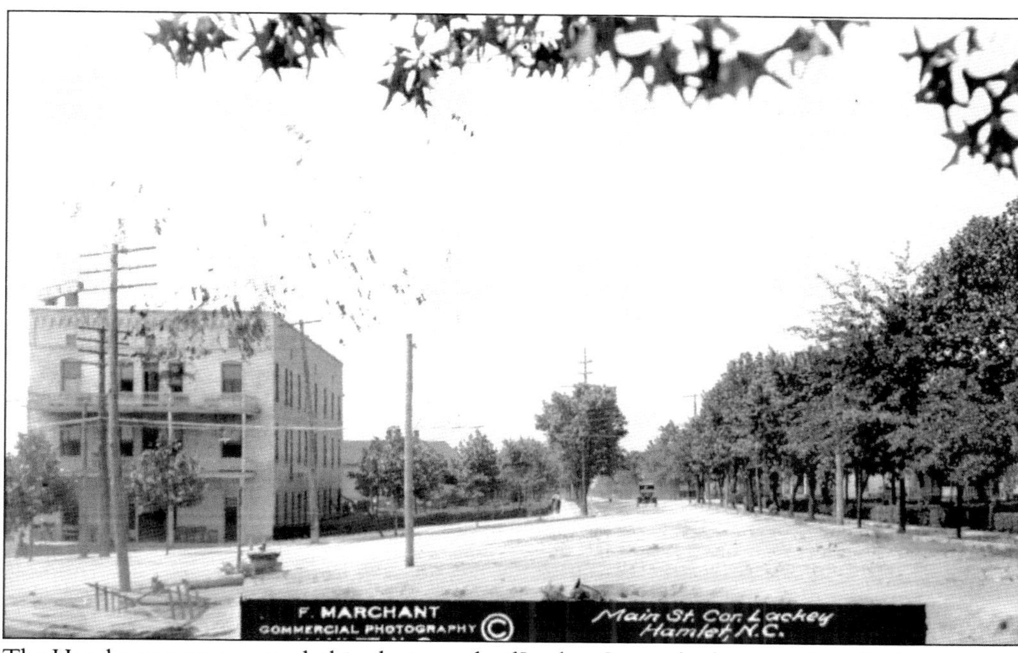

The Hamlet cameraman took this photograph of Lackey Street, looking south at the intersection of Main Street, in the late 1910s. At left is the Central Hotel. (Courtesy A&H.)

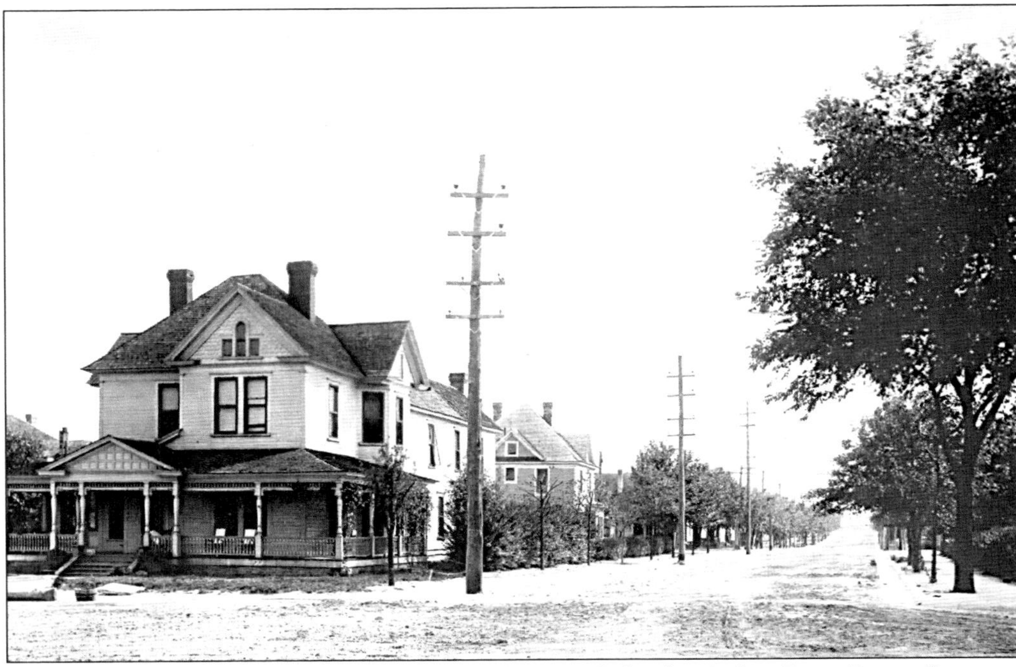

On April 24, 1918, Marchant fashioned this photograph for the Yadkin River Power Company to show its new 22,000-volt line on Chamberlain Street (later Champlain Street) in Hamlet. The utility company was formed about 1910 to complete construction of Blewett Falls Dam on the Pee Dee River. (Courtesy A&H.)

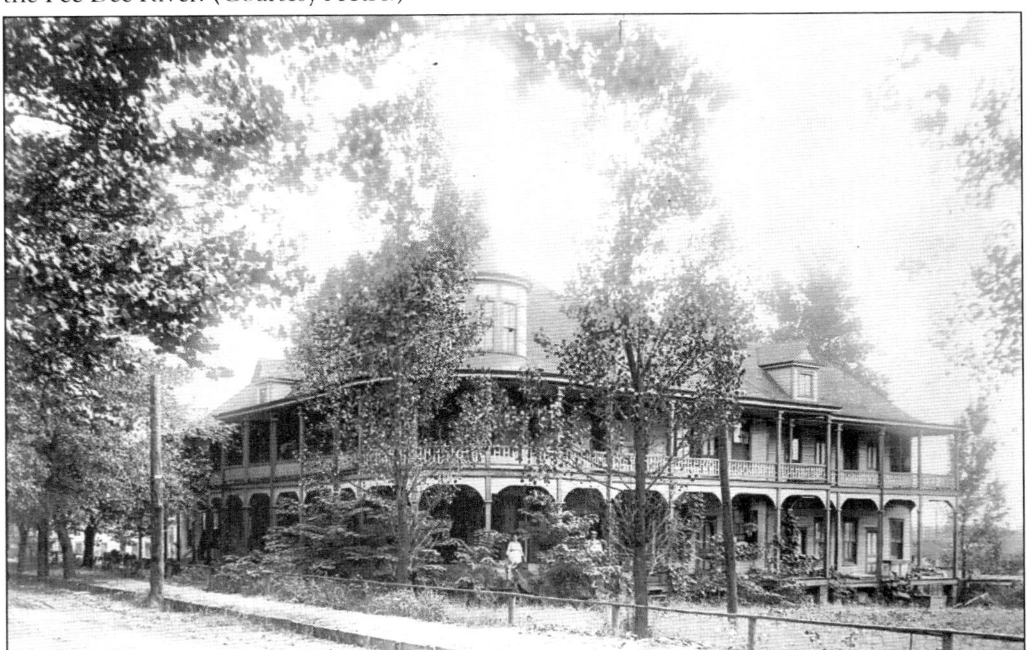

This large boardinghouse on Charlotte Street was known in the late 1910s as the Seaboard Hotel Annex in Hamlet. (Courtesy A&H.)

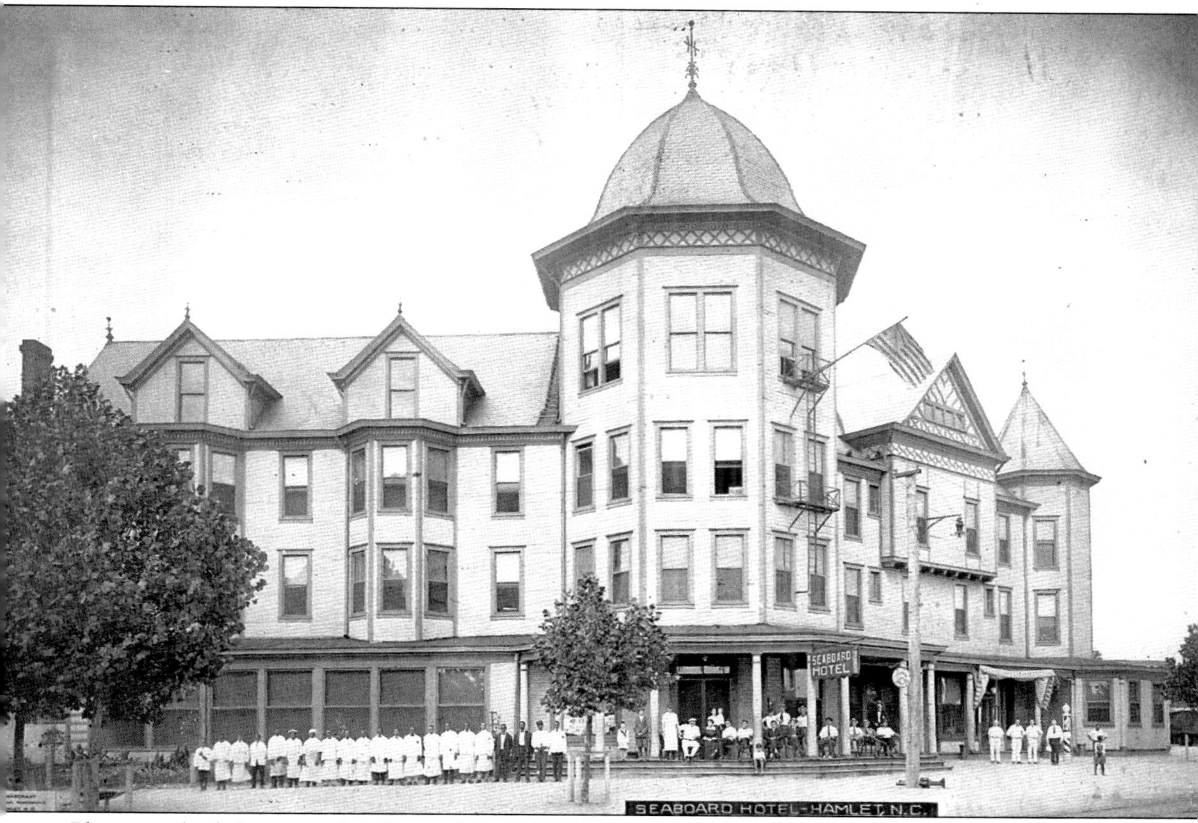

Photographed during its heyday is the Seaboard Hotel, located adjacent to the railroad depot in Hamlet. Hotel employees form a line in front of the building, probably in the spring or summer of 1911. The hotel opened on April 1, 1900, and had 45 rooms for guests. (Courtesy Dan Hicks.)

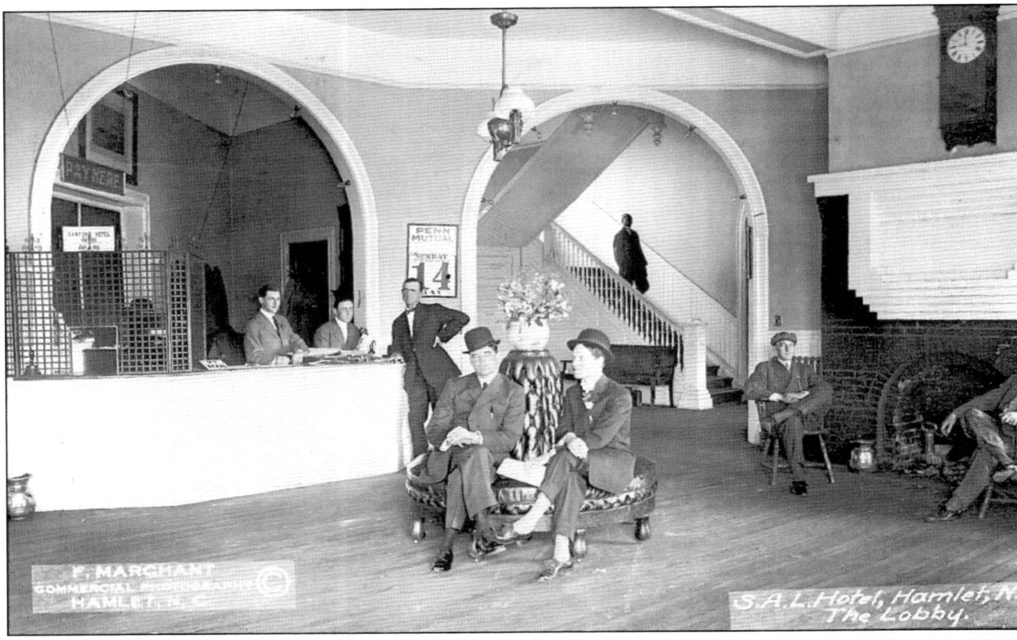

Hotel personnel and guests pose in the lobby of the Seaboard Hotel on Sunday, May 14, 1911. The man to the right of the archway leading to the stairs is John Bruce Gibson. The wall calendar helps to date the photograph. (Courtesy A&H.)

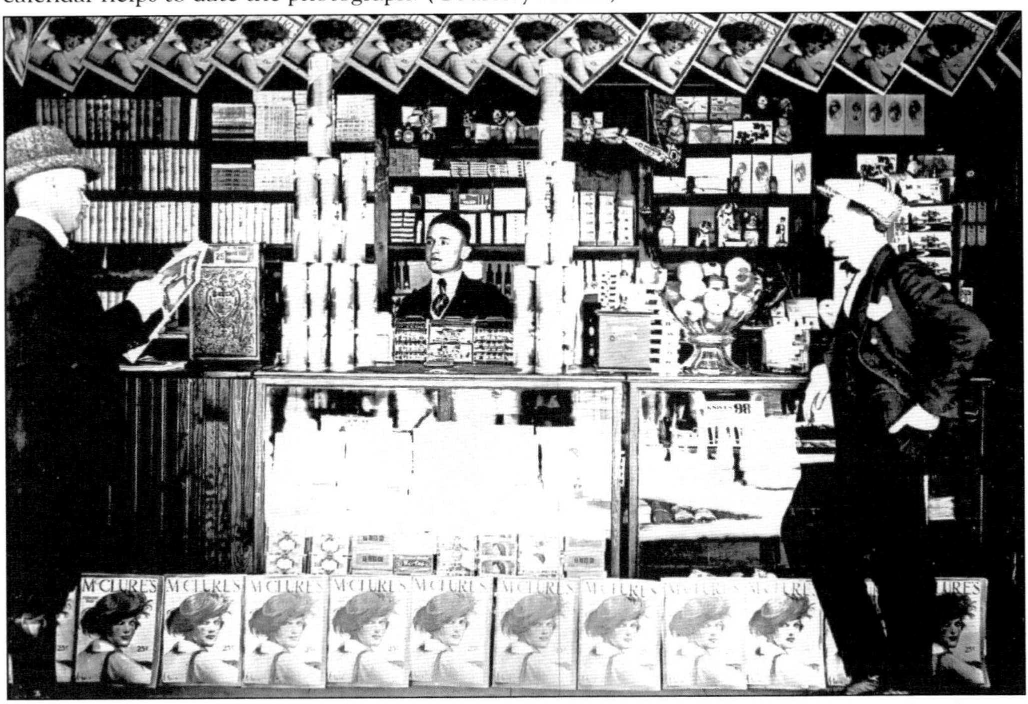

In February 1920, Marchant stepped inside the hotel to photograph the newsstand and store. This view includes customers flanking a clerk and merchandise such as magazines, peaches, and postcards. (Courtesy A&H.)

This photograph documents the construction of a stylish opera house on Main Street in Hamlet about 1913. The caption indicates that the cost of the building was $30,000. (Courtesy Durwood Barbour.)

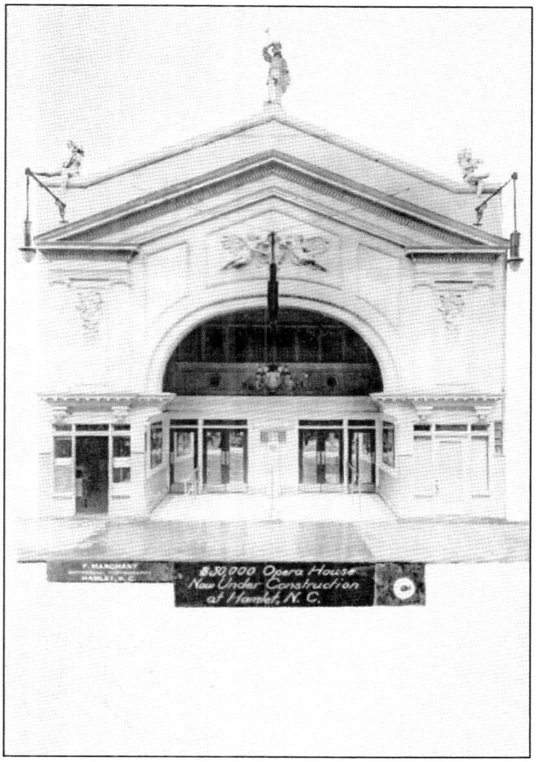

Shown here is a rare interior view of actors on the stage of the opera house during the production of *Al Martin's Country Store*, presented by the Auxiliary Railroad YMCA on April 28, 1914. Identified actors from left to right are as follows: L. Lorena Folkes (Mrs. W.N. Cosby Sr.), Isadora Kinsman, eight unidentified actors, Thomas G. Bagwell, six unidentified actors, Dr. I. McPhail, and two unidentified actors. (Courtesy Hamlet Public Library.)

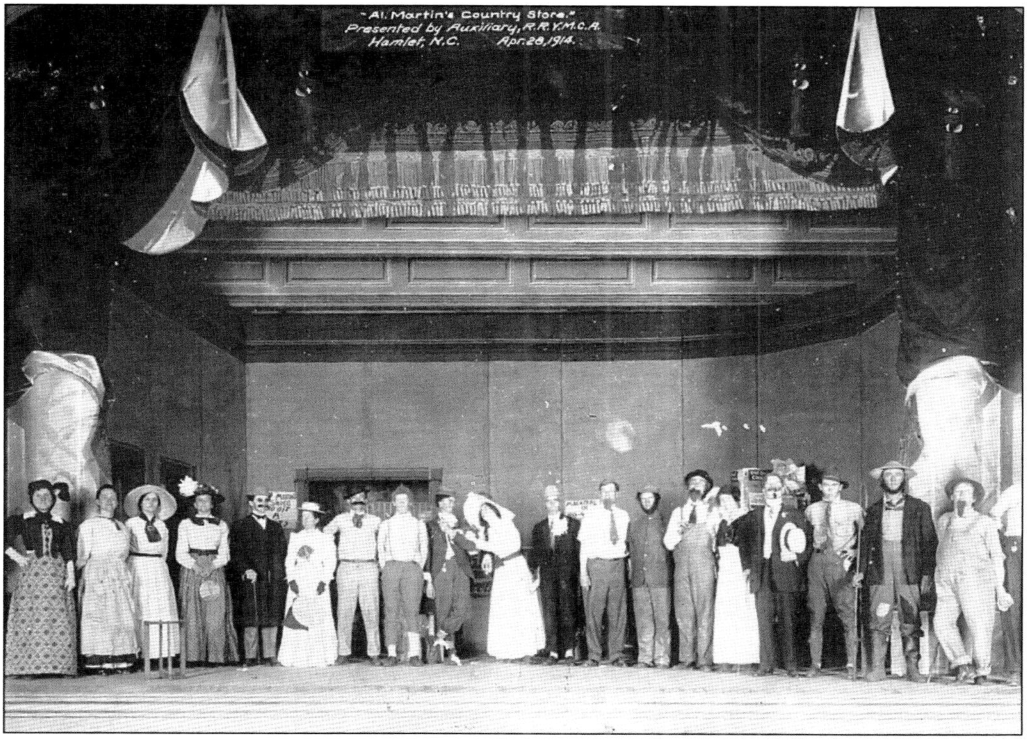

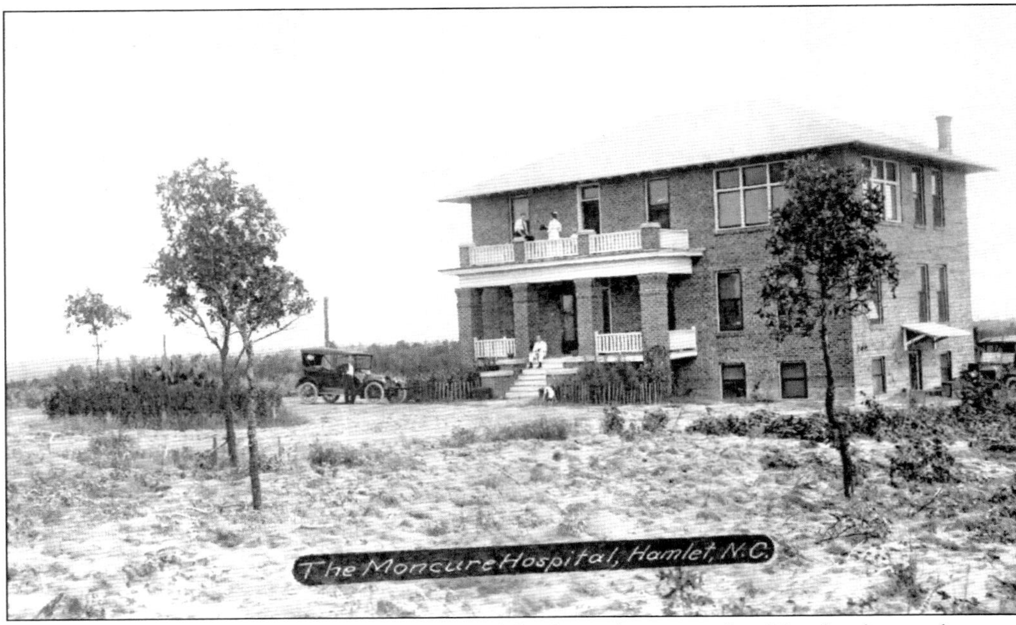

The Moncure Hospital was one of two medical facilities that existed in Hamlet during the years prior to World War I. It opened in 1914 on a tract of land located at the end of Henderson Street and closed in 1930. (Courtesy Durwood Barbour.)

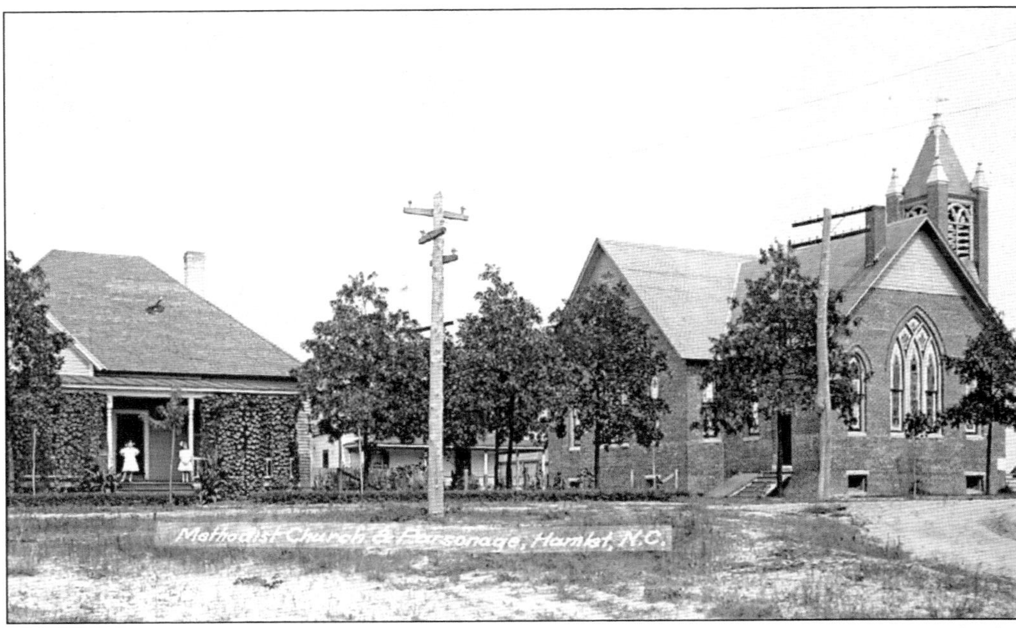

At left is the church parsonage that in 1911 was situated next to the First United Methodist Church in Hamlet. The church itself, located at the corner of Charlotte and High Streets, was completed about 1907. (Courtesy C. Vernon Vallance.)

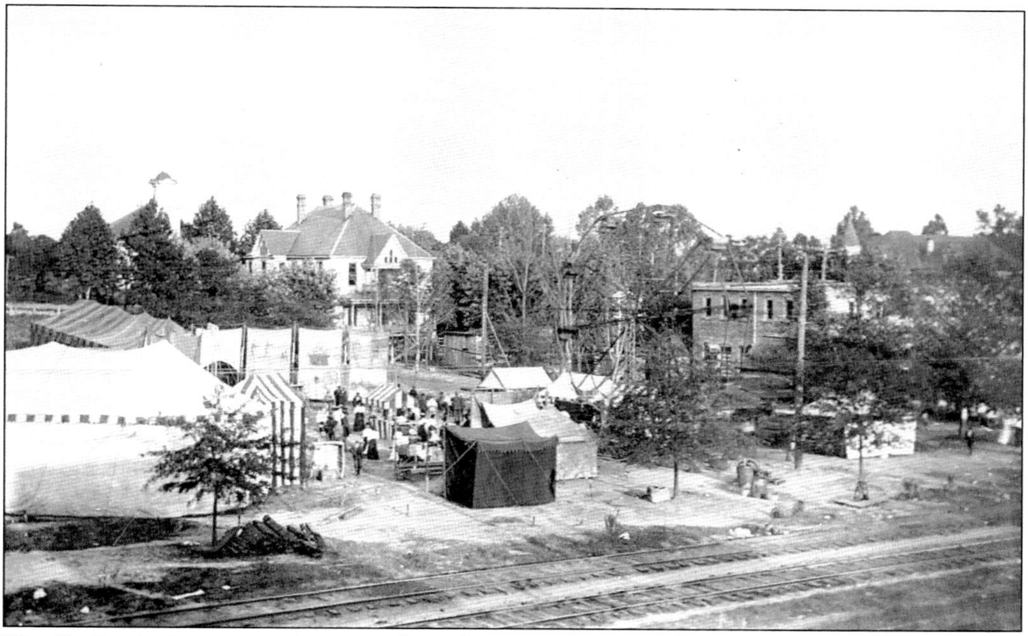

The St. Louis Attraction Company brought its street carnival to Hamlet on October 21–26, 1907. The show was set up alongside the railroad tracks in an area not far from the intersection of Raleigh and Charlotte Streets. This is one of the earliest surviving photographs taken by Marchant in Richmond County. (Courtesy A&H.)

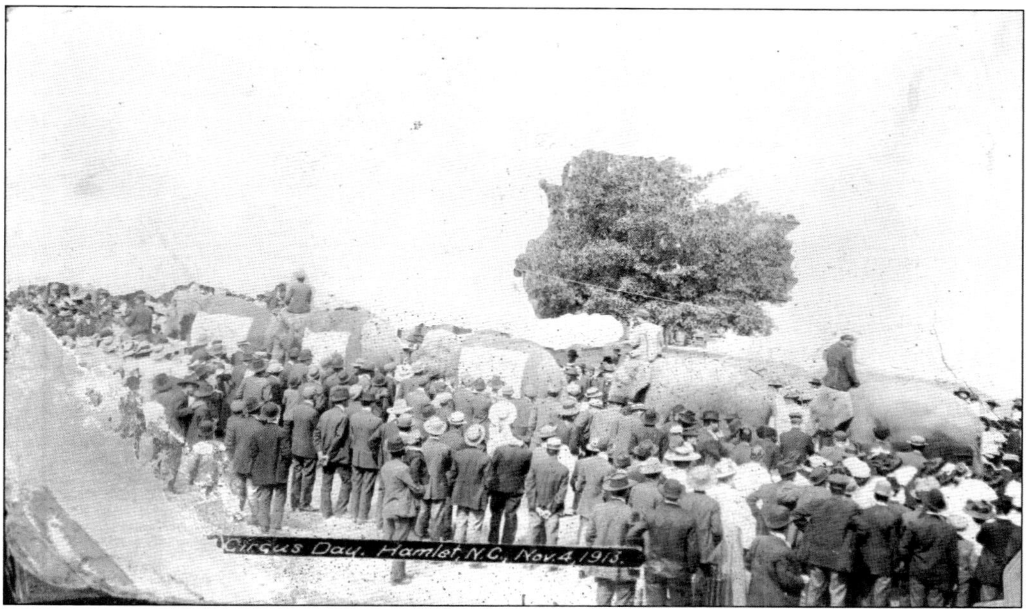

Spectators watch elephants trooping in a "Circus Day" parade at Hamlet on November 4, 1913. (Courtesy A&H.)

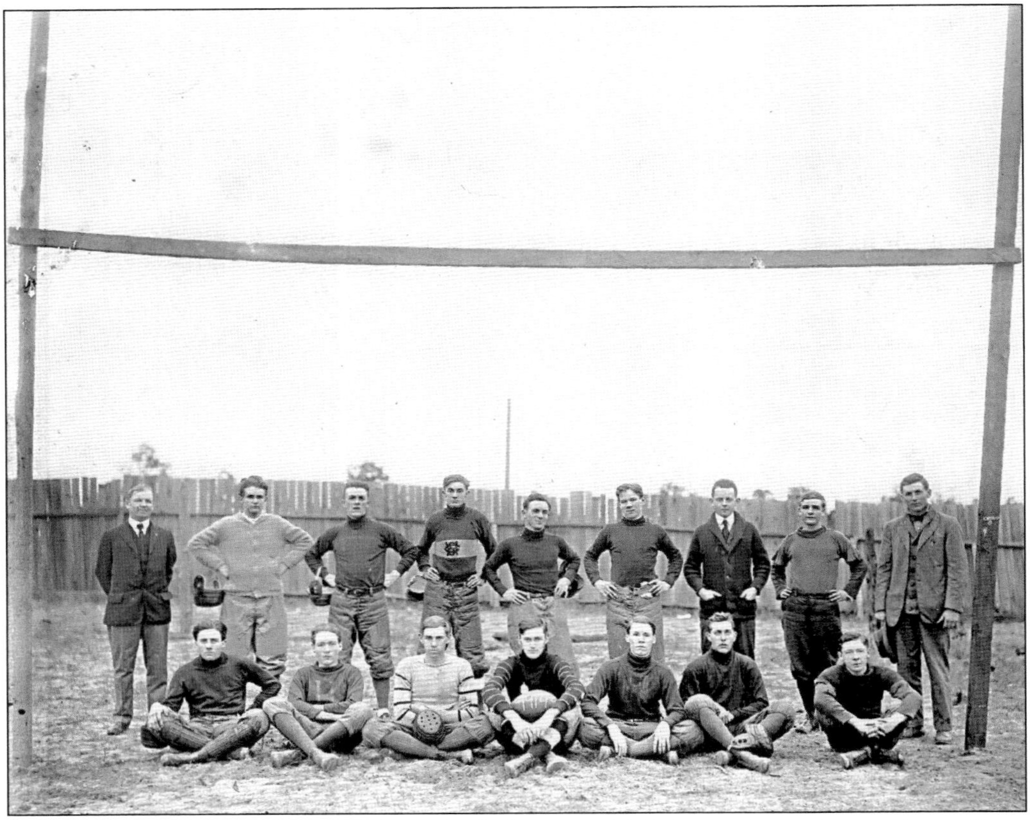

Members of the Hamlet High School football team of 1914 pose beneath a goalpost. From left to right, are (seated) ? Gribbs; Jake Lackey; Bob Smith; B. Tuttle; Louis McDonald; Clyde Medlin; and Bruce Hogan; (standing) ? Fuller, director of the local YMCA; Wade Pritchard; Shem Blackley, halfback; Lloyd Hill, halfback; Dan McDonald, fullback; Clarence McDonald, quarterback; Red Parish; Ray Turner; and George Byers, coach. (Courtesy A&H.)

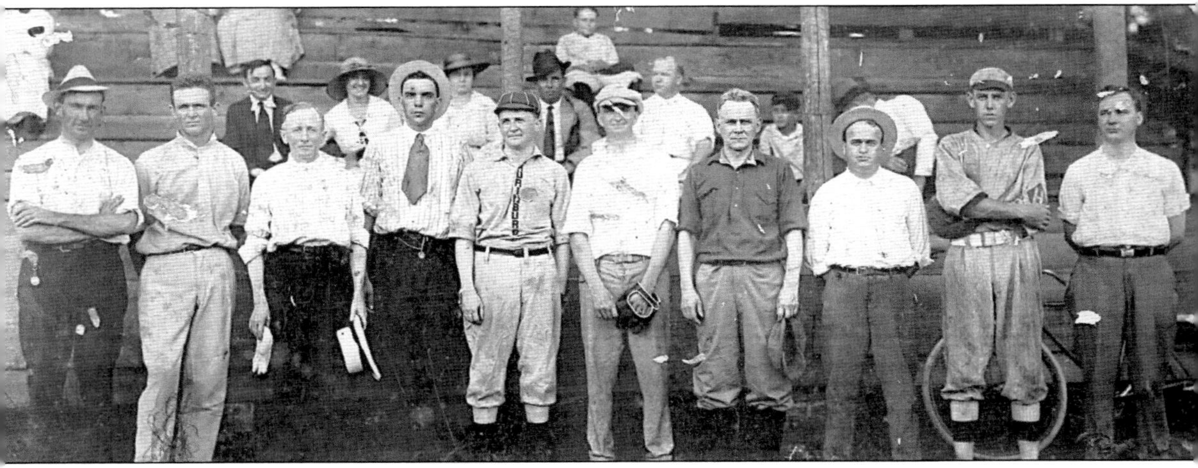

These baseball players and fans pose for Marchant at James's Field in Hamlet about 1920. (Courtesy A&H.)

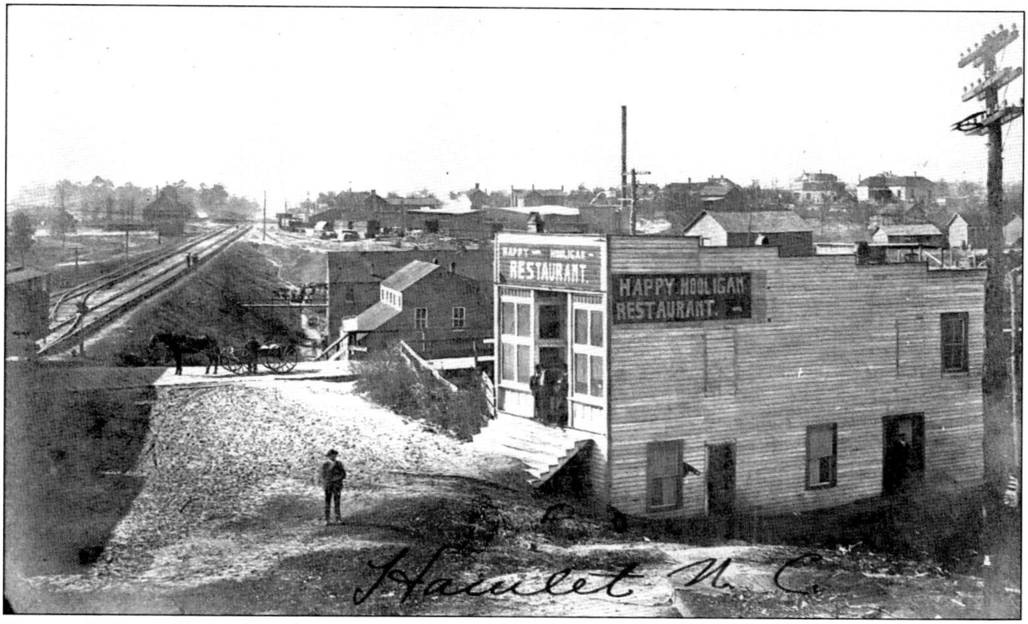

Situated along the railroad tracks in the manufacturing district of Hamlet about 1907 is the Happy Hooligan Restaurant. It was a popular establishment for good food and drink. (Courtesy Aubrey T. Haddock.)

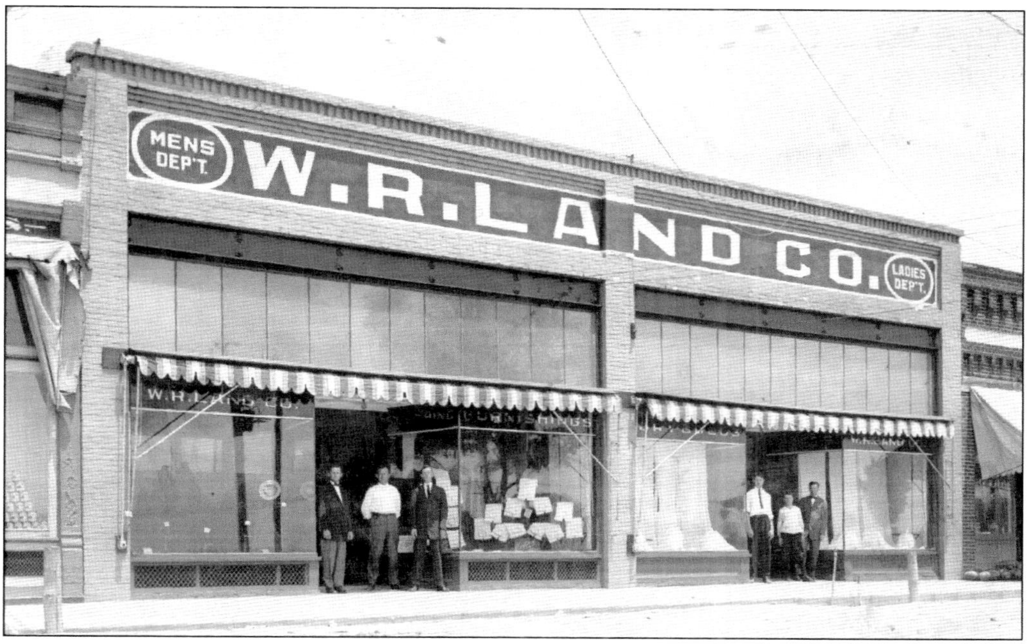

William Raines Land Sr. (1877–1945) operated one of the largest clothing stores in Hamlet. In 1911, Land and other employees posed at the entrance to the Front Street department store, which had sections for men and women. (Courtesy North Carolina Collection, University of North Carolina Library at Chapel Hill.)

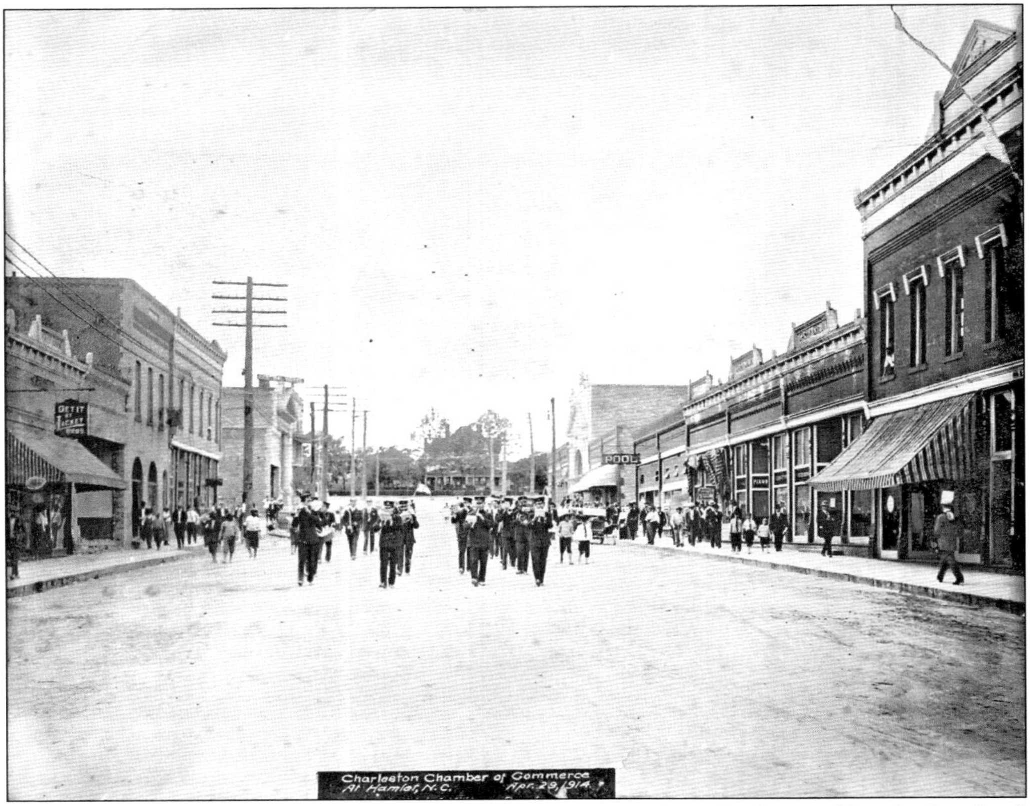

Marchant took this view of the Metz Military Band of the Charleston (South Carolina) Chamber of Commerce performing on Main Street in Hamlet on April 29, 1914. (Courtesy Dan Hicks.)

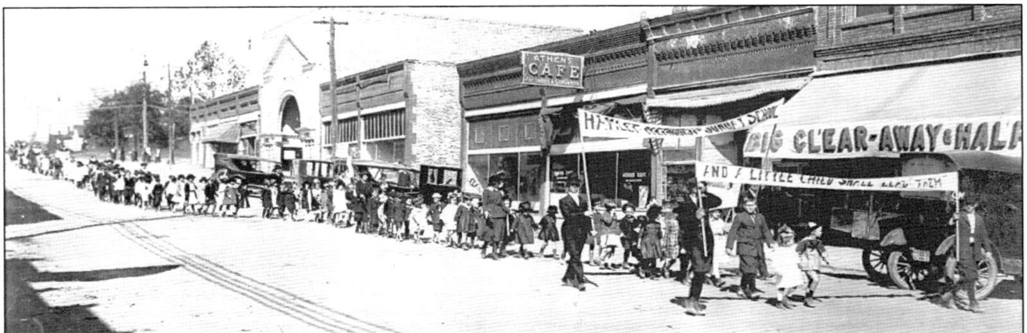

Members of Hamlet's First United Methodist Church march down Main Street about 1923. A hand-held banner at the head of the parade reads "And a Little Child Shall Lead Them." The participants are moving past the opera house and the Athens Café. (Courtesy A&H.)

Two

ROCKINGHAM

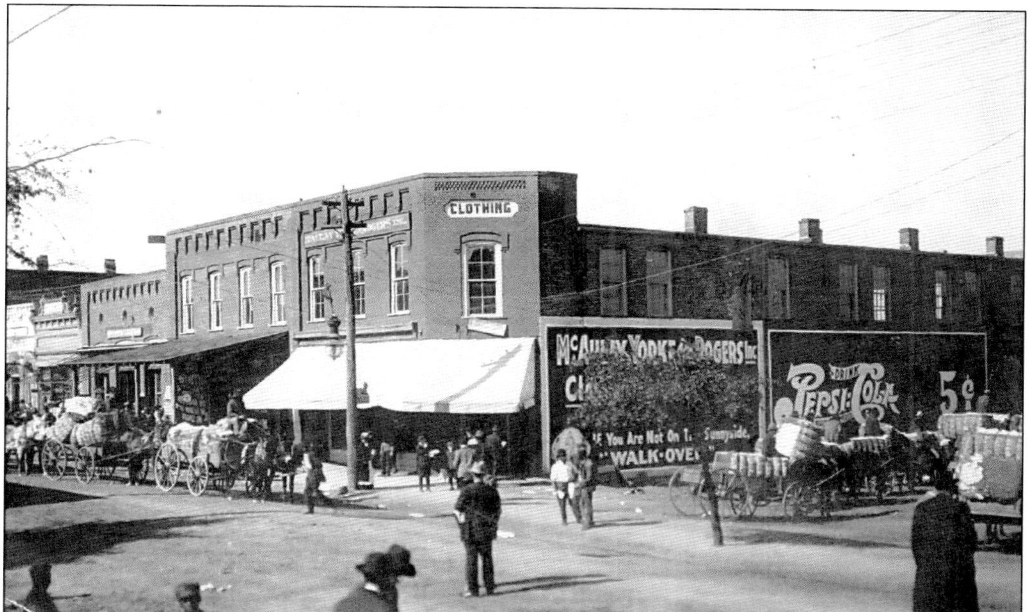

Cotton wagons and pedestrians fill the business district of Rockingham in this photograph taken about 1909. At center is McAulay, Yorke & Rogers clothing store facing Washington Street. (Courtesy C. Vernon Vallance.)

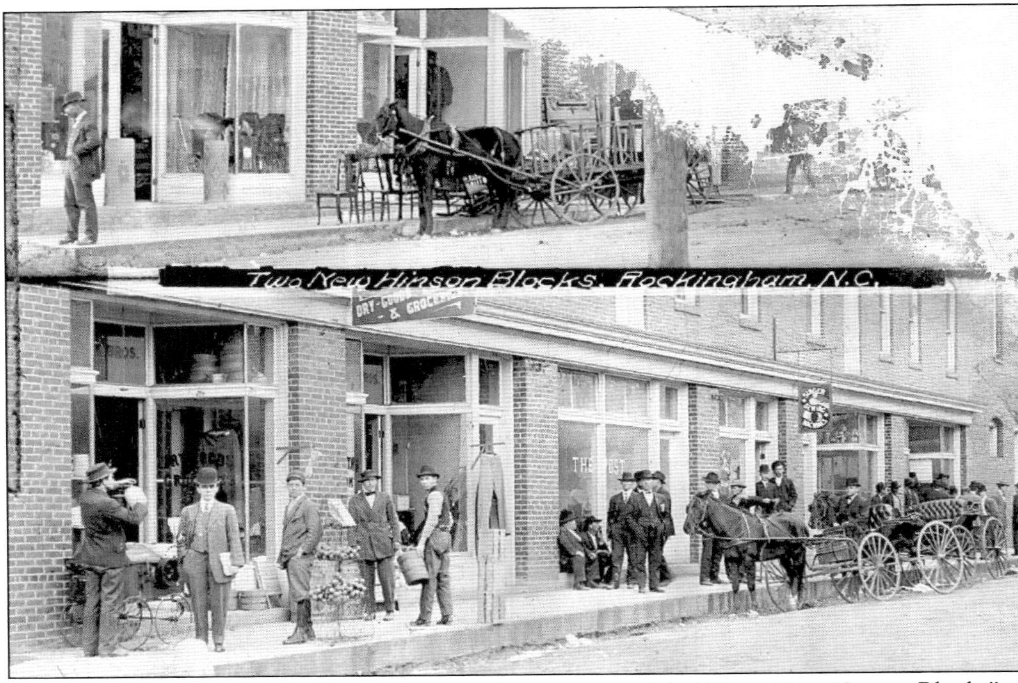

Reproduced here from a double-view postcard are pictures titled "Two New Hinson Blocks" in Rockingham about 1909. The Hinson name likely refers to Marion Lee Hinson (1864–1912), Richmond County sheriff and prominent businessman, who owned valuable real estate in Rockingham. (Courtesy A&H.)

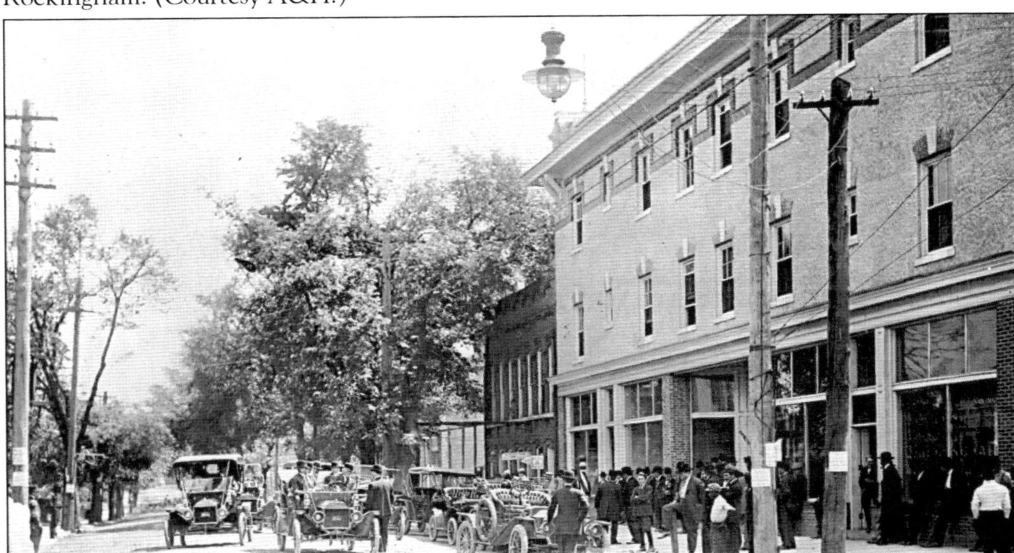

Here is a view looking toward the corner of Hancock and Washington Streets in Rockingham, date unknown. The gathering of automobiles and onlookers suggests a special occasion. The building on the right is the Rockingham Hotel, which faced Hancock Street. (Courtesy A&H.)

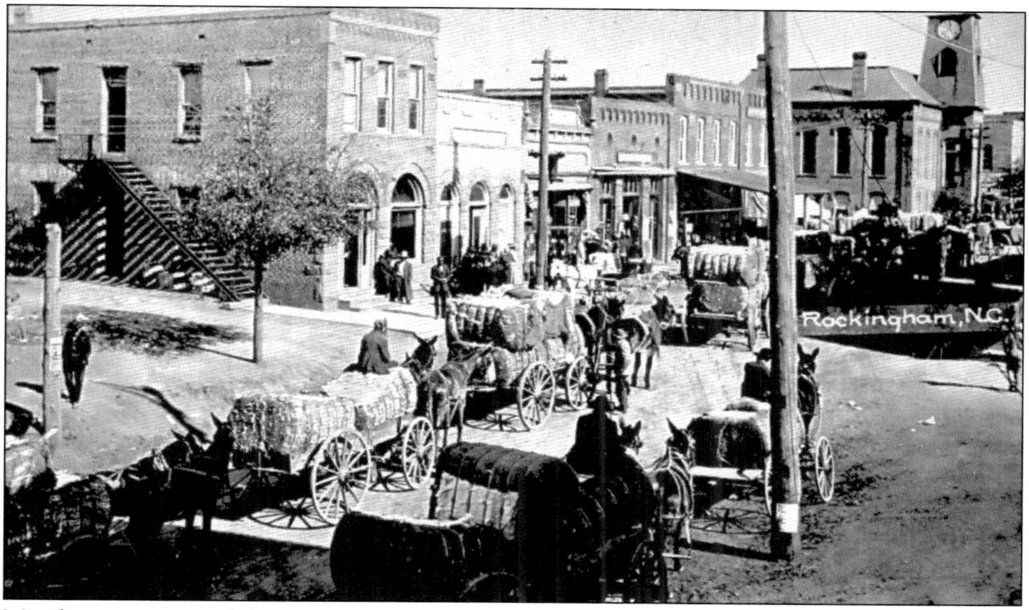

Marchant positioned his camera at a slightly elevated spot along Washington Street to photograph a line of wagons filled with cotton bales in Rockingham about 1911. The building with the clock tower at right is the Richmond County Courthouse. (Courtesy A&H.)

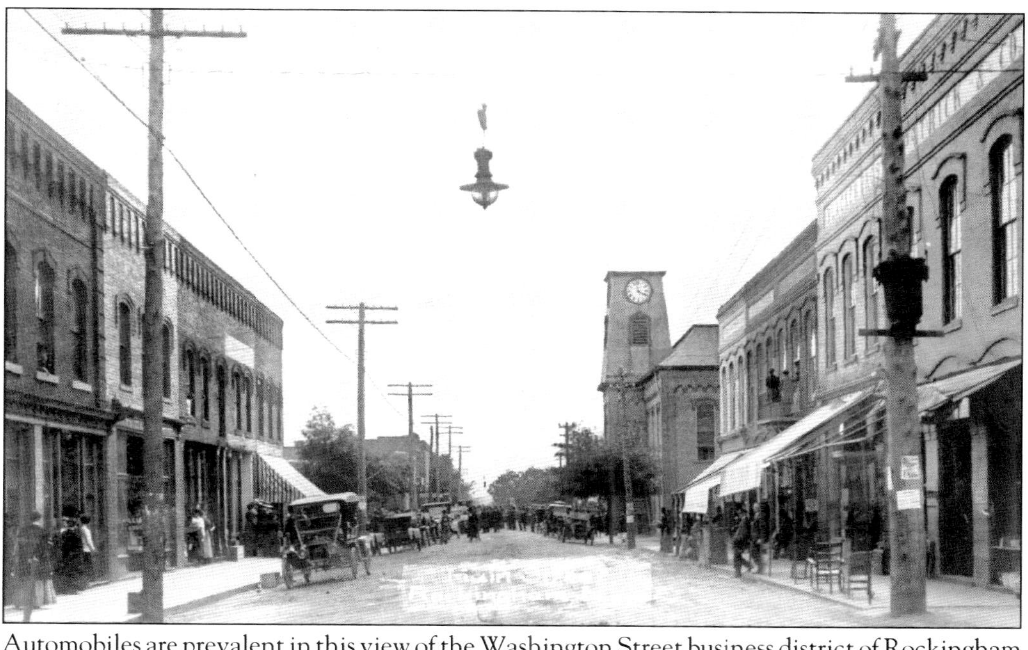

Automobiles are prevalent in this view of the Washington Street business district of Rockingham in the late 1910s. Again, the tower of the county courthouse is prominently visible in the distance. (Courtesy C. Vernon Vallance.)

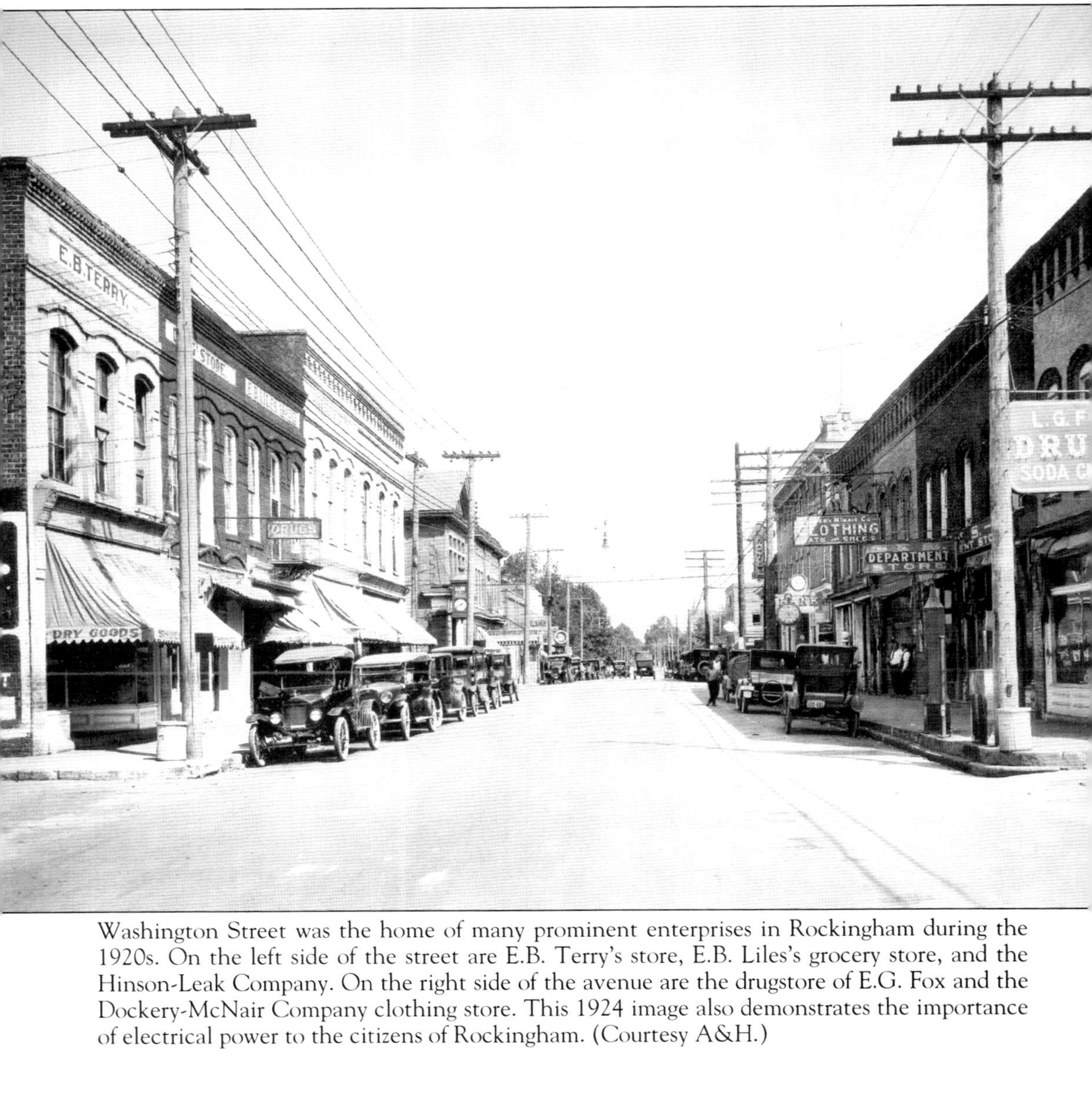

Washington Street was the home of many prominent enterprises in Rockingham during the 1920s. On the left side of the street are E.B. Terry's store, E.B. Liles's grocery store, and the Hinson-Leak Company. On the right side of the avenue are the drugstore of E.G. Fox and the Dockery-McNair Company clothing store. This 1924 image also demonstrates the importance of electrical power to the citizens of Rockingham. (Courtesy A&H.)

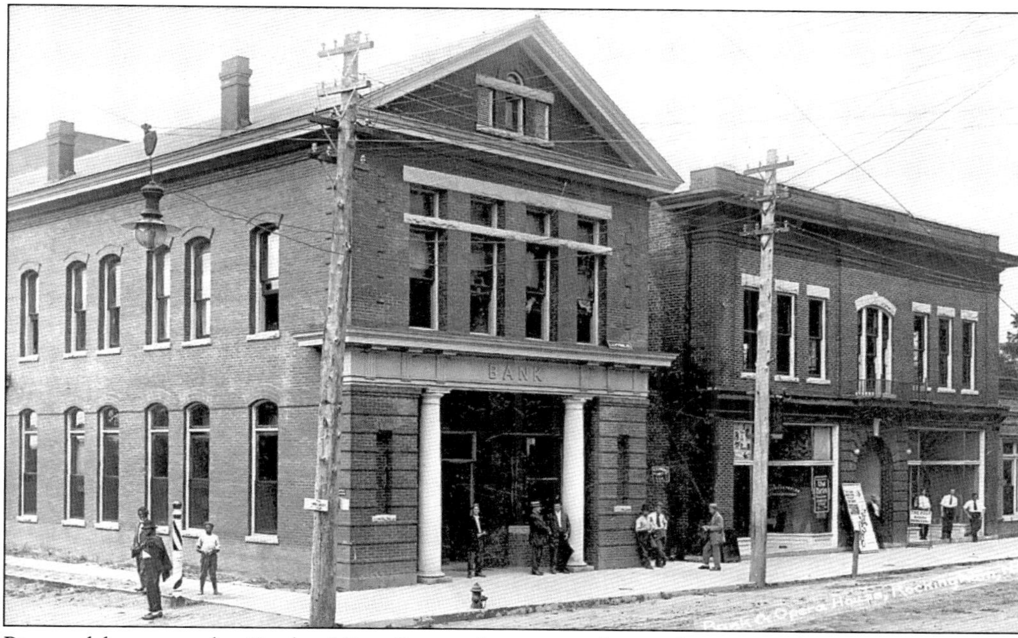

Pictured here are the Bank of Pee Dee and an opera house facing Washington Street at its intersection with Hancock Street, date unknown. (Courtesy Wayne Chapman.)

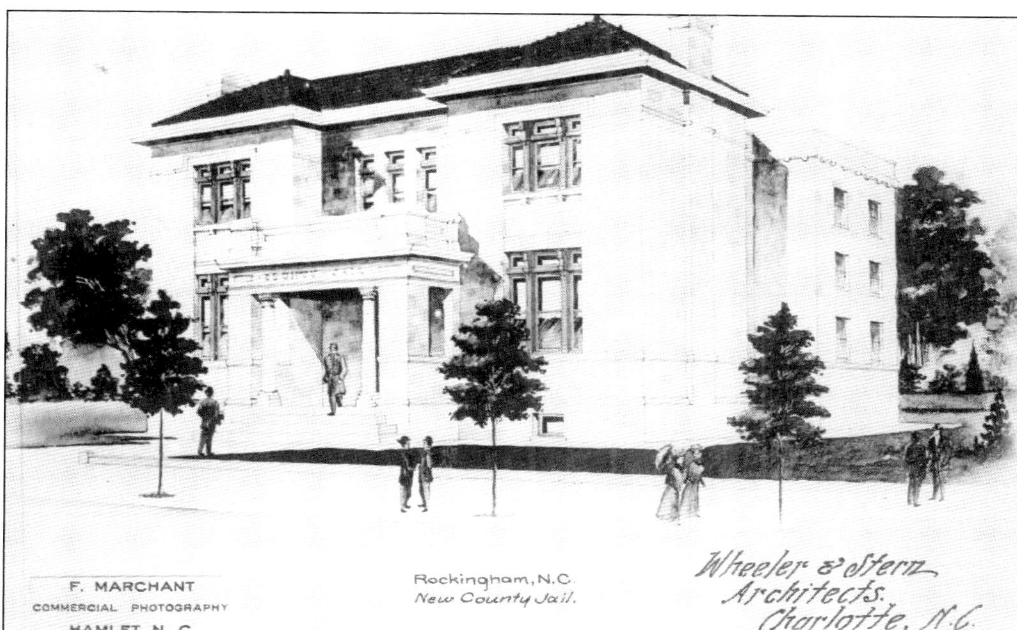

About 1912, Marchant published as a postcard this architectural rendering by Wheeler & Stern, architects in Charlotte, of a proposed new jail in Rockingham. (Courtesy Durwood Barbour.)

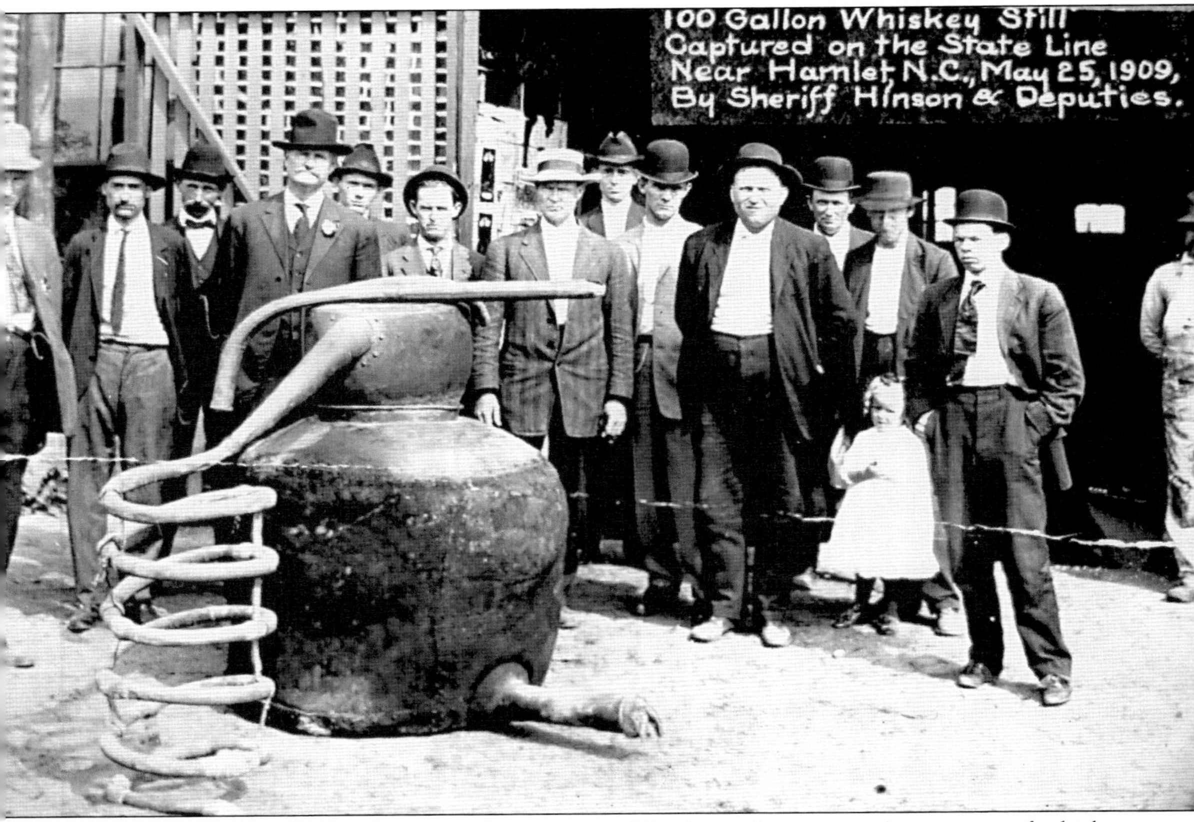

In the three views on these two facing pages, Marchant documents the capture of whiskey stills in the area in 1909. A popular social movement in North Carolina at that time called for the prohibition of all "spirituous liquors." Here, Richmond County sheriff Marion Lee Hinson, fourth from left, and his deputies pose behind a 100-gallon still they have confiscated near the North Carolina–South Carolina border on May 25, 1909. (Courtesy A&H.)

From left to right, Deputy Sheriff Carl Shores, Sheriff Hinson (with hands on Lonnie Cole), Dan Nuttall, Robert "Bob" Ledbetter Johnson, Ben Palmer, and L.J. Bell view captured stills destroyed at the courthouse in Rockingham in June 1909. (Courtesy A&H.)

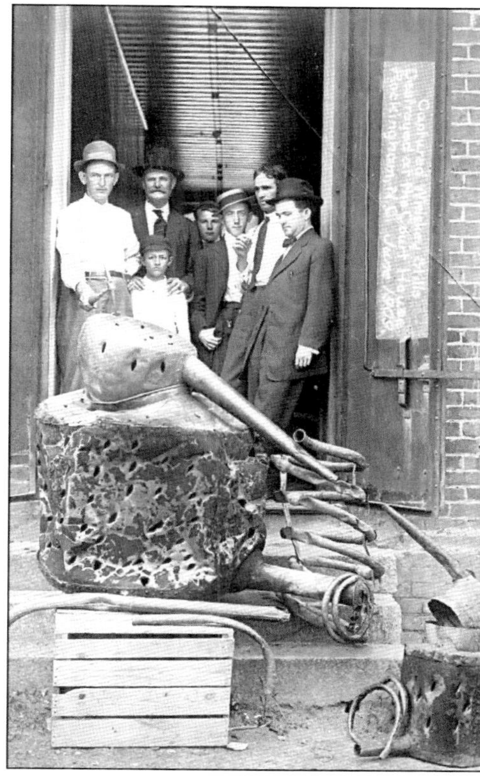

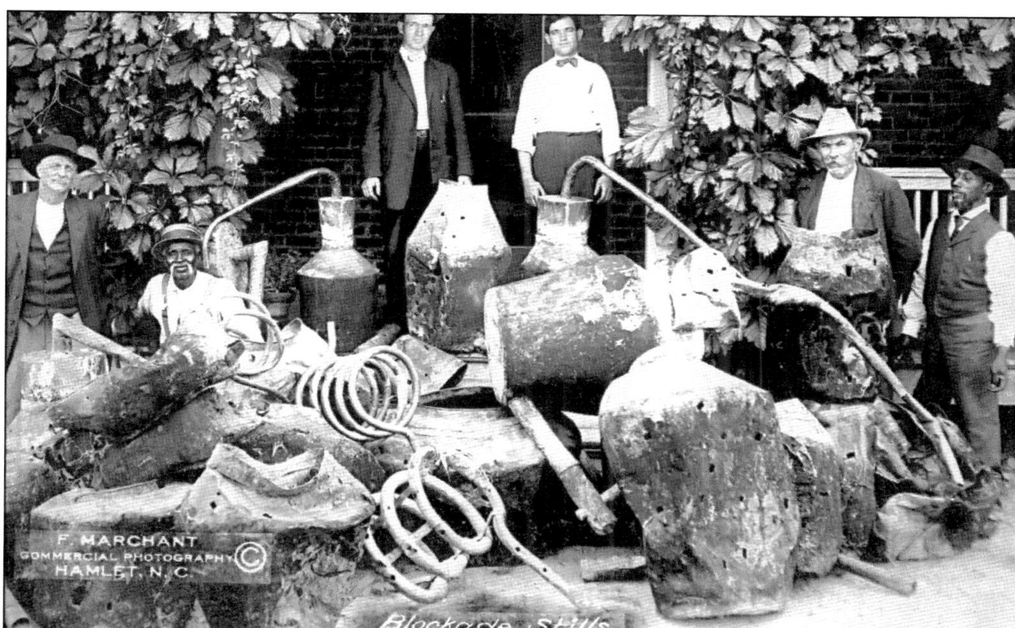

Here, Sheriff Hinson and others surround a pile of portions of dismantled liquor stills at the county seat, date unknown. (Courtesy A&H.)

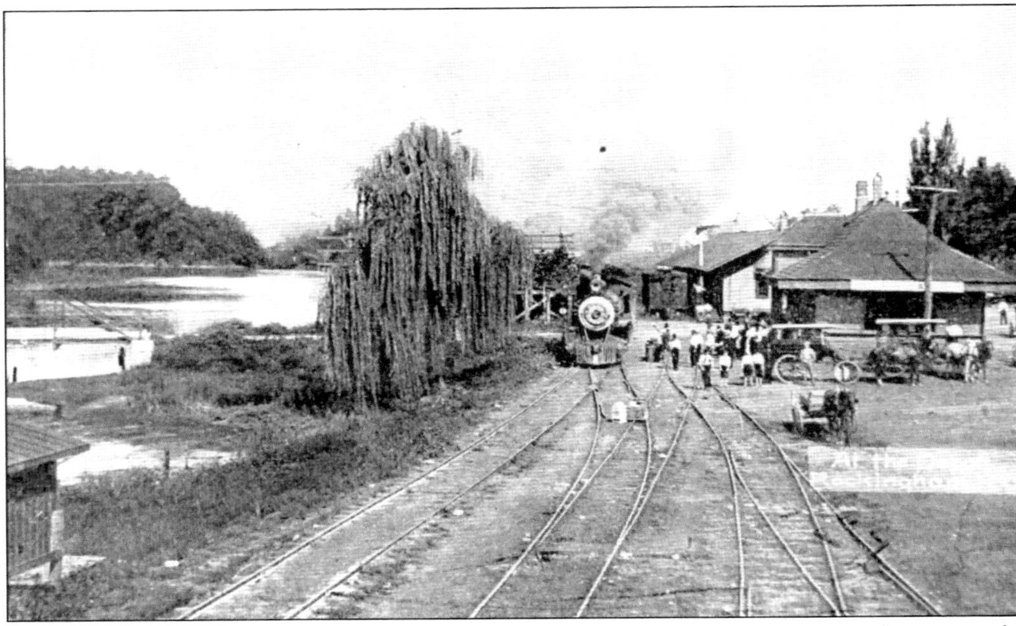

Marchant stood at an elevated position along the railroad tracks to achieve this view of a steam engine at the Seaboard Air Line Railway Depot at Rockingham about 1910. (Courtesy Durwood Barbour.)

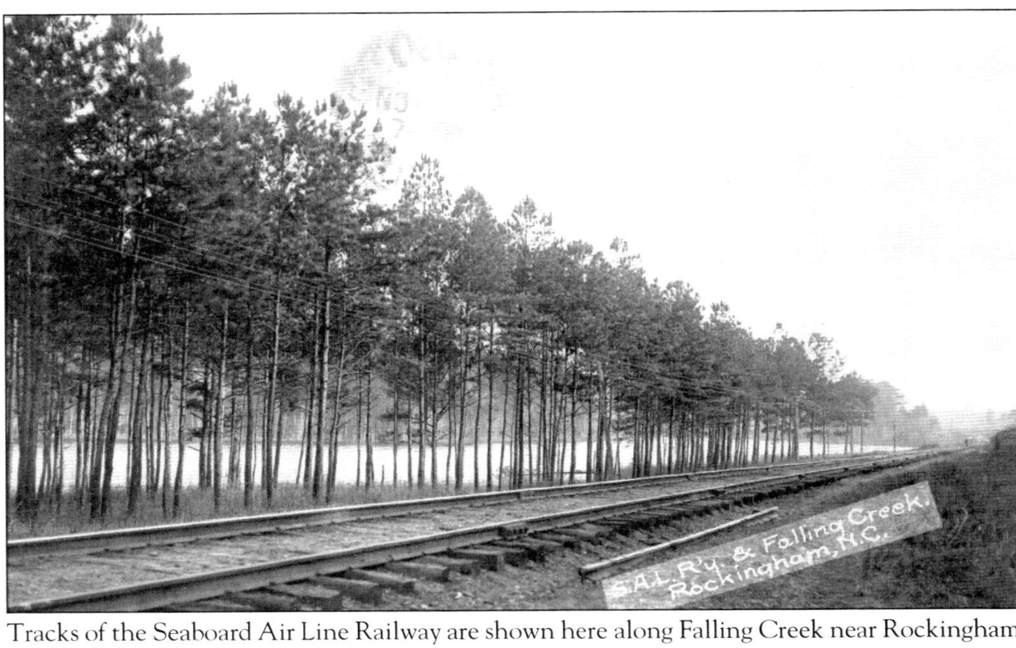

Tracks of the Seaboard Air Line Railway are shown here along Falling Creek near Rockingham. (Courtesy A&H.)

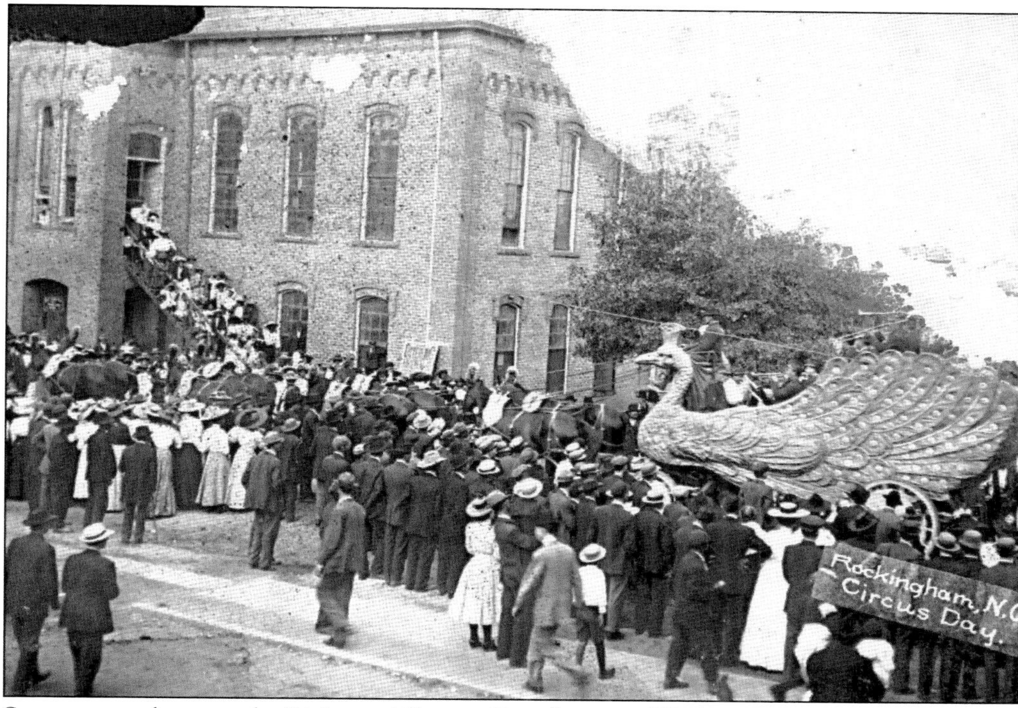

Spectators gather near the Richmond County Courthouse on Washington Street in Rockingham to see a circus parade, date unknown. The horse-drawn peacock float carries musicians who are entertaining the crowd. (Courtesy A&H.)

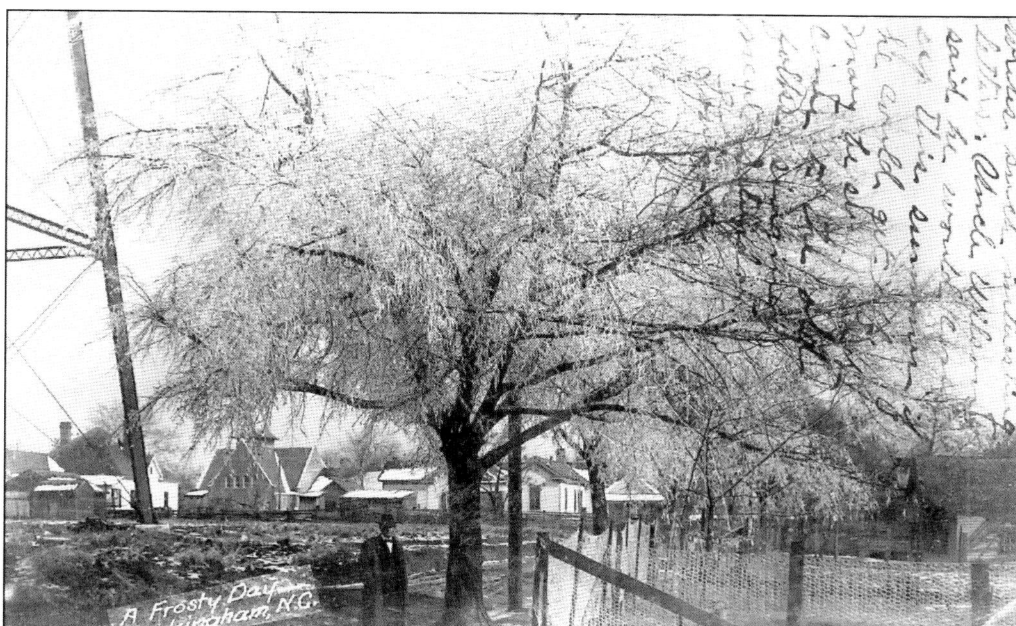

Marchant enjoyed photographing winter scenes and publishing them as postcards. He identified this 1910 view as a "Frosty Day in Rockingham." (Courtesy Wayne Chapman.)

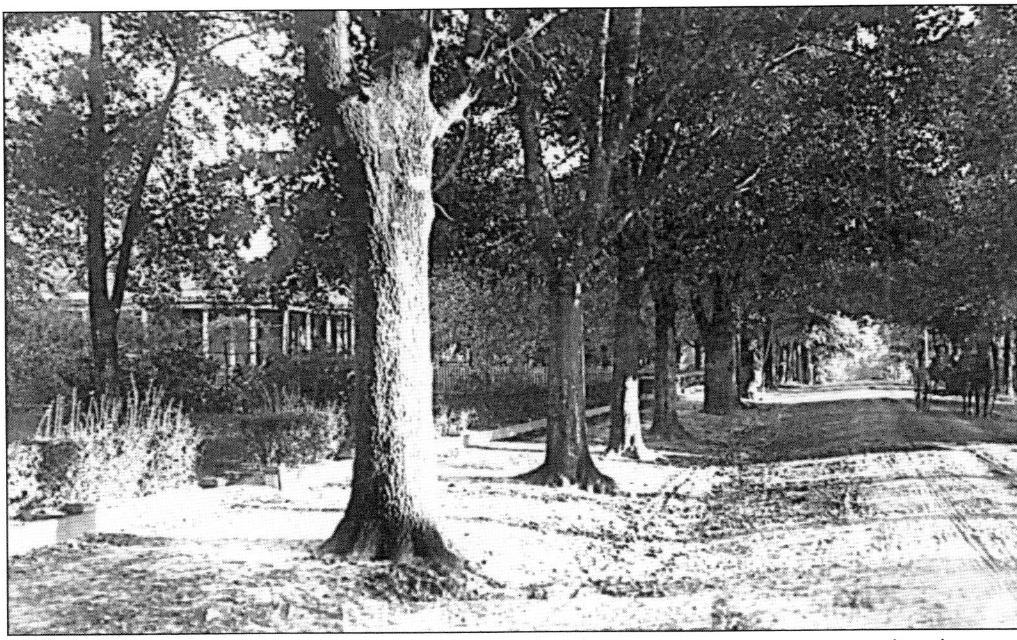

Shown here in the summer of 1910 is one of Rockingham's more picturesque tree-lined streets, Fifth Avenue. A horse and buggy travels along the dirt road in the direction of the camera. (Courtesy Stephen E. Massengill.)

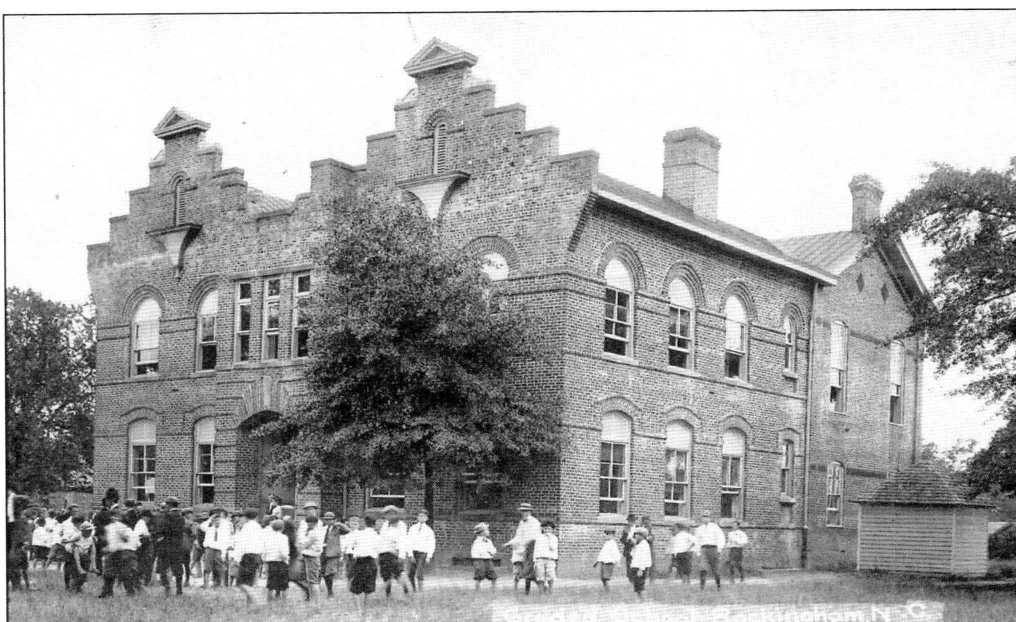

These children play on the grounds of the graded school at Rockingham about 1912. The building's entrance faced Washington Street. (Courtesy Wayne Chapman.)

Three

The Seaboard Air Line Railway

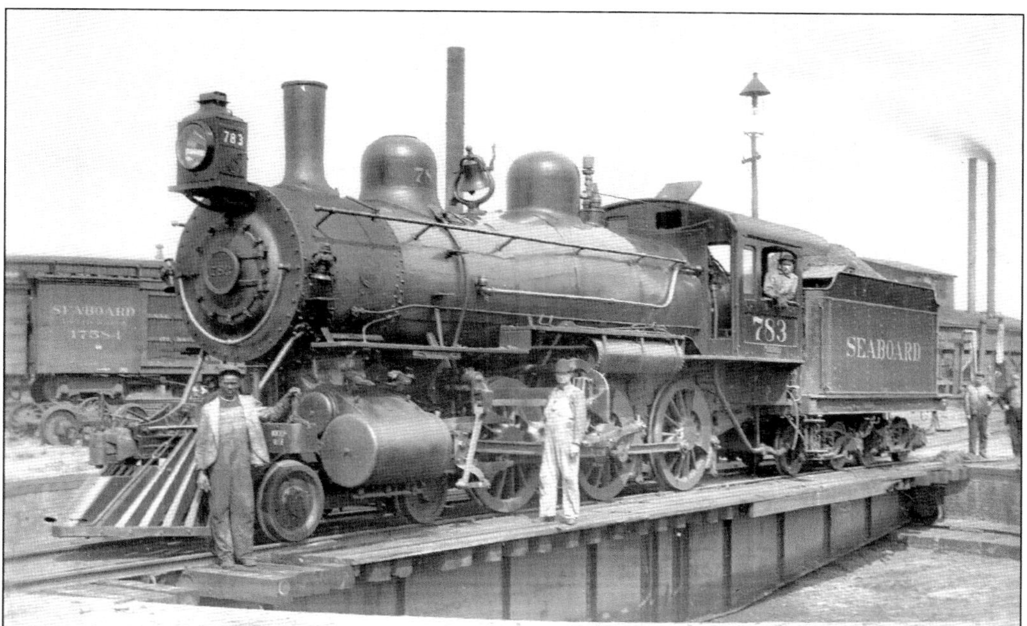

Employees of the Seaboard Air Line Railway roundhouse at Hamlet pose here with Engine No. 783 on the 100-foot-long, electrically powered turntable. (Courtesy A&H.)

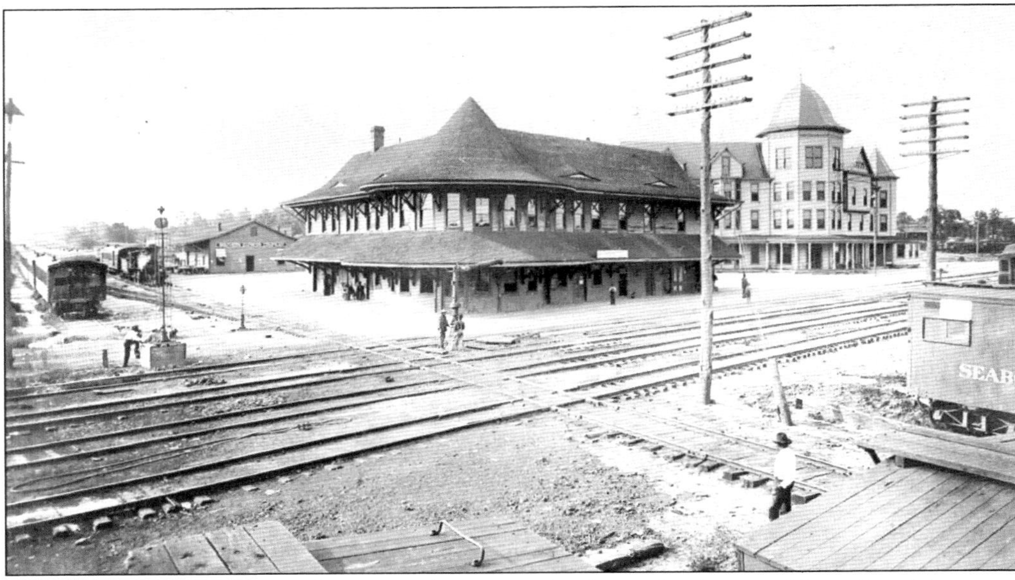

One of Marchant's most popular postcard images is this distant landscape of the railroad depot and the Seaboard Hotel at Hamlet, likely taken before 1910. The photograph also includes the junction of the north-south and east-west lines at the station. (Courtesy Stephen E. Massengill.)

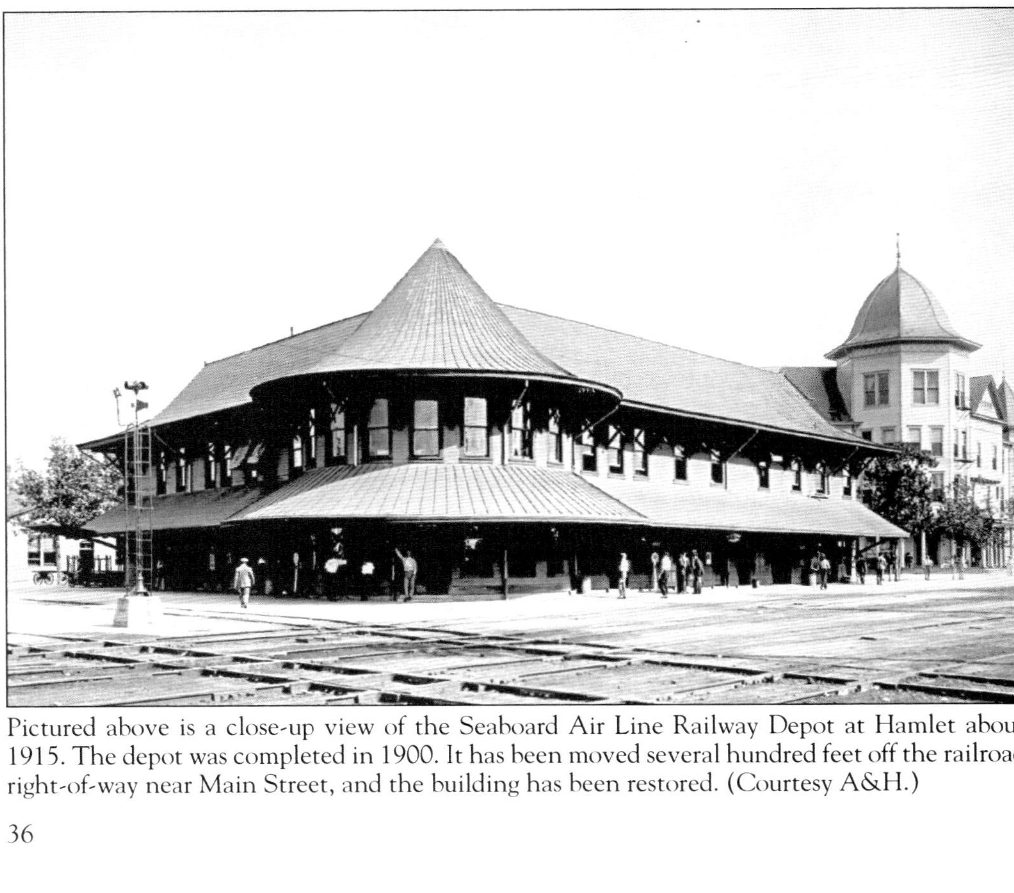

Pictured above is a close-up view of the Seaboard Air Line Railway Depot at Hamlet about 1915. The depot was completed in 1900. It has been moved several hundred feet off the railroad right-of-way near Main Street, and the building has been restored. (Courtesy A&H.)

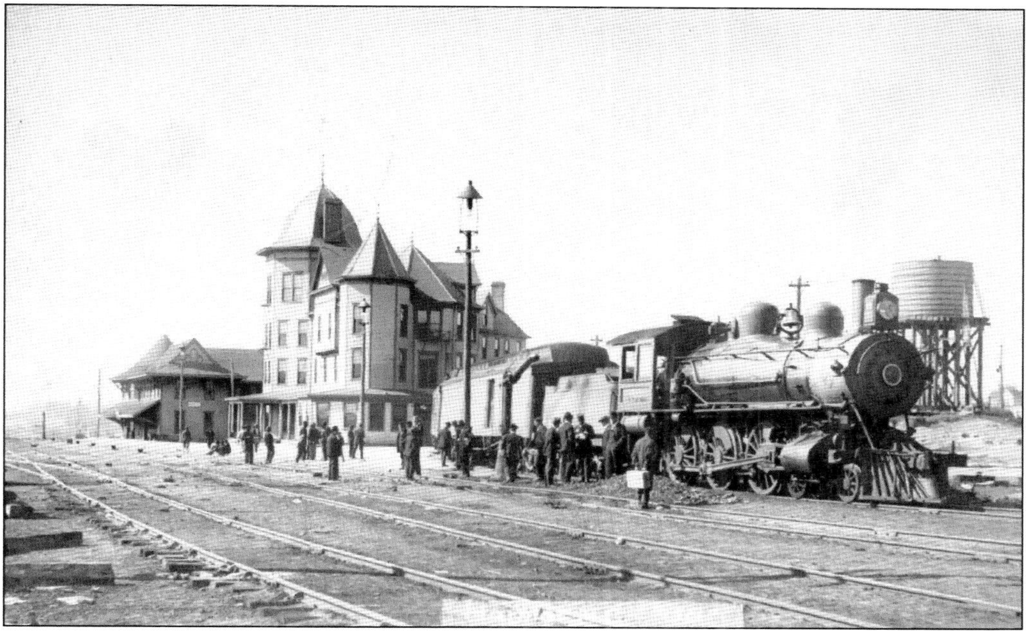

Passengers wait to board the train pulled by Engine No. 51 at Hamlet about 1911. Just south of the passenger cars are the Seaboard Hotel and the railroad depot. (Courtesy Stephen E. Massengill.)

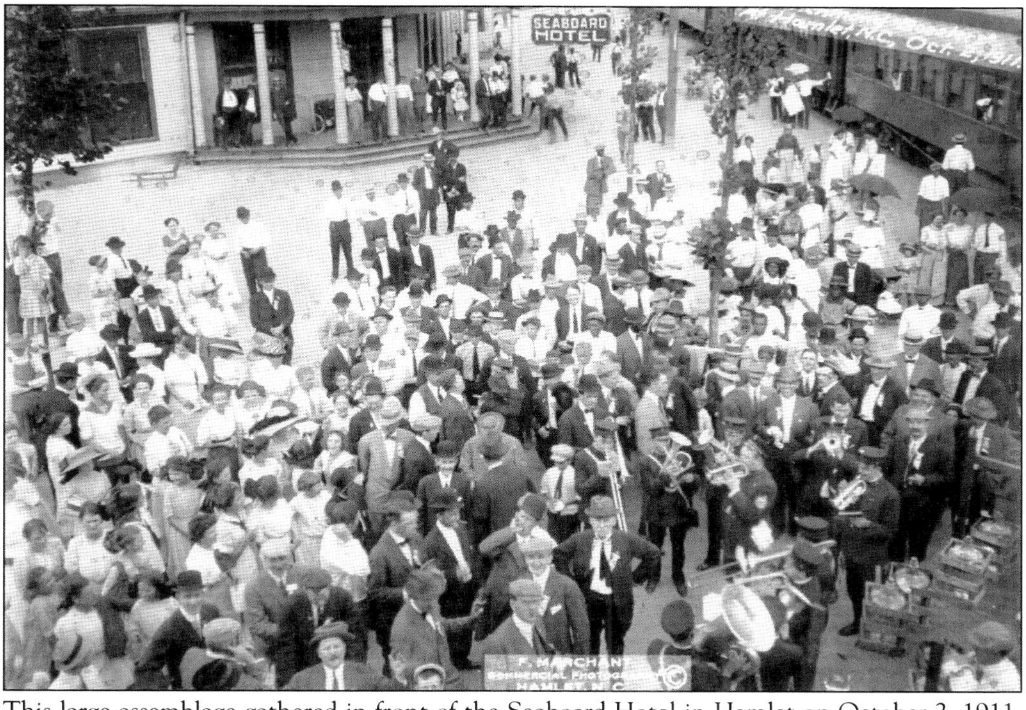

This large assemblage gathered in front of the Seaboard Hotel in Hamlet on October 2, 1911, is identified as the Richmond "Boosters." The group, which includes musicians, appears to be greeting a passenger train. (Courtesy Hamlet Public Library.)

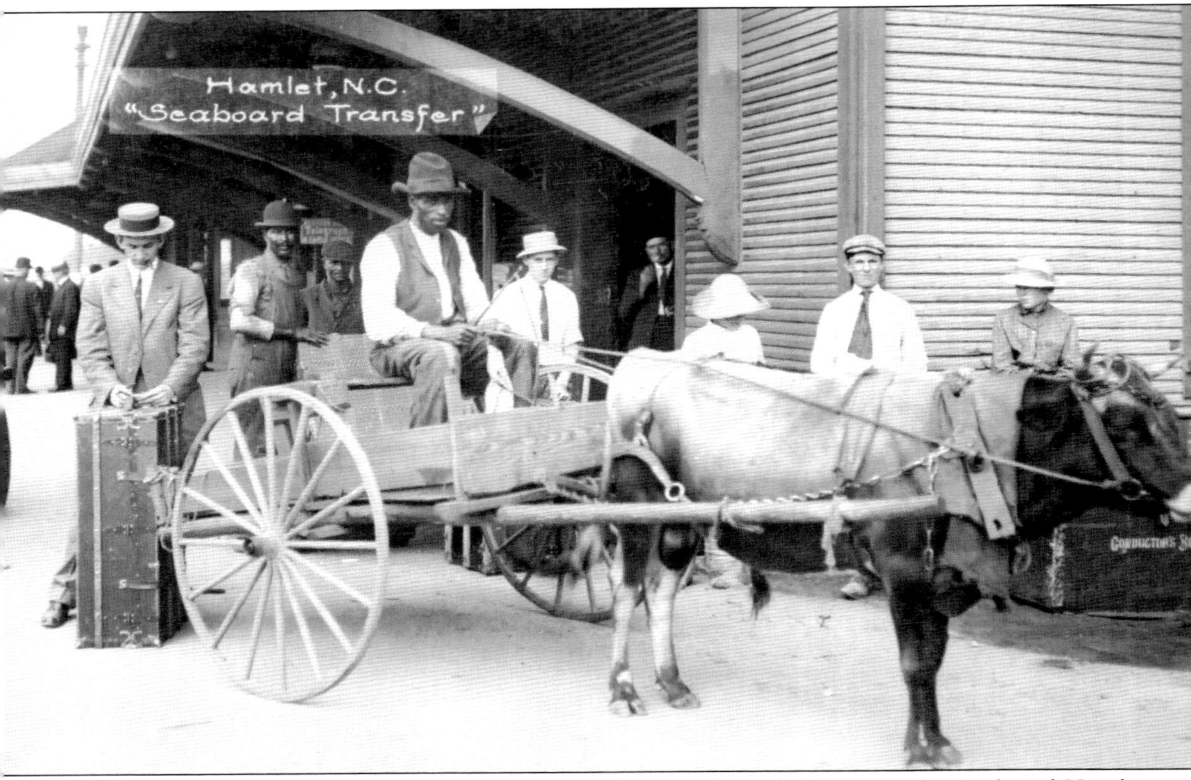

This bull-drawn cart hauled trunks and heavy baggage from the depot to the Seaboard Hotel and back before the advent of the automobile. The identified people in this 1909 photograph are Henry Page, railroad clerk, who is checking baggage at left; Harrison Ewing, the driver of the cart; Bruce Leviner, man under wooden beam in the distance; ? Leviner, boy with the large hat; Albert Hubbard Sr., man with derby and tie; and Clinton Moring, located behind the head of the bull. (Courtesy Durwood Barbour.)

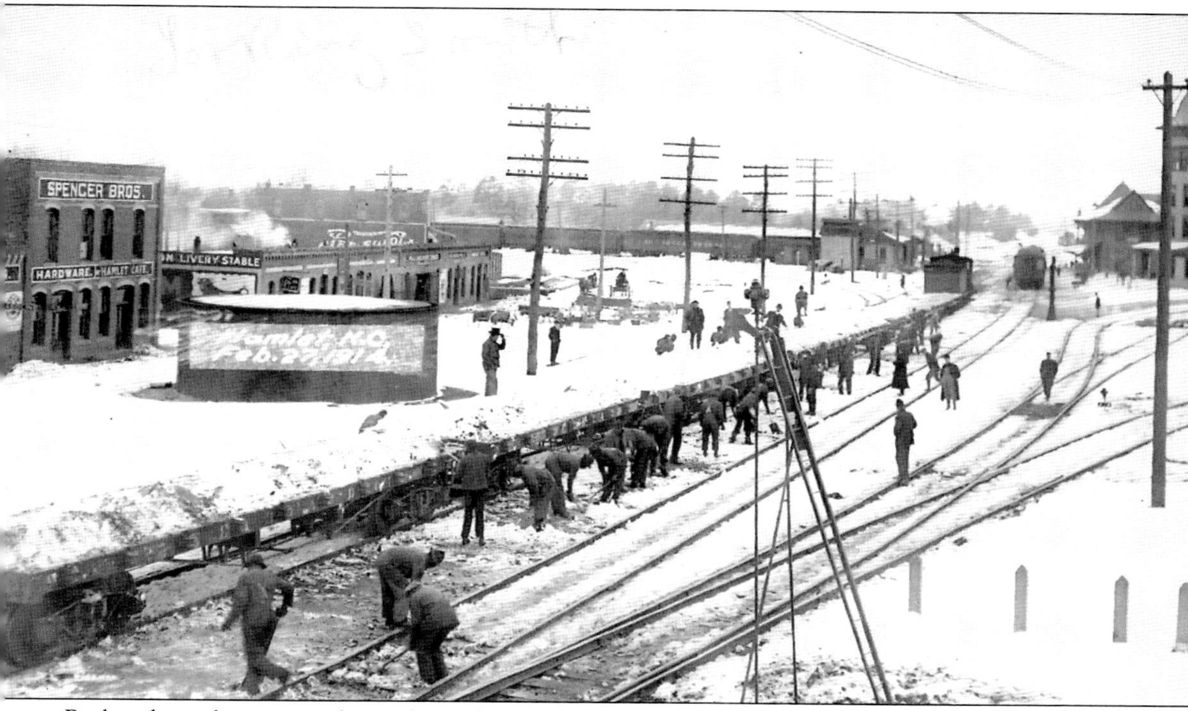

Railroad employees are shown here shoveling snow near the hotel and depot in Hamlet on February 27, 1914. Businesses visible at left are Spencer Brothers Hardware, the Hamlet Café, the Palace Café, and a livery stable. (Courtesy Wayne Chapman.)

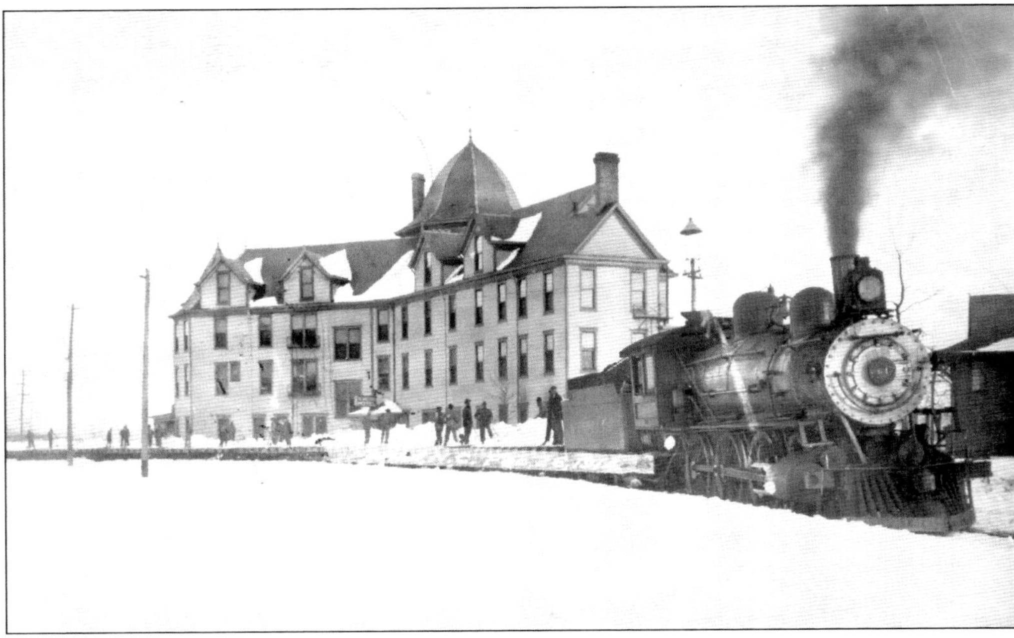

Marchant's camera was the source of many postcard views of infrequent snowfalls in Richmond County. These two views were taken in Hamlet following the storm of late February 1914 and show steam engines on the frozen tracks. (Above, courtesy Sarah M. Pope; below, courtesy Wayne Chapman.)

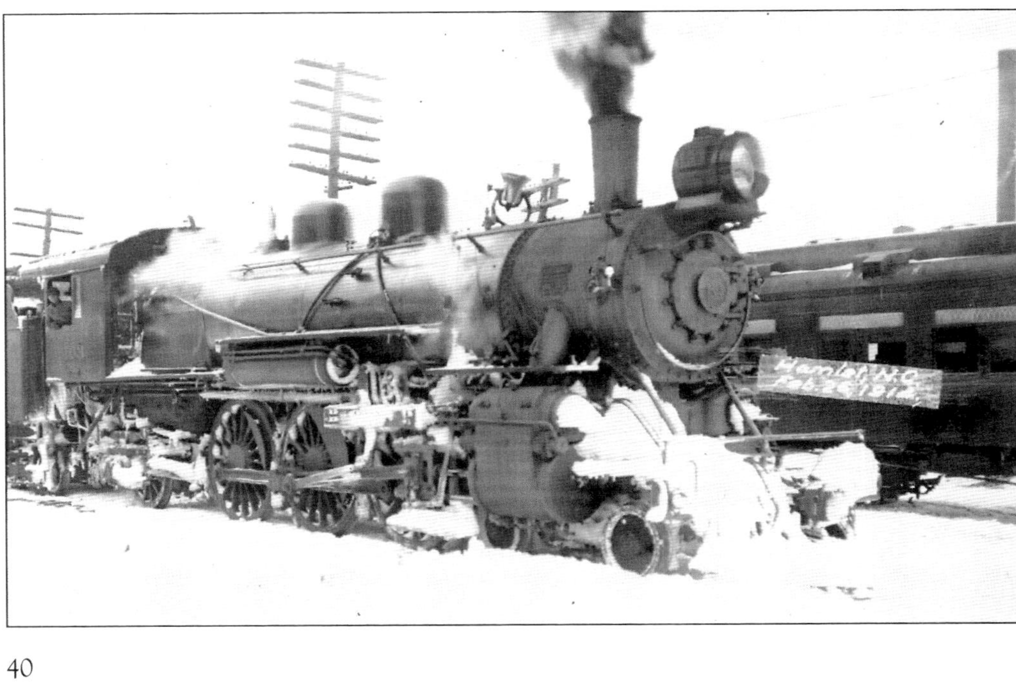

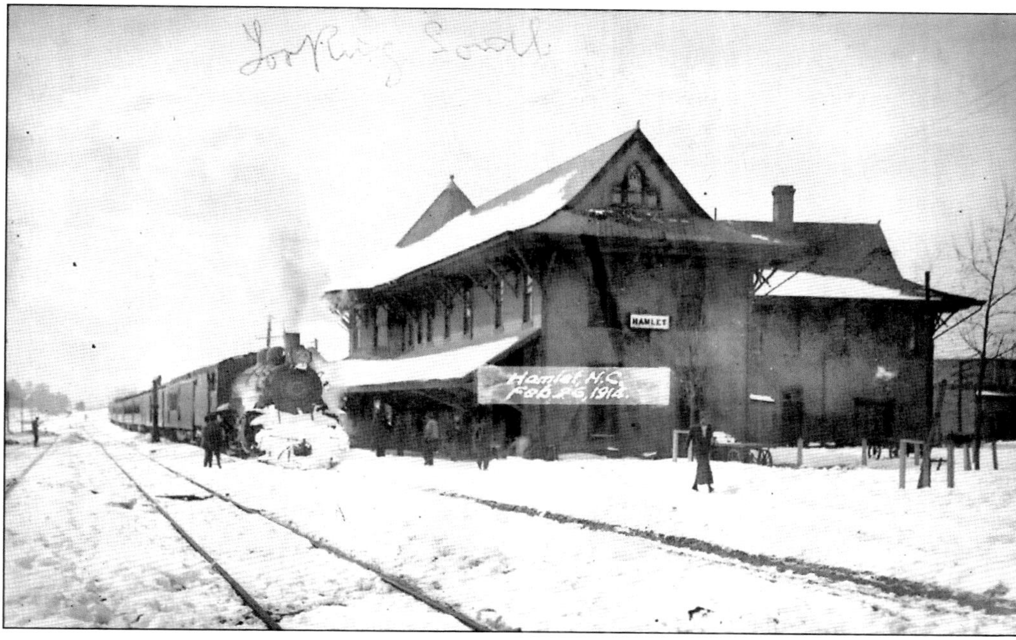

Marchant documented the aftermath of several winter storms in Hamlet between 1910 and 1914. These two views were also taken after the snowfall in February 1914 and show the Seaboard Air Line depot (top) and the hotel and depot (bottom). (Above and below, courtesy Wayne Chapman.)

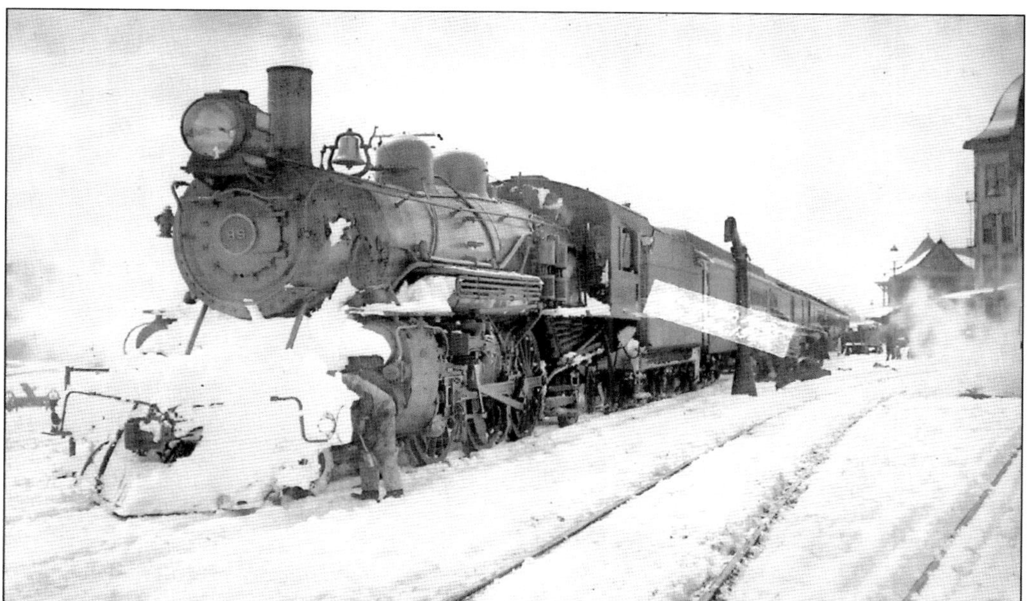

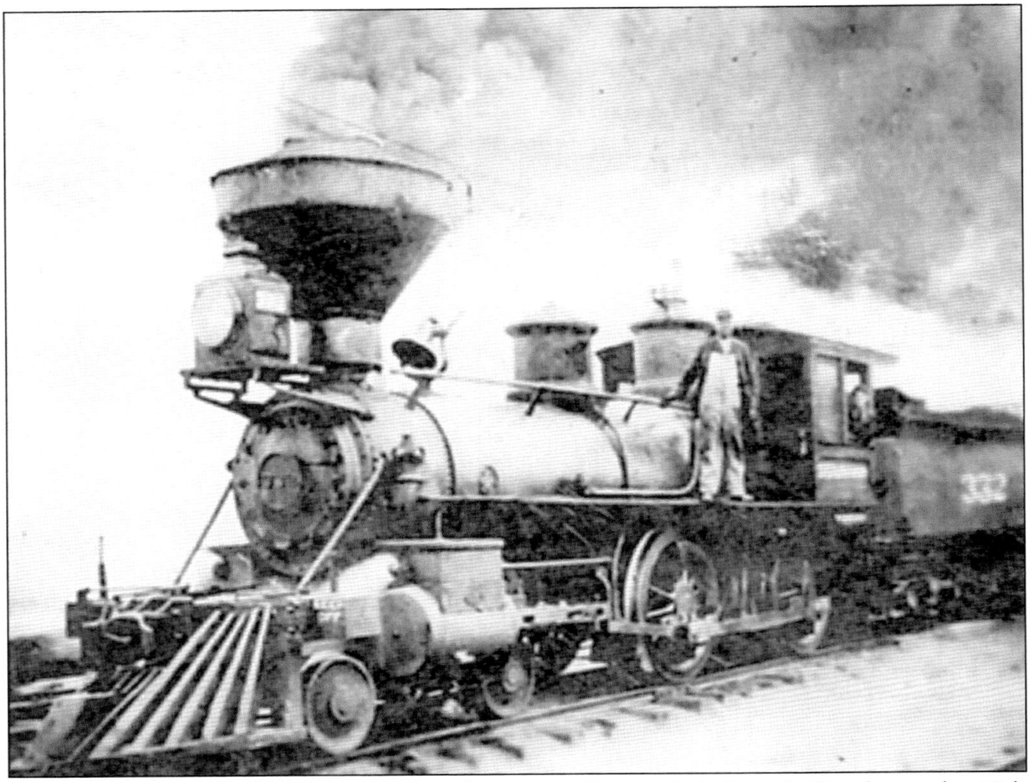

Pictured above is an older steam engine that originally traveled through Hamlet in the 19th century. (Courtesy Durwood Barbour.)

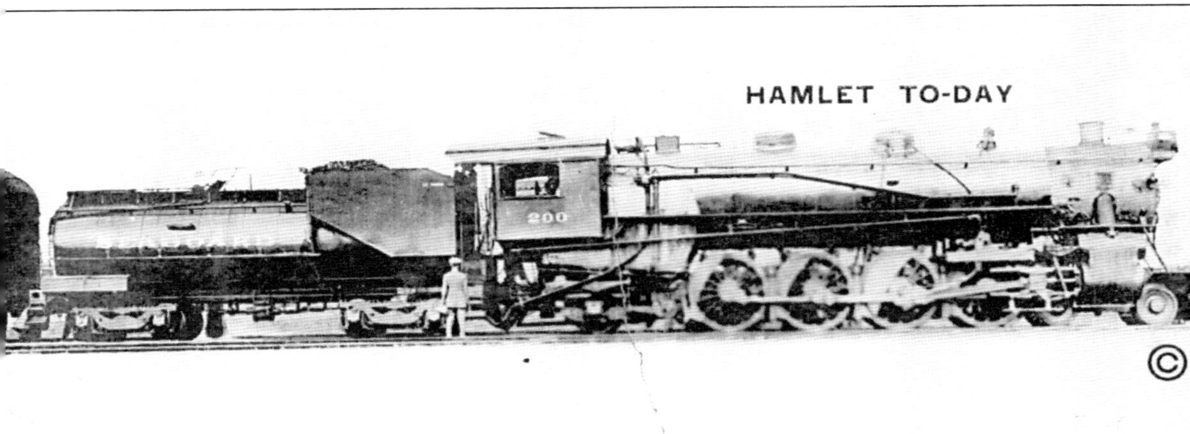

Here is a Marchant photograph of a railroad steam engine and tender that he titled "Hamlet To-day." The Seaboard Air Line Railway train of 1916 vintage is being powered by Engine No. 200. The Hamlet photographer applied for and received a copyright for this image. (Courtesy Durwood Barbour.)

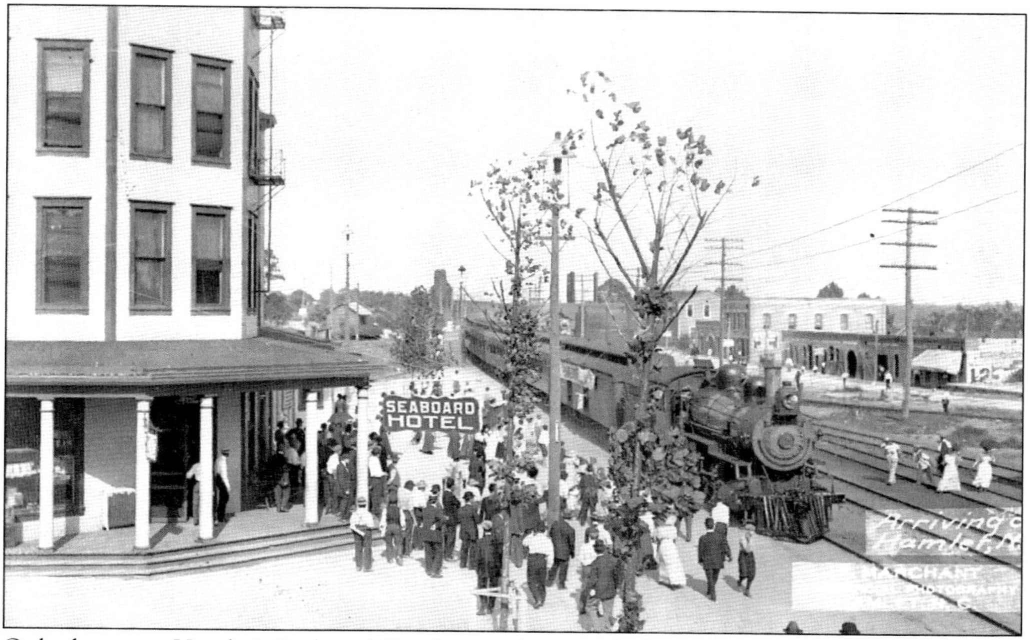

Onlookers near Hamlet's Seaboard Hotel await the arrival of a passenger train. The photograph, the date of which is unknown, was secured from the second floor of the railroad depot. (Courtesy Wayne Chapman.)

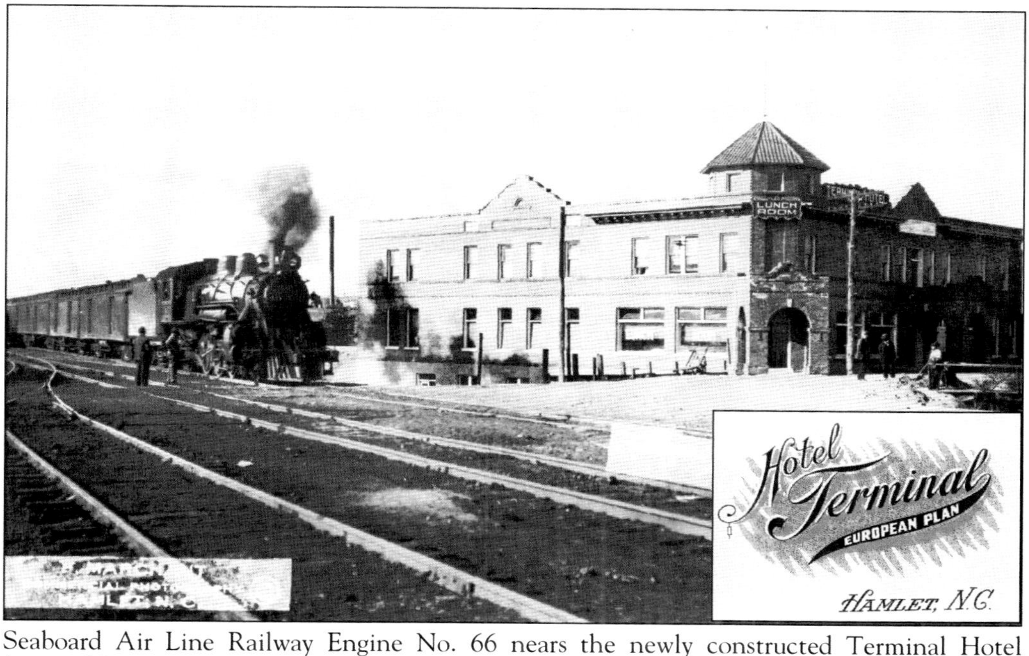

Seaboard Air Line Railway Engine No. 66 nears the newly constructed Terminal Hotel (opened January 1, 1912) in Hamlet. The locomotive was built in 1905 in Richmond, Virginia. (Courtesy Wayne Chapman.)

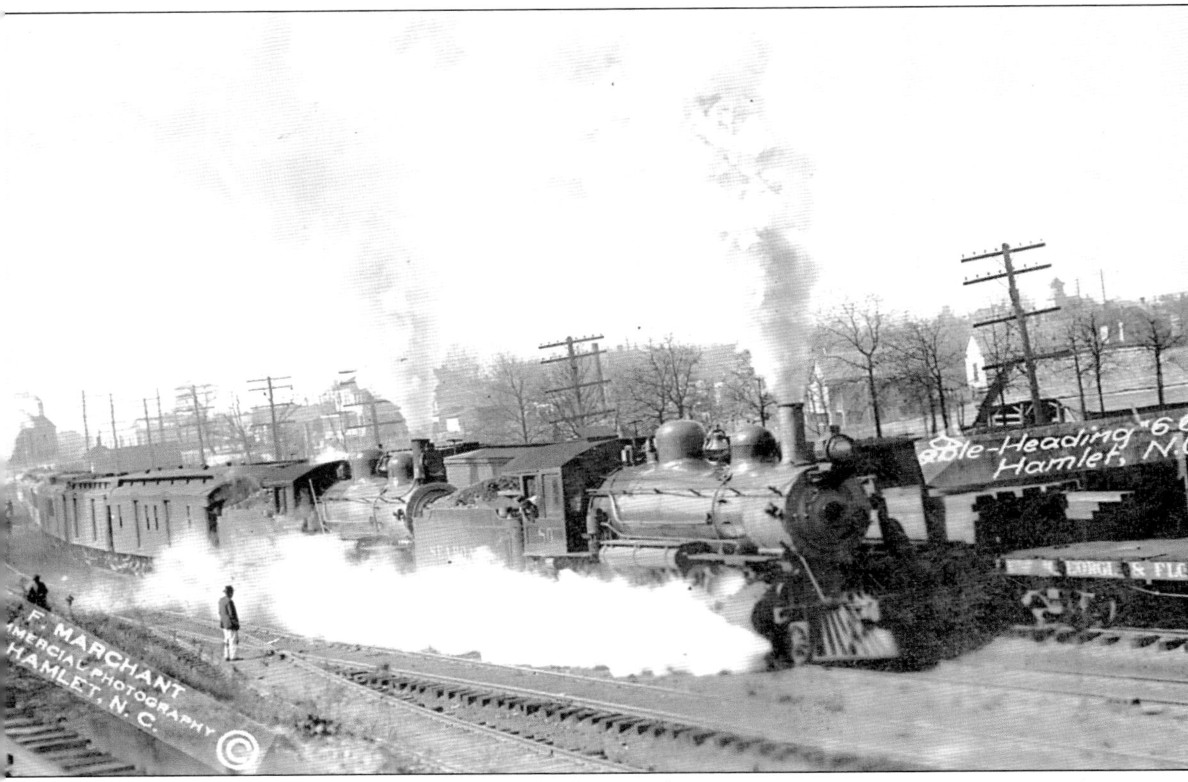

Marchant titled this postcard "Double-Heading 66" because two engines are powering a train at Hamlet in 1911. (Courtesy C. Vernon Vallance.)

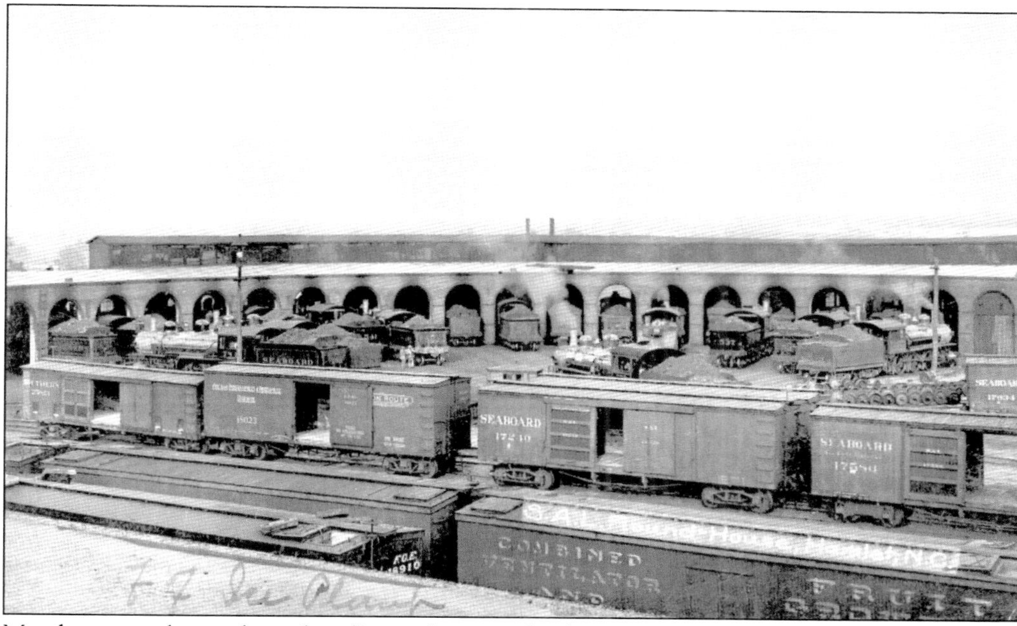

Marchant stood atop the railroad's ice plant to take this elevated view of the Seaboard Air Line Railway roundhouse at Hamlet in 1910. Almost all of the structure's 20 stalls are visible. The railroad company demolished the roundhouse in the 1950s. (Courtesy Wayne Chapman.)

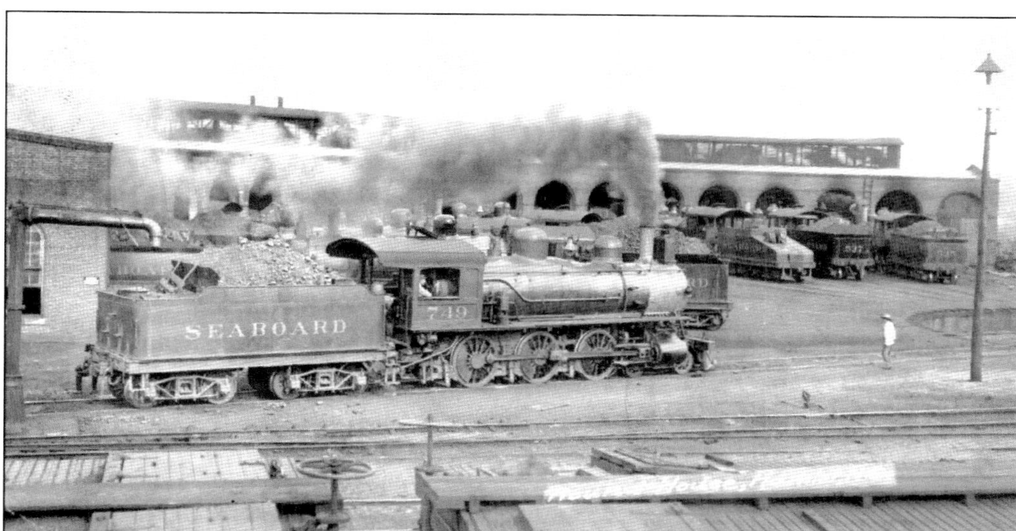

This ground-level postcard view of the roundhouse at Hamlet features Engine No. 749 in the foreground. The card was mailed in 1918, and the sender wrote the following lines: "I received the card you gave me to write on. Will stay here about 10 hrs. I guess. [B]ought me a good dinner here for 30 [cents]." (Courtesy Stephen E. Massengill.)

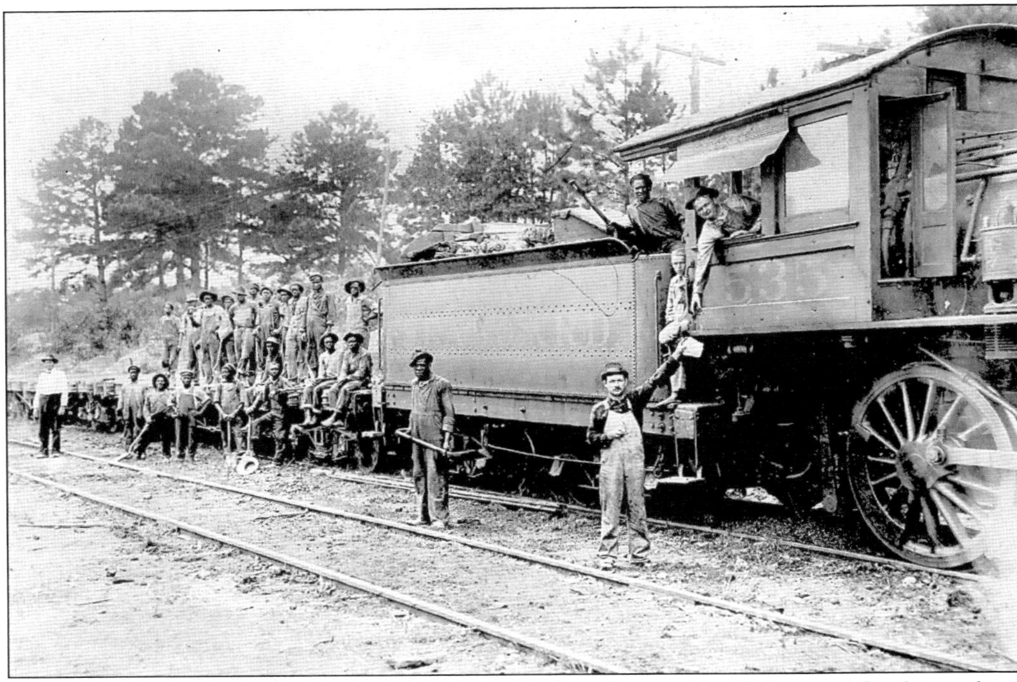

The crew and work detail of Seaboard Air Line Railway Engine No. 535 paused for this undated photograph while repairing tracks at an unidentified location. (Courtesy A&H.)

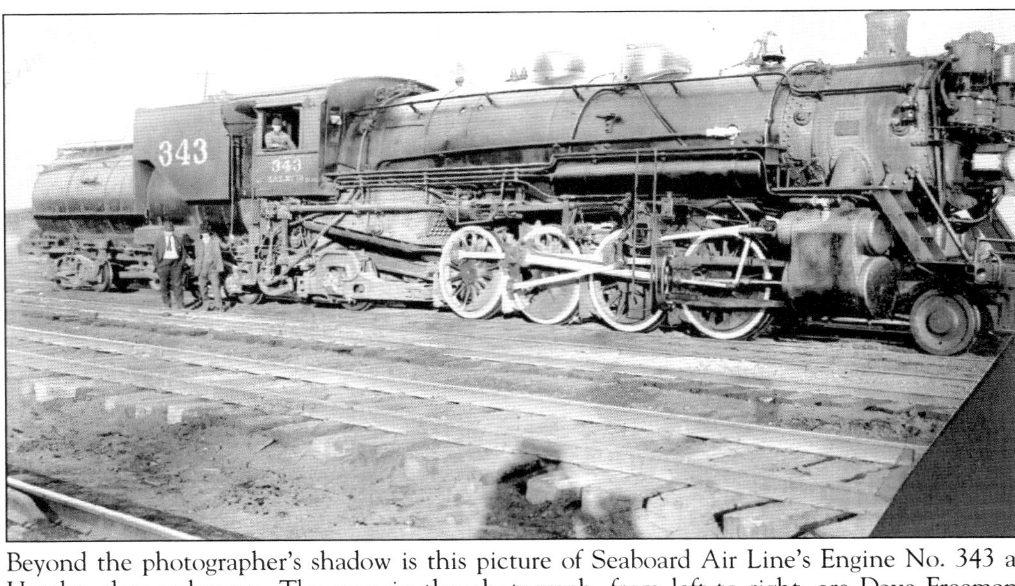

Beyond the photographer's shadow is this picture of Seaboard Air Line's Engine No. 343 at Hamlet, date unknown. The men in the photograph, from left to right, are Dave Freeman, master mechanic; H.L. Barrett, engineer; and Earl Knight, fireman. (Courtesy A&H.)

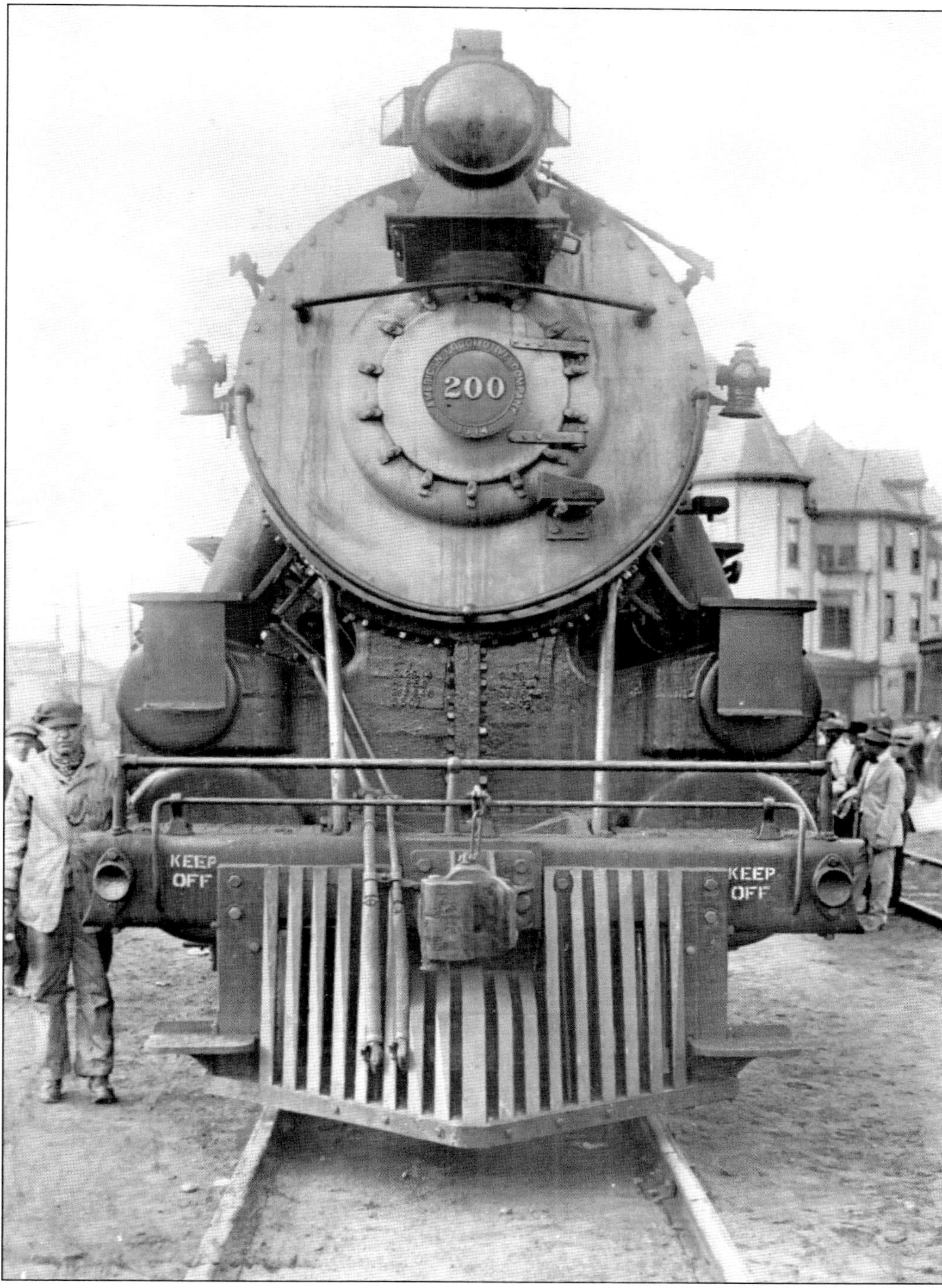

Marchant took this frontal view of Seaboard Air Line Engine No. 200 at Hamlet about 1914. The man at left is probably the engineer, and the Seaboard Hotel is partially visible in the background. The identification plate on the steam locomotive reveals that the American Locomotive Company of Richmond, Virginia, built the engine in 1914. (Courtesy Wayne Chapman.)

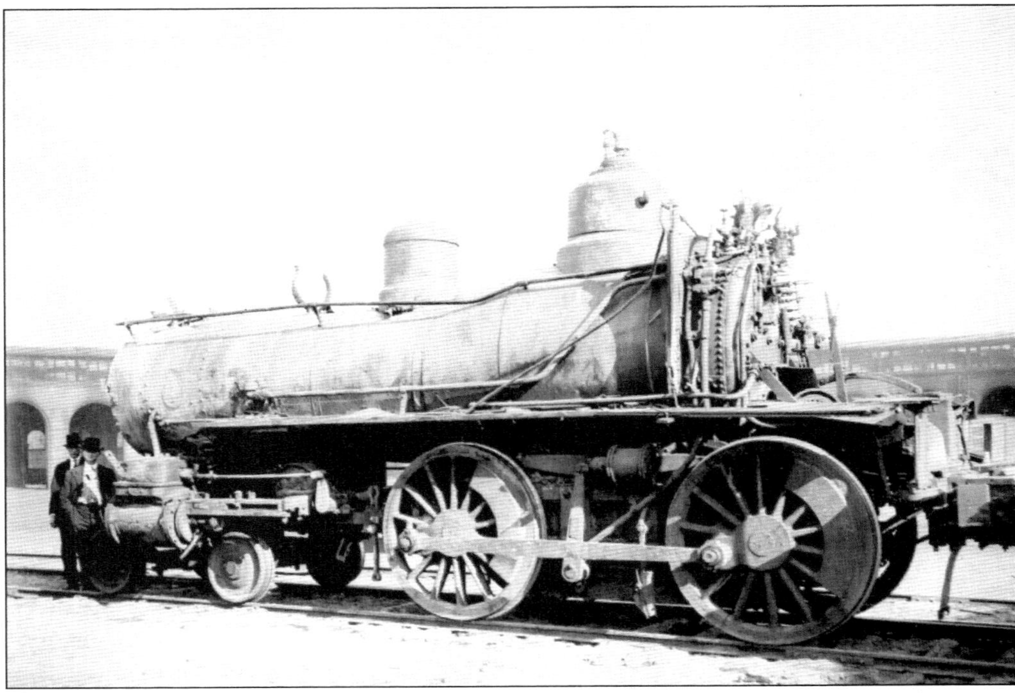

Two men pose beside an unidentified engine with its cab removed at the Seaboard Air Line Railway roundhouse at Hamlet, date unknown. (Courtesy A&H.)

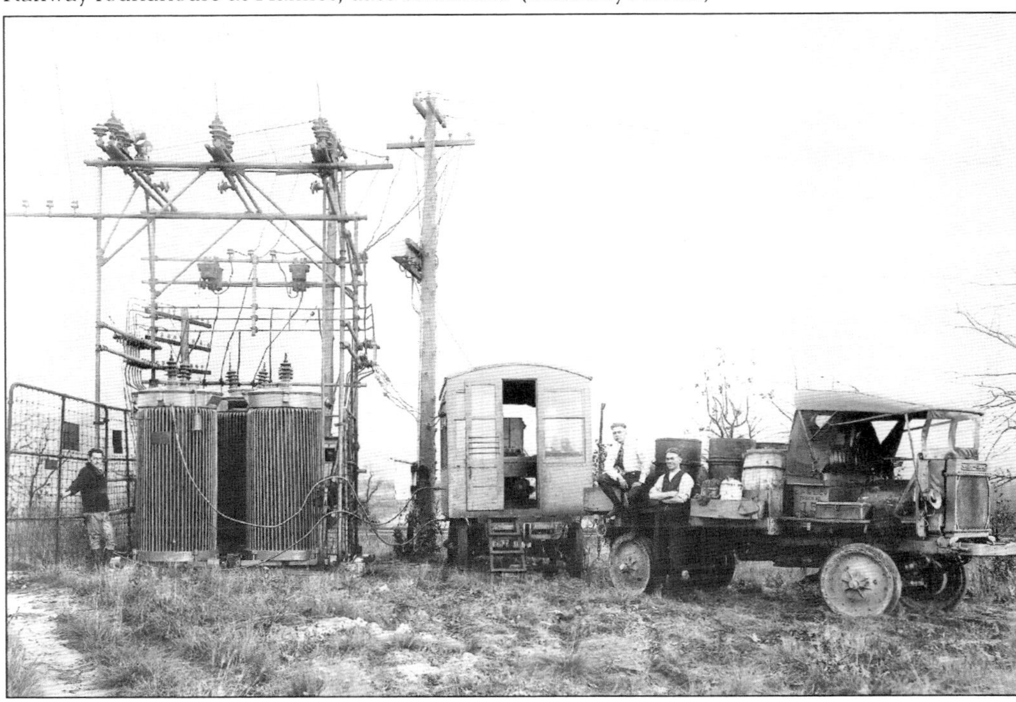

Workers pose with a truck at the Seaboard Air Line Railway electrical power plant at the shops near Hamlet in 1921. (Courtesy A&H.)

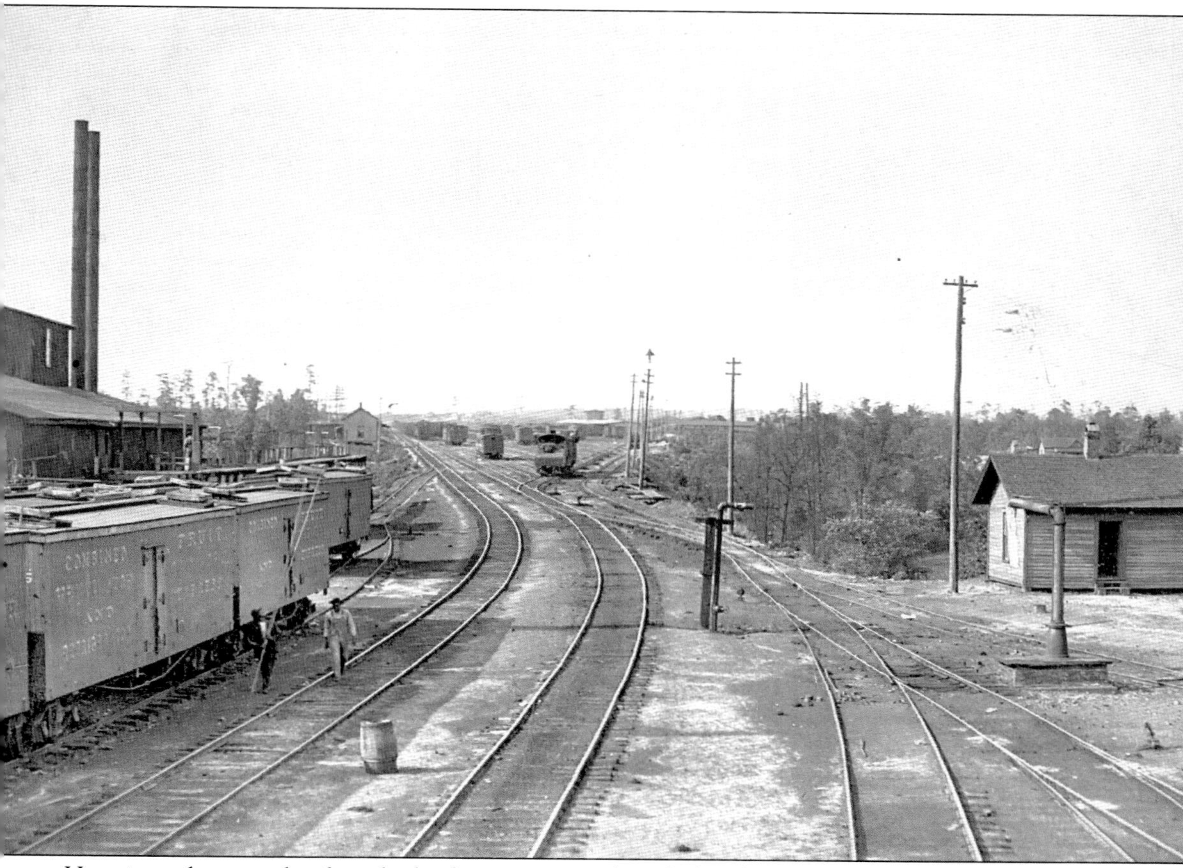

Here is a photograph of tracks leading to an unidentified railroad yard. At left is possibly a sawmill. This undated image perhaps shows a portion of the Seaboard Air Line Railway yard at Hamlet. (Courtesy A&H.)

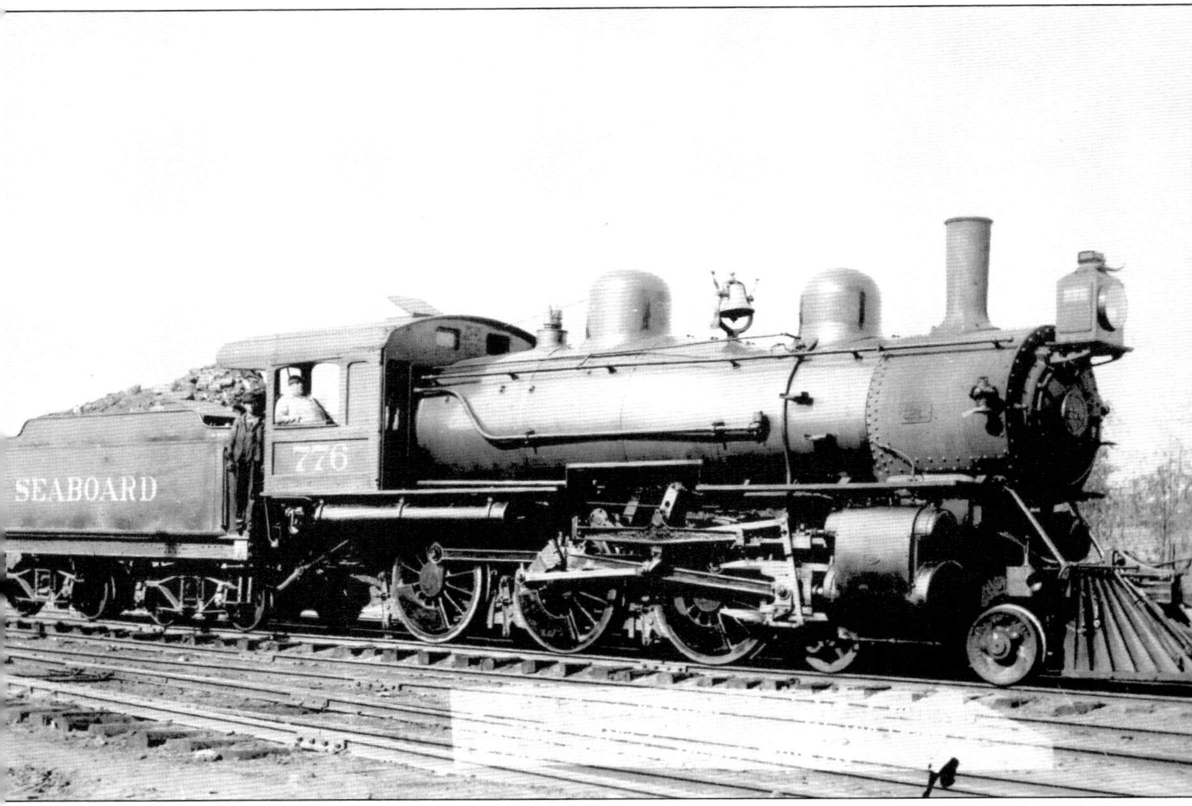

Marchant traveled the rails to Norlina, North Carolina, to obtain this view of Seaboard Air Line's ten-wheel Freight Engine No. 776 about 1911. Seated in the cab is engineer P.B. Bishop, and standing is fireman Ellis Horton. (Courtesy Phil Perkinson.)

Four

Wrecks and Derailments

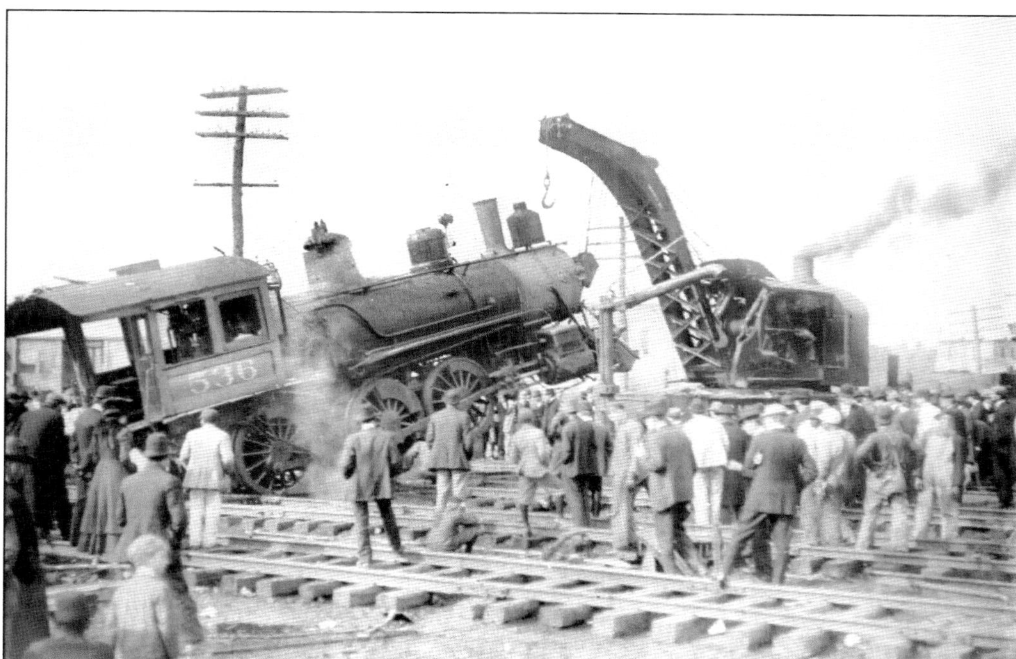

Observers watch Seaboard Air Line Engine No. 536 being lifted back onto the tracks by a steam-powered derrick, date and place unknown. (Courtesy A&H.)

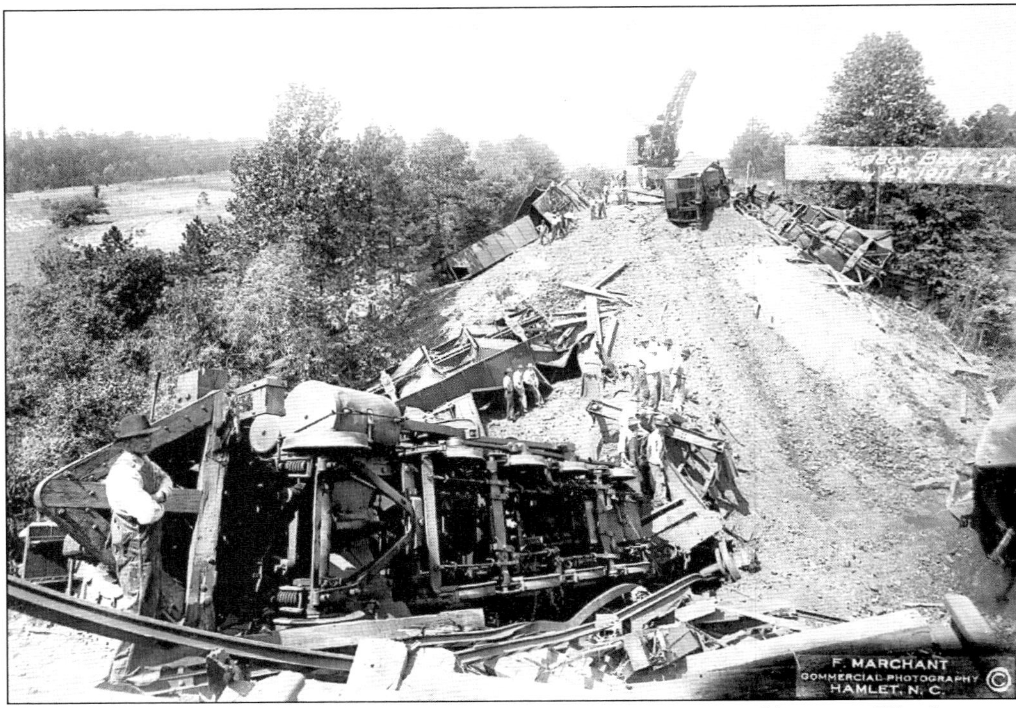

These photographs show the aftermath of a train wreck that occurred between Ellenboro and Bostic in Rutherford County, North Carolina. The site of the accident was the Watkins Creek trestle. The wooden bridge apparently collapsed under the weight of a double-header Seaboard Air Line Railway coal train. (Courtesy A&H.)

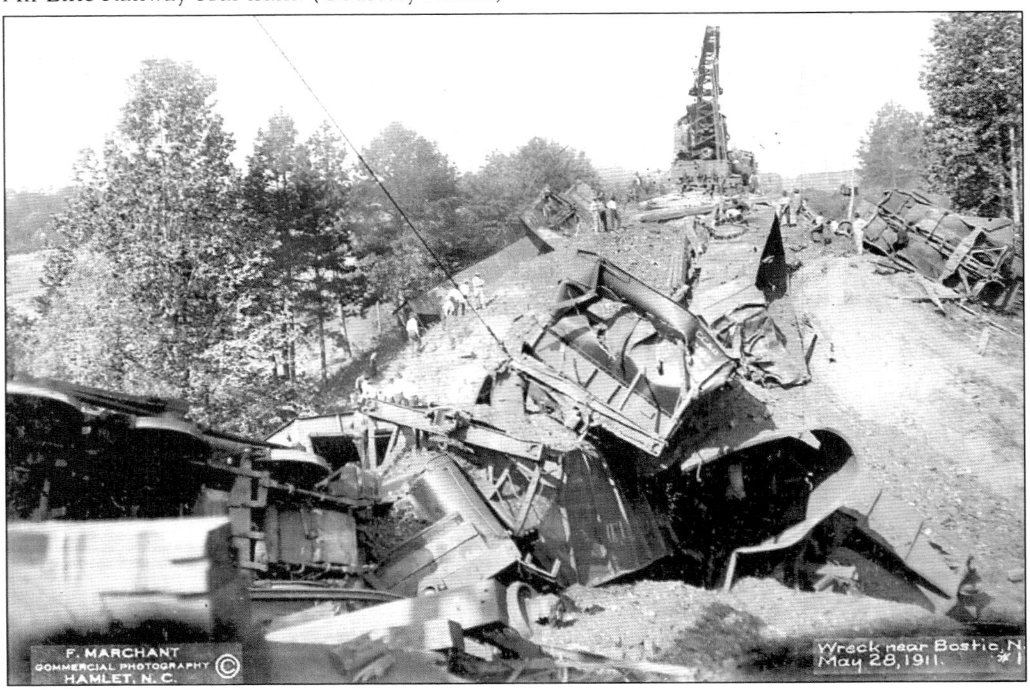

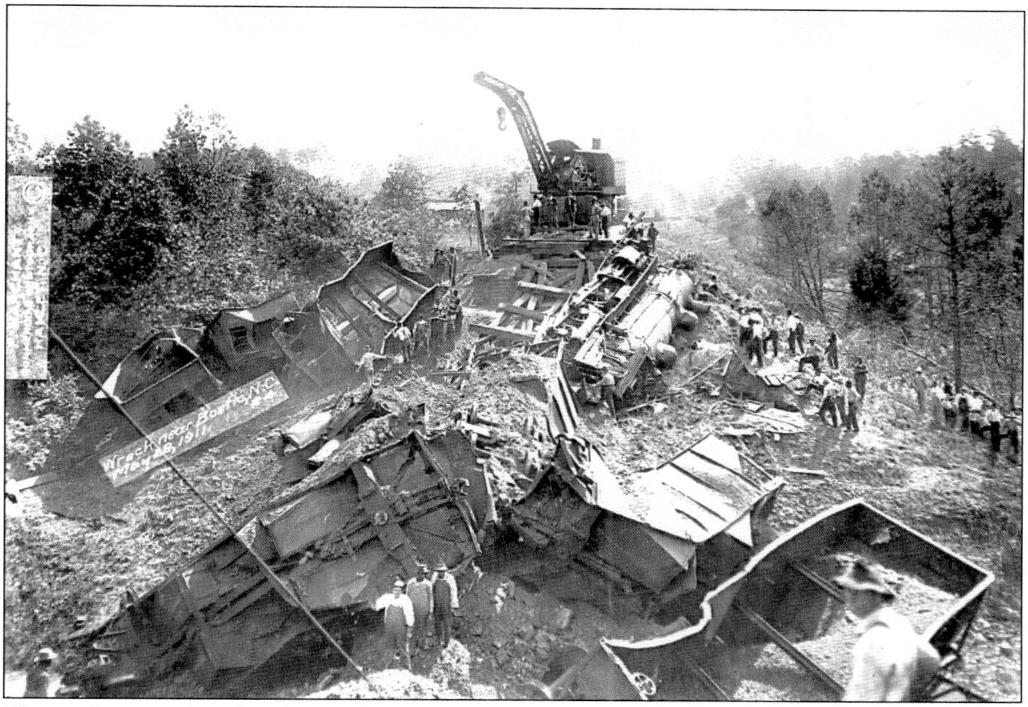

These photographs also depict the train wreck in Rutherford County. Both engines of the eastbound train plummeted 40 feet into the creek bed and were buried under the coal cars. Three of the train's crewmen were killed, and two were seriously injured. A railroad derrick was employed to assist with the cleanup of the wreckage. (Courtesy A&H.)

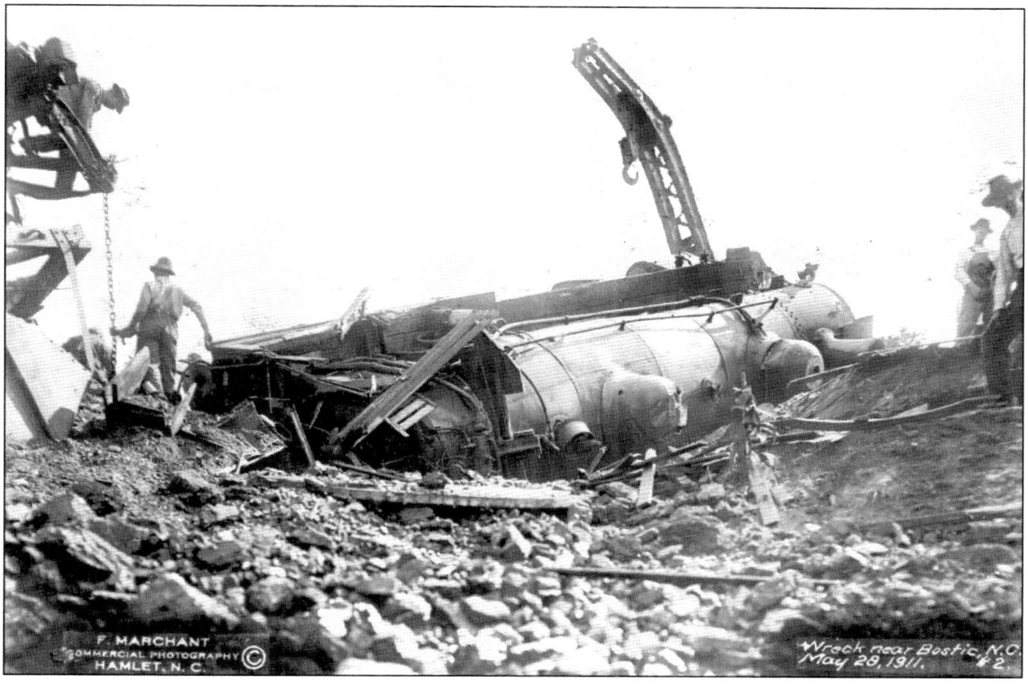

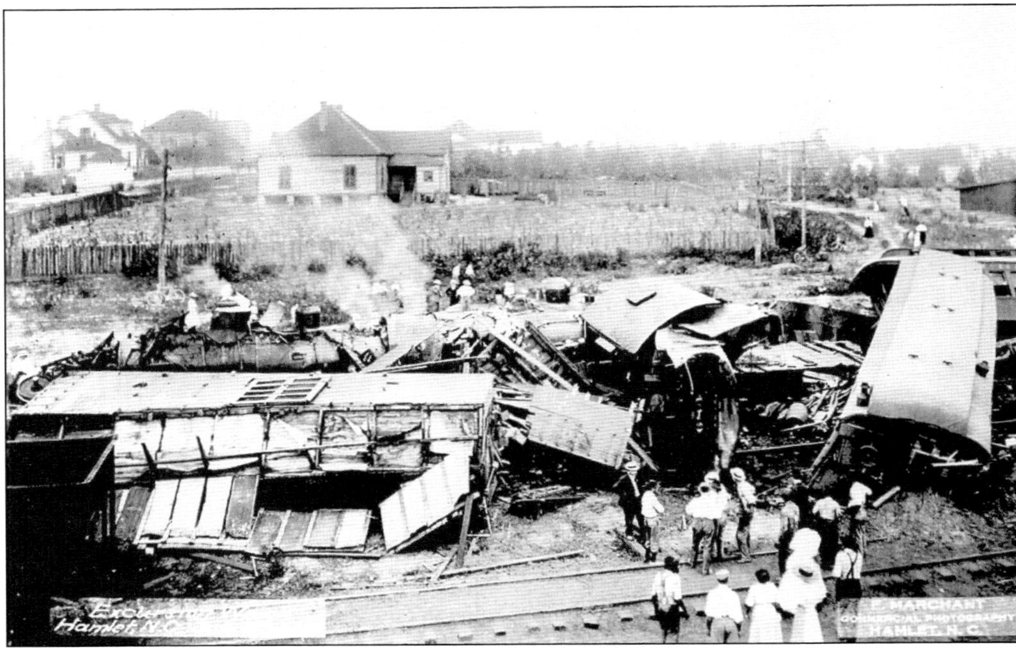

One of the worst railroad accidents in the history of Richmond County took place in Hamlet on July 27, 1911. Marchant and his camera were quickly on the scene, and the following eight photographs graphically document the tragedy. (Courtesy A&H.)

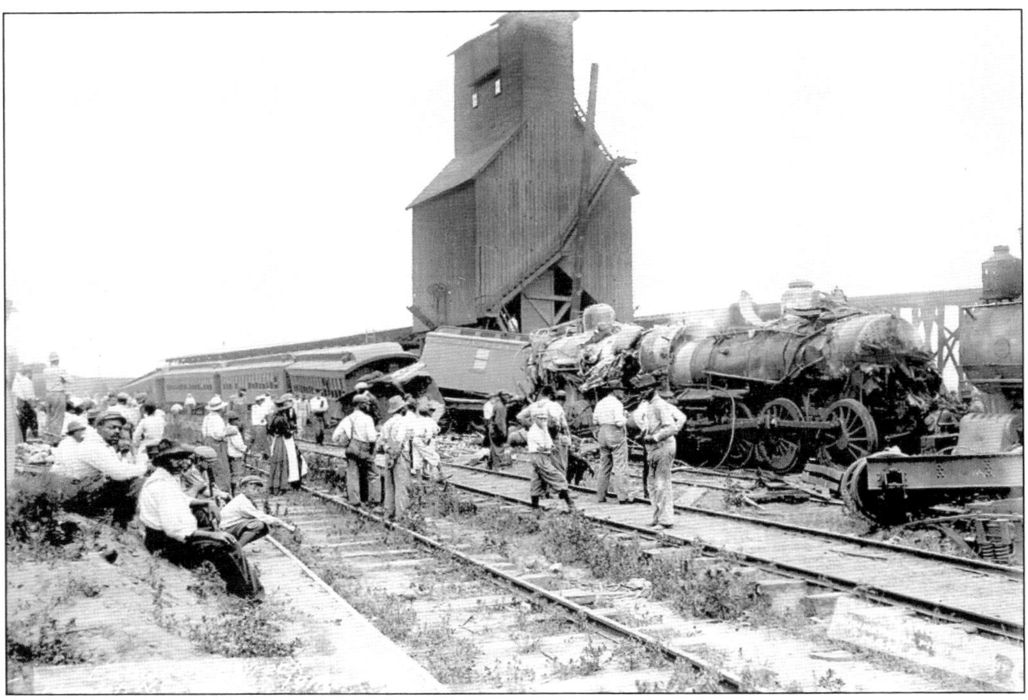

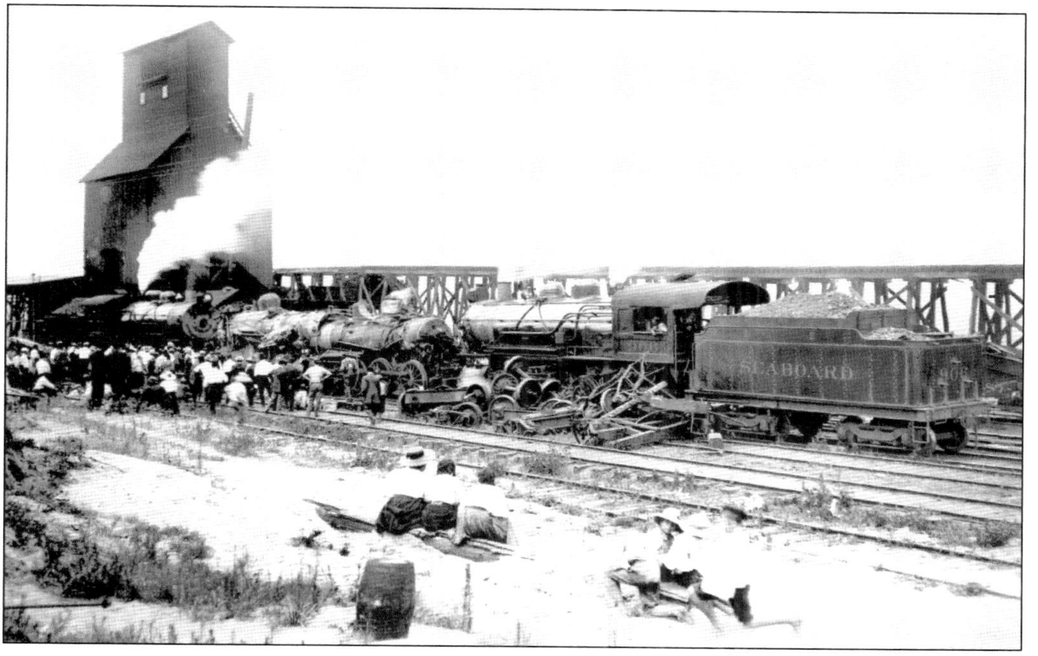

The accident occurred when an excursion train from Durham, bound for Charlotte, collided head-on with a slowly moving freight train near the roundhouse at Hamlet. (Courtesy A&H.)

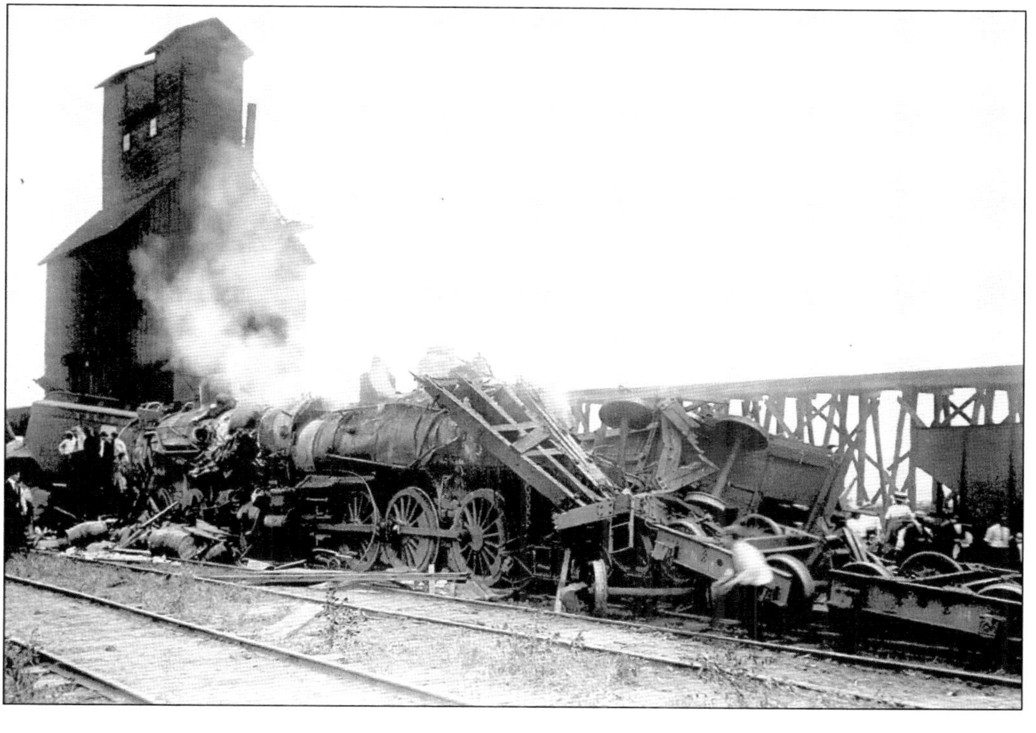

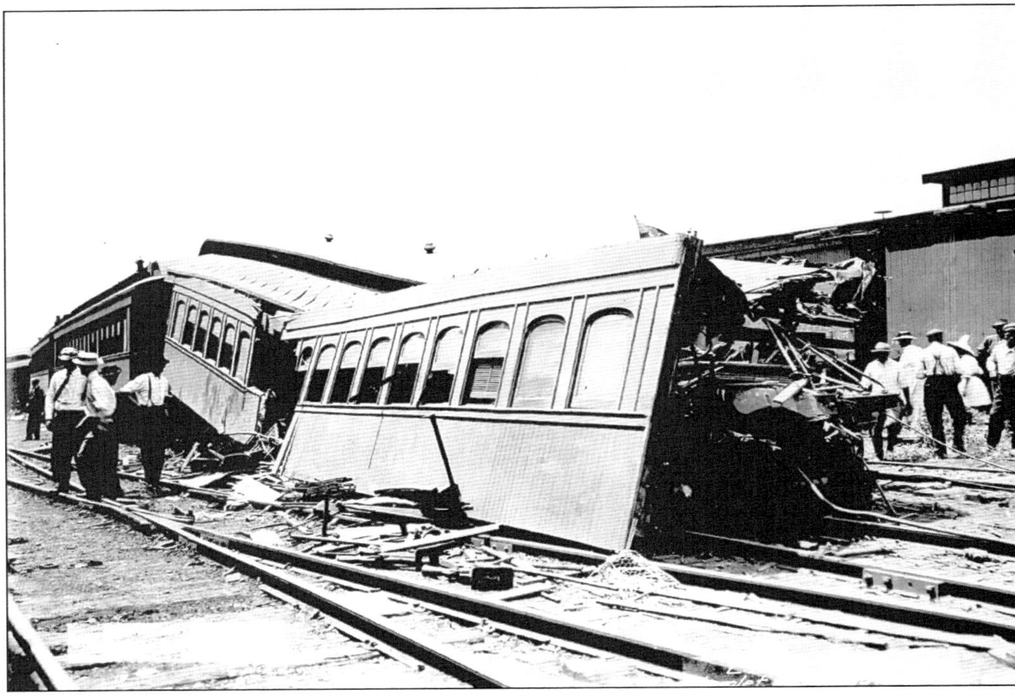

These photographs also depict the train accident from July 27, 1911. More than 900 passengers were packed aboard the train, which was transporting them on a religious outing sponsored by St. Joseph's African Methodist Episcopal Church in Durham. (Courtesy A&H.)

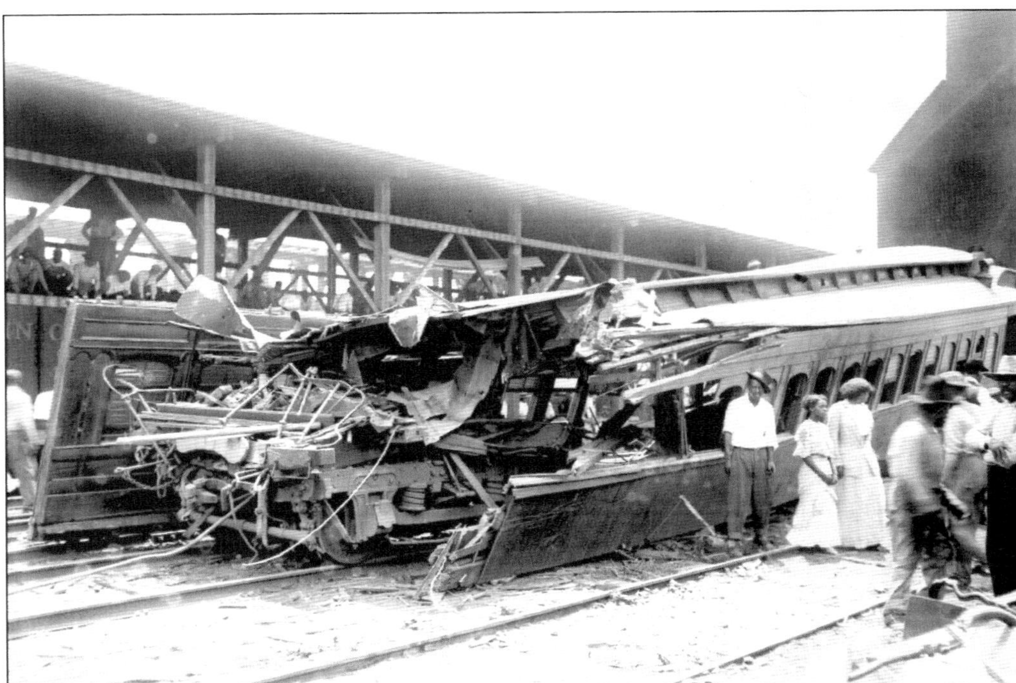

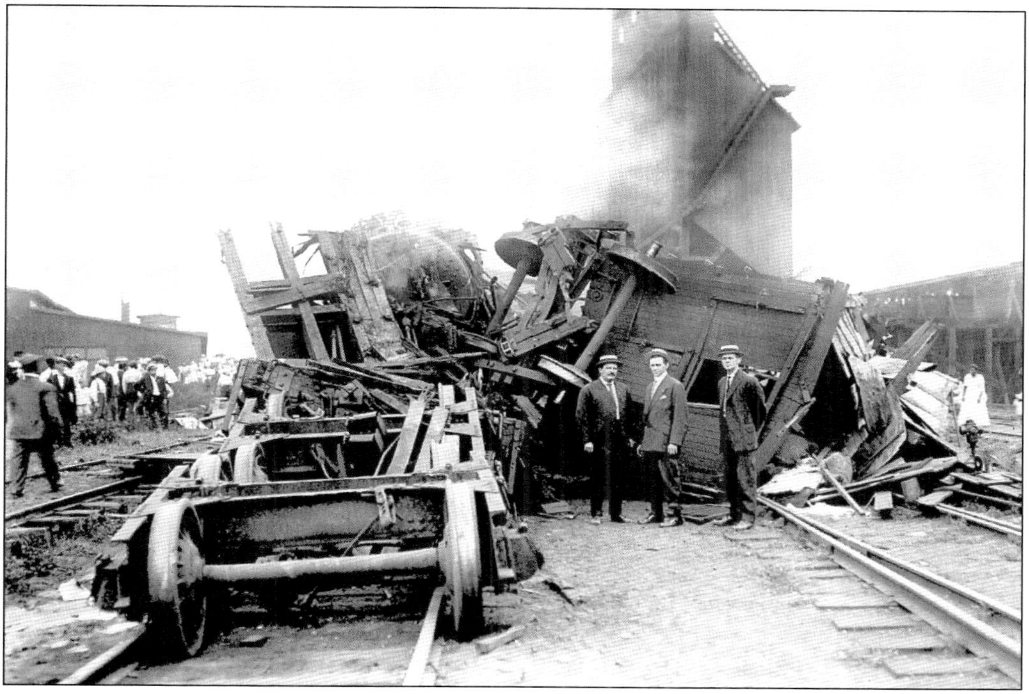

Eleven people were killed and 75 were seriously injured in the Richmond County accident from 1911. (Courtesy A&H.)

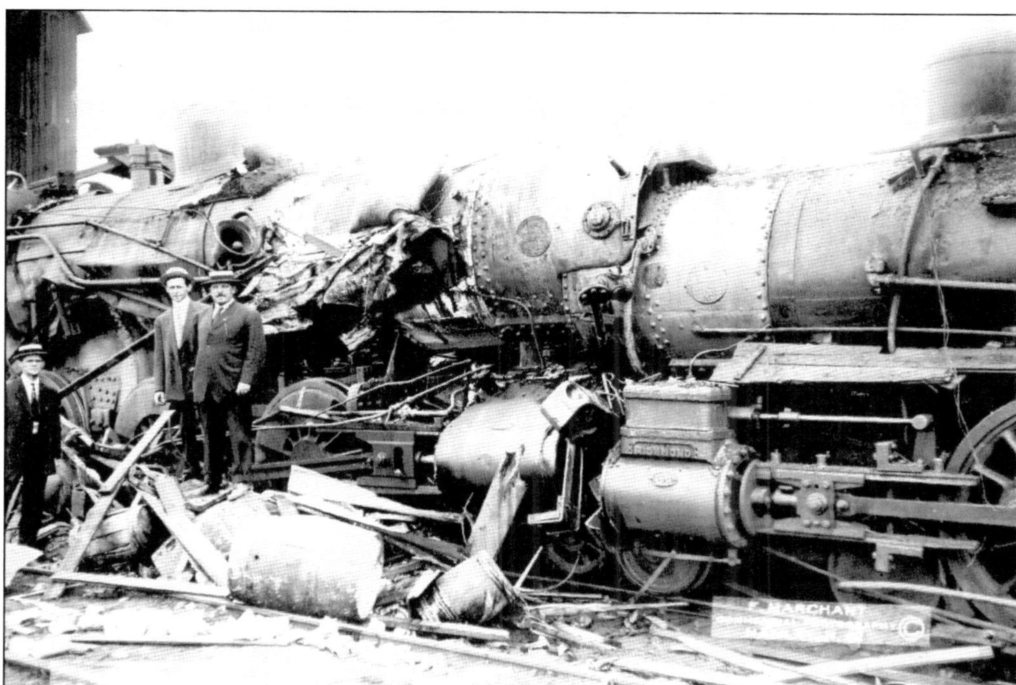

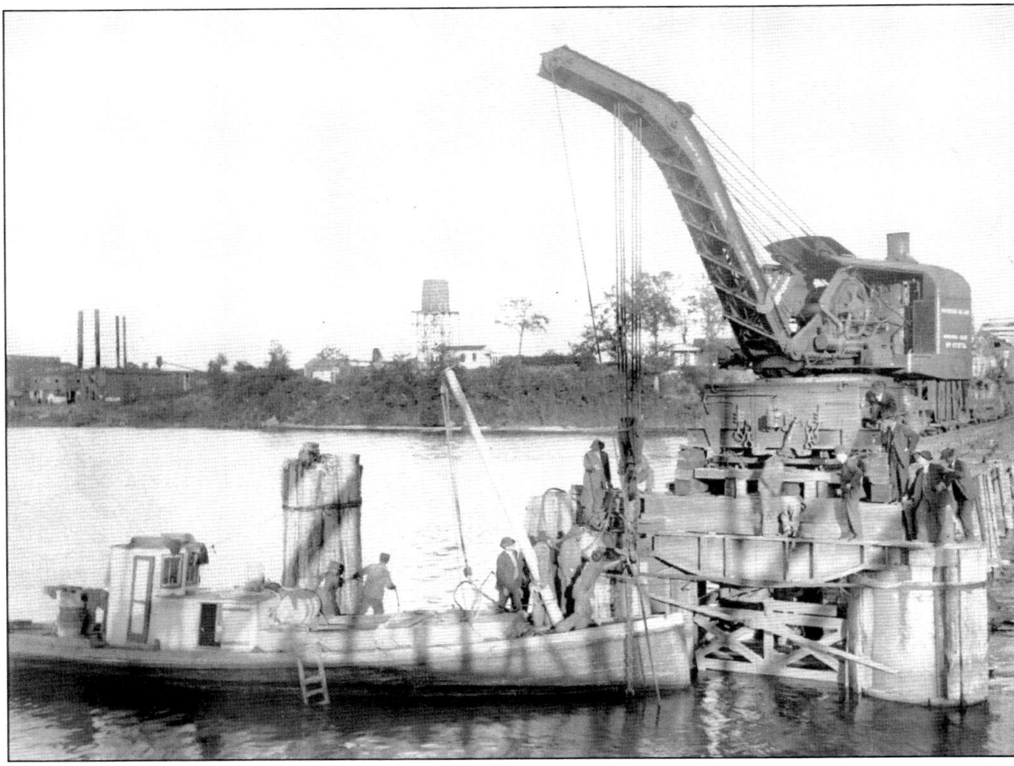

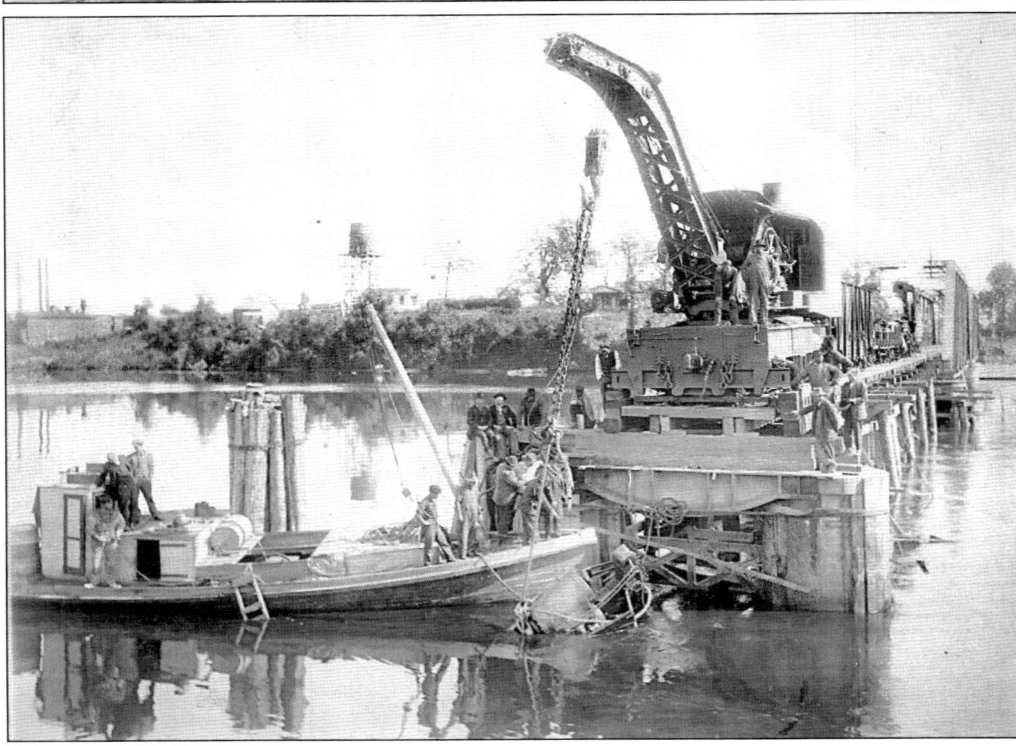

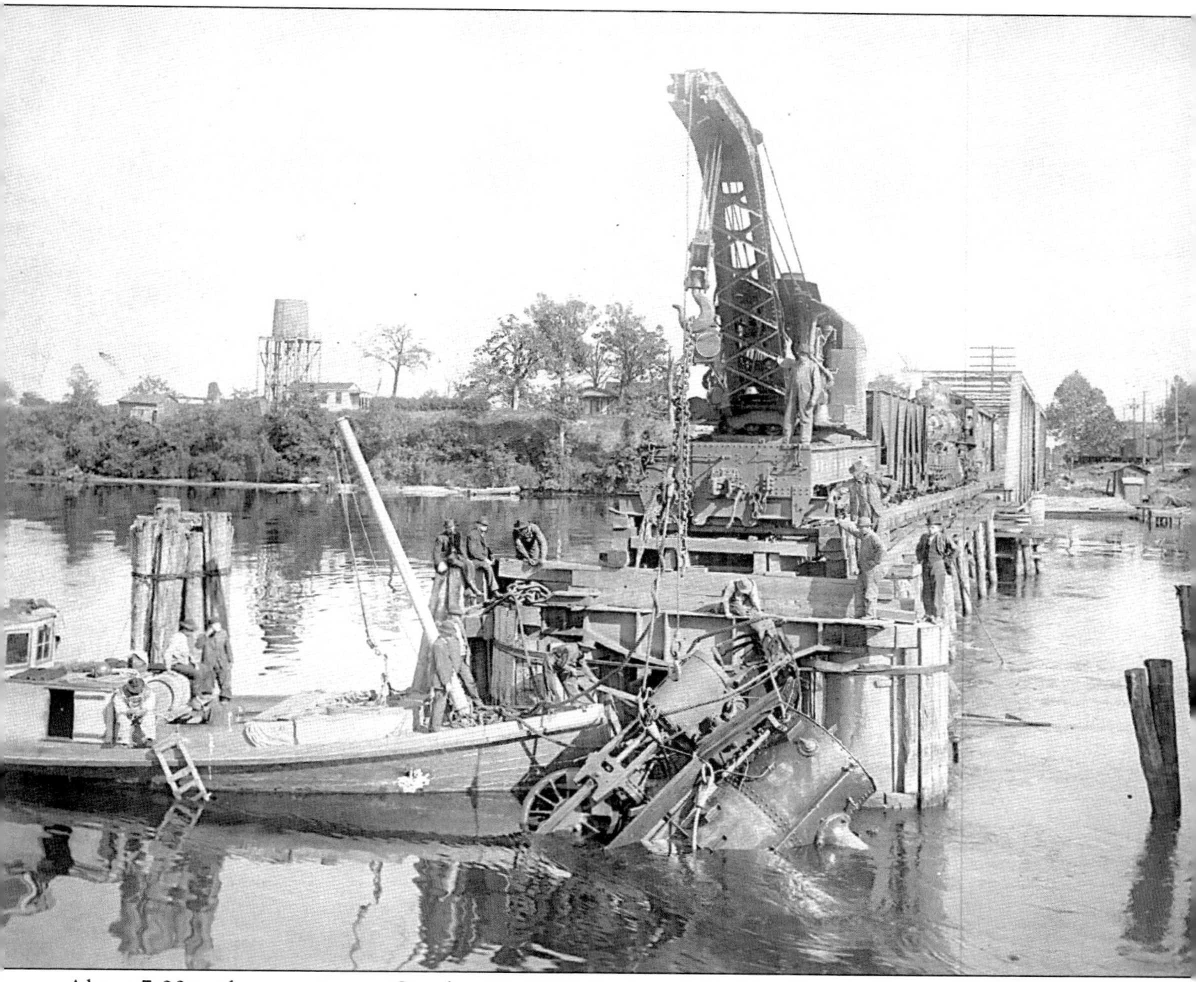

About 7:00 in the morning on October 29, 1914, Seaboard Air Line Freight Engine No. 733 was outward bound from Wilmington, pulling a string of cars. As the train neared the Hilton Bridge over the Cape Fear River, heavy fog prevented the engineer from seeing that the drawbridge was open. The engineer applied the brakes but could not prevent the engine from plunging into the river. It twisted loose from the tender and other cars and sank some nine feet to the bottom of the river.

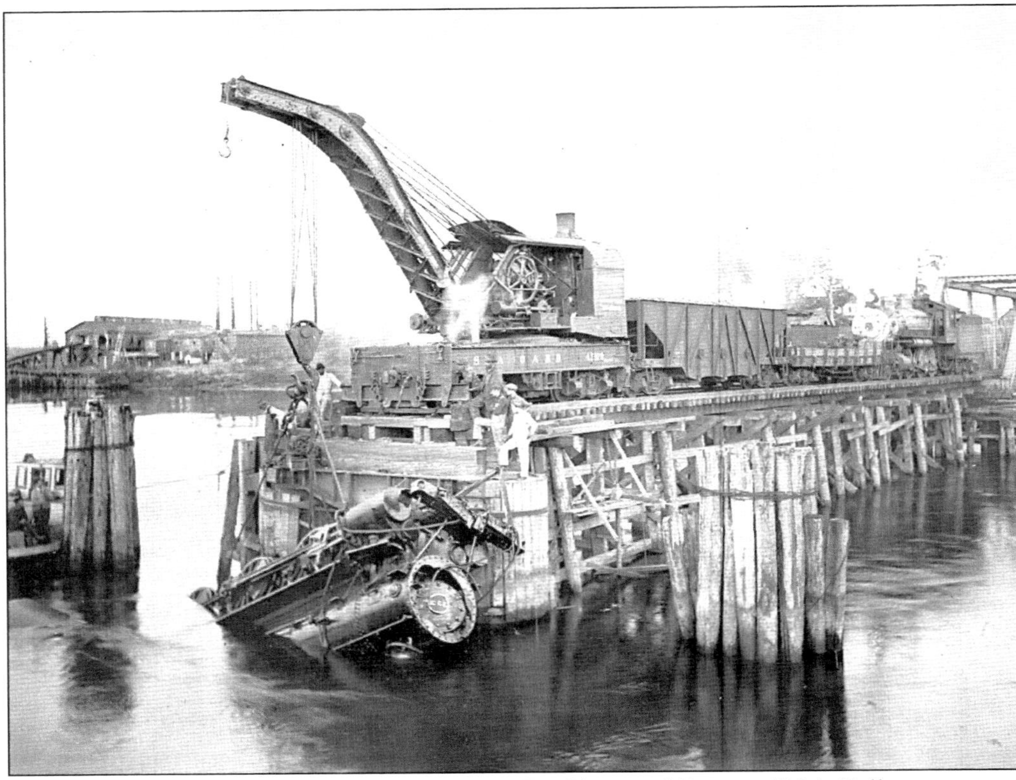

In the wreck of Engine No. 733, Engineer C.D. Bradshaw and Fireman R.M. Galloway escaped injury by jumping to the tender before the engine fell into the water. A fertilizer company's boat was towing a barge through the opening. The images on pages 58 through 60 show a railroad derrick lifting the engine from the river. (Courtesy A&H.)

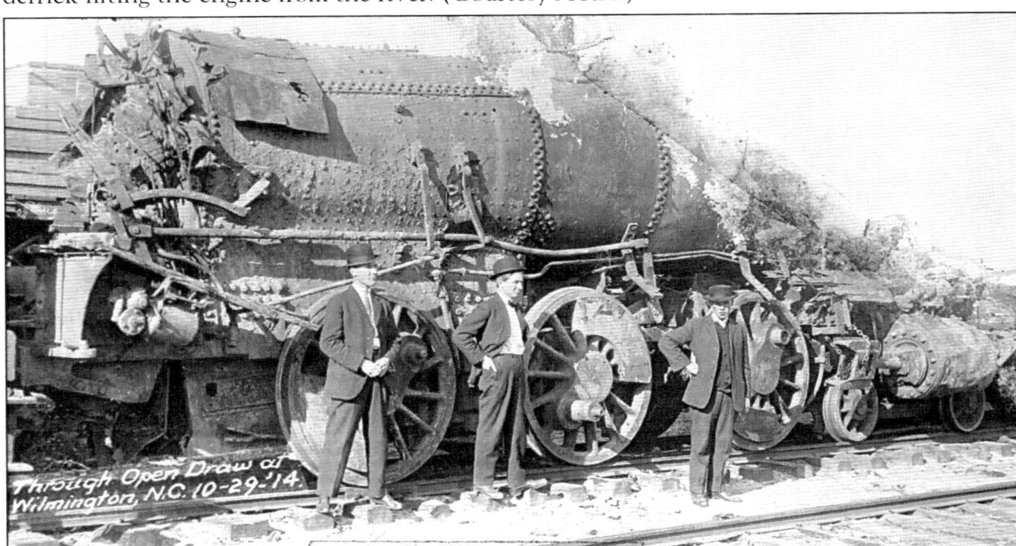

Several unidentified men posed with the damaged engine after it had been hoisted upon the tracks. (Courtesy A&H.)

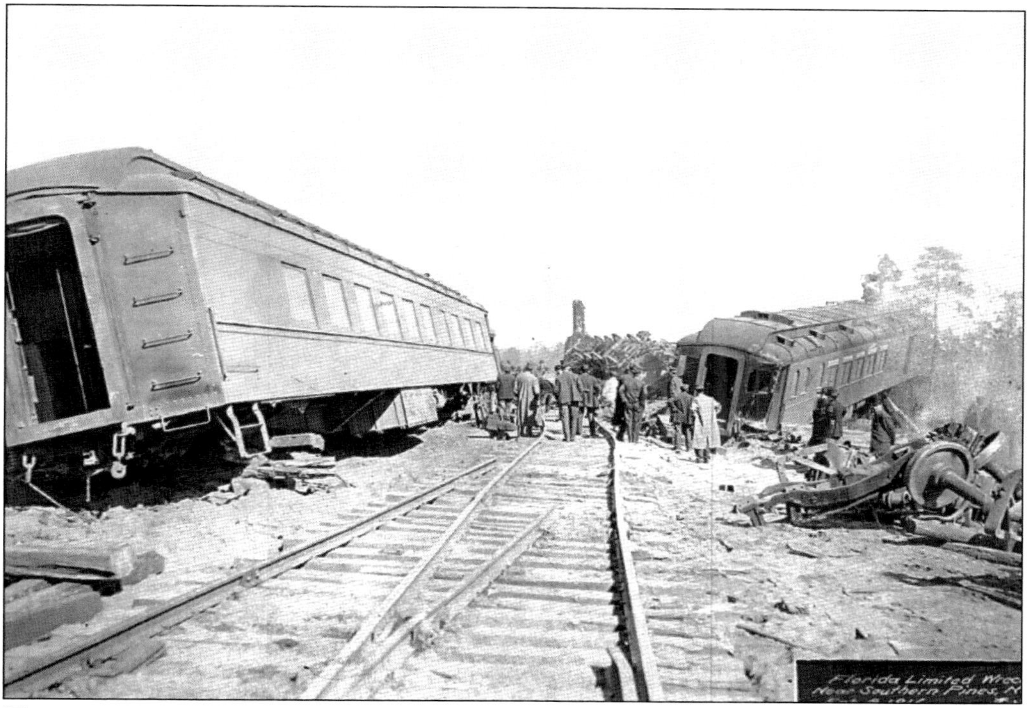

These two images are part of a series of photographs taken by Marchant at the scene of the wreck of the *Florida Limited* (Seaboard Air Line Passenger Train No. 10) near Southern Pines, North Carolina, on February 8, 1916. The train was en route to Richmond, Virginia, from Jacksonville, Florida, when the engine, a dining car, and a Pullman car derailed in the early hours of the morning. Engineer David K. Albright was killed in the accident, which occurred about one mile north of the Moore County village of Niagara. (Courtesy A&H.)

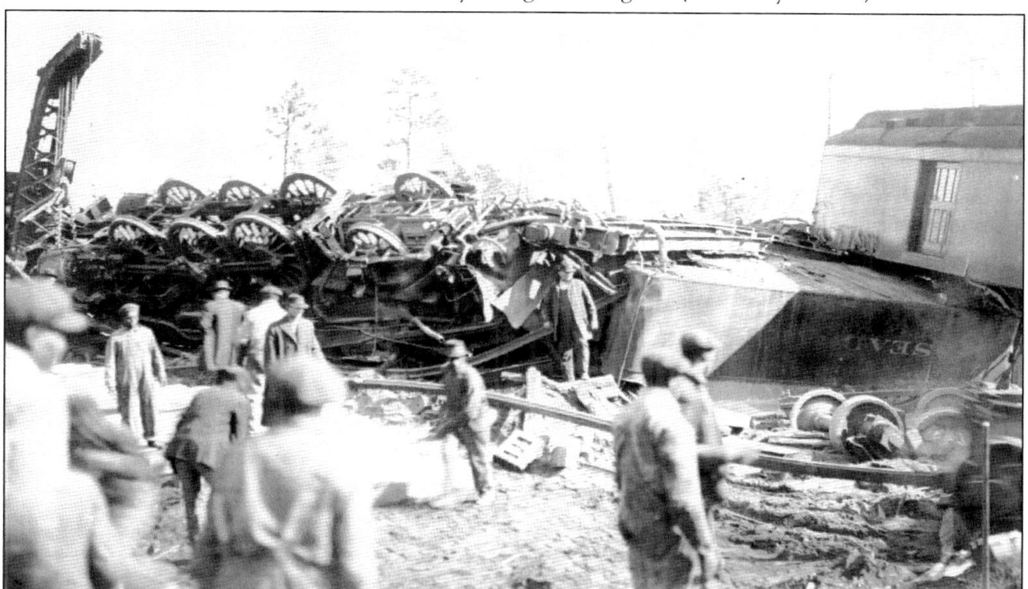

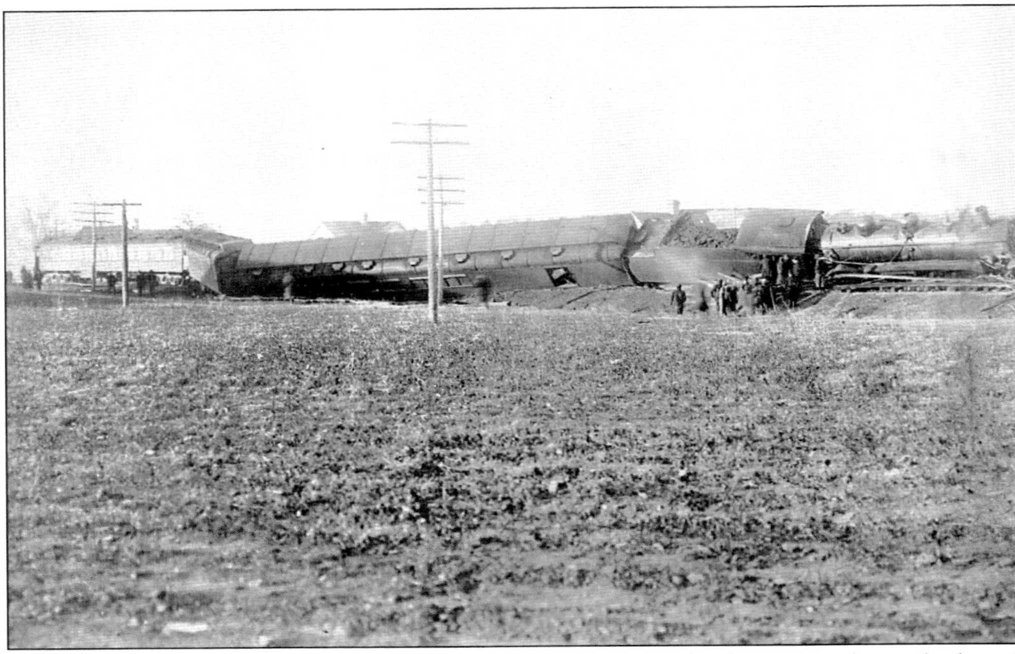

A week later, a second Florida Limited passenger train was involved in an accident, which took the life of another railroad employee. Fireman Jim Holloway was crushed to death when the northbound train collided with a freight train at Franklinton, North Carolina, on February 15, 1916. The freight train was backing onto a siding at the north switch near the Franklin County town. The freight engine had not quite cleared the main track when it was struck by the fast-moving passenger train. Photographs show the derailed sections of the passenger train and the position of the tender when the fireman was killed. (Courtesy A&H.)

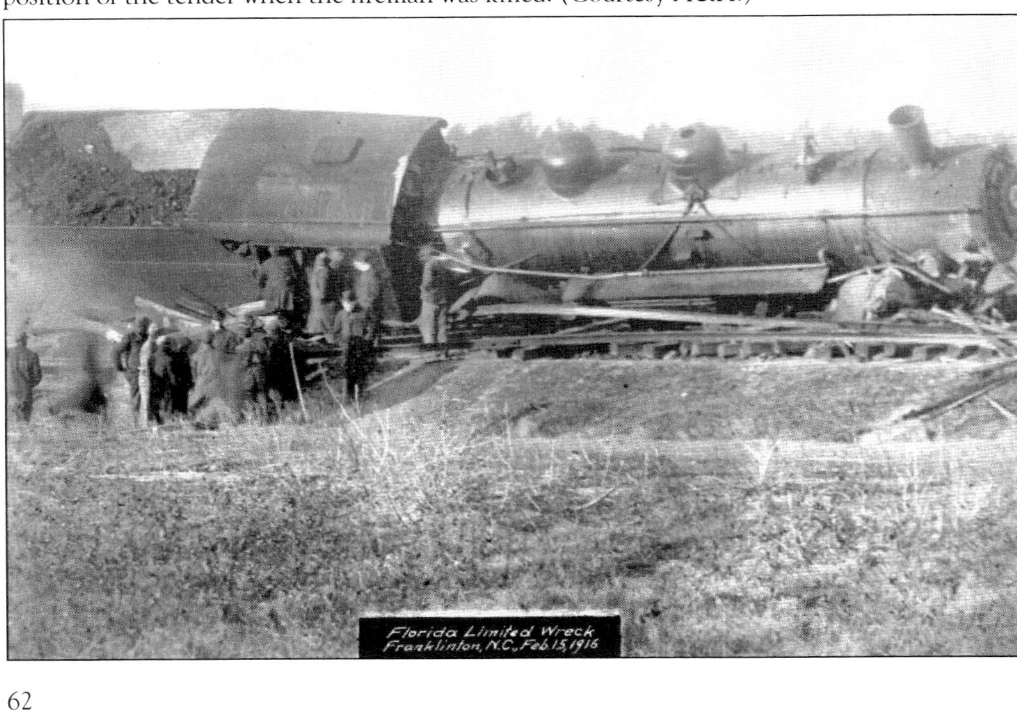

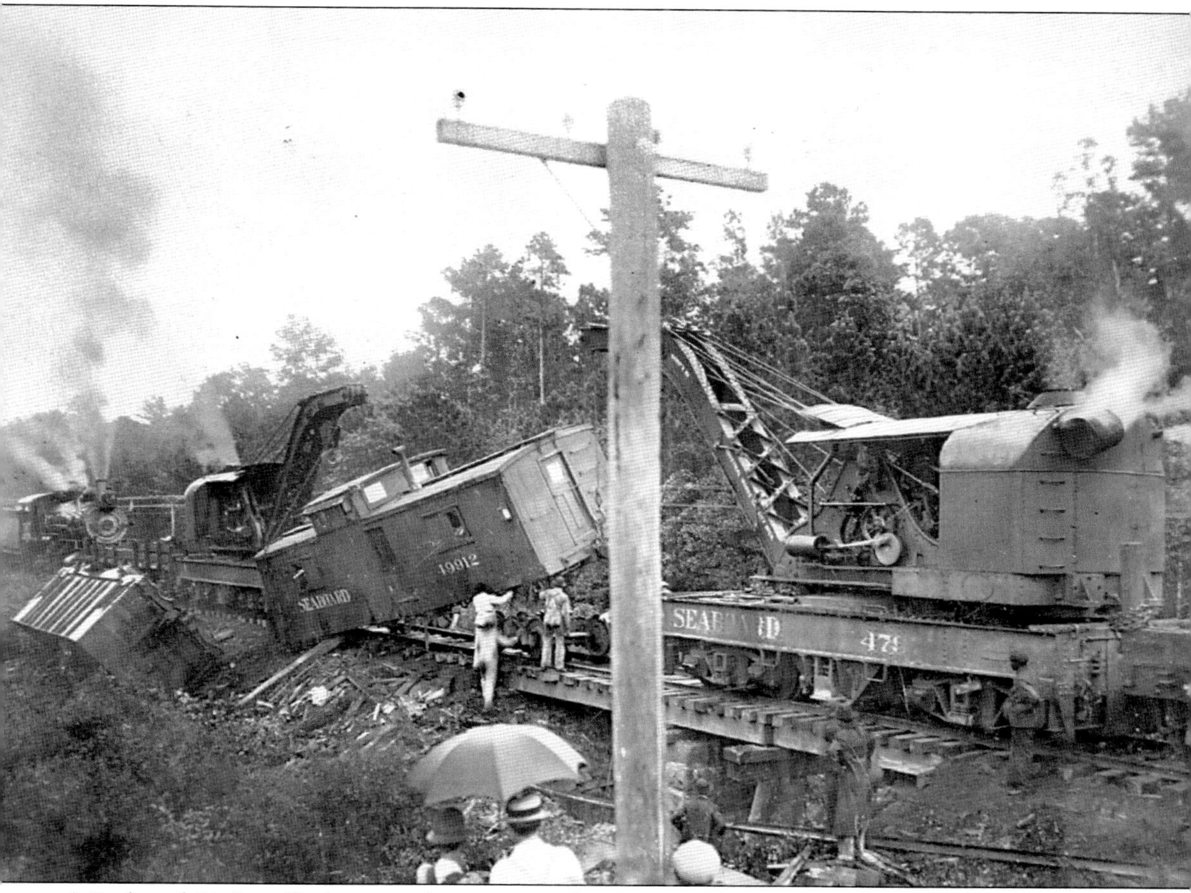

A Seaboard Air Line Railway wrecking crew used two steam-powered derricks to pull this caboose back onto the tracks. The date and place of the derailment are unknown. (Courtesy A&H.)

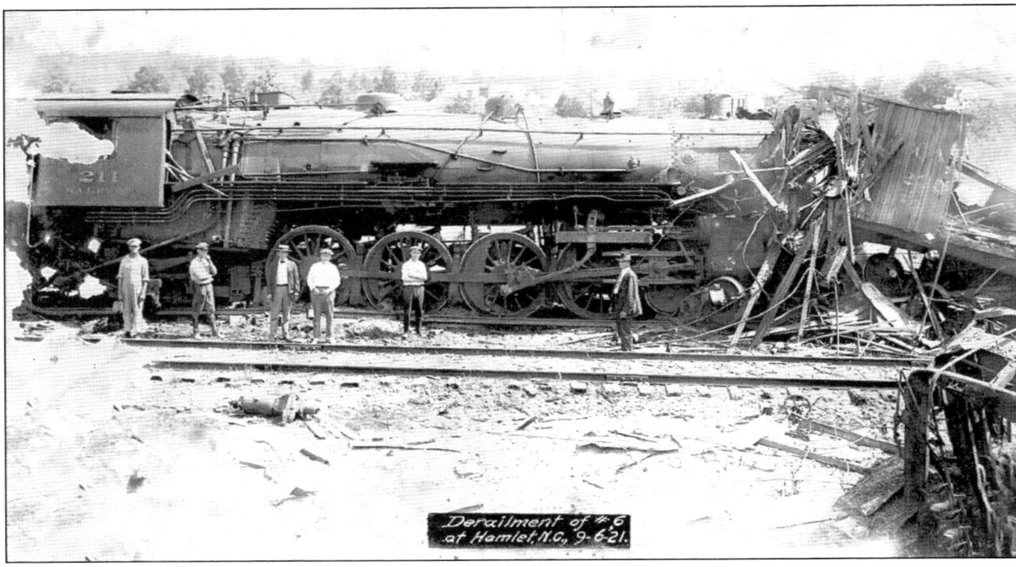

These men stand in front of the wrecked engine of Seaboard Fast Train No. 6 at Hamlet on September 6, 1921. The train, en route from Atlanta to Washington, D.C., rammed into a string of empty boxcars in the Hamlet yard. Investigators later revealed that the accident resulted when an unidentified party surreptitiously threw a switch, which diverted the train from its regular course. No one was injured in the mishap, but five boxcars were destroyed. The names of three of the men viewing the wreckage are (third from left) ? Poindexter, (fifth from left) John Watts Freeman, and (far left) C.C. Jones. (Courtesy A&H.)

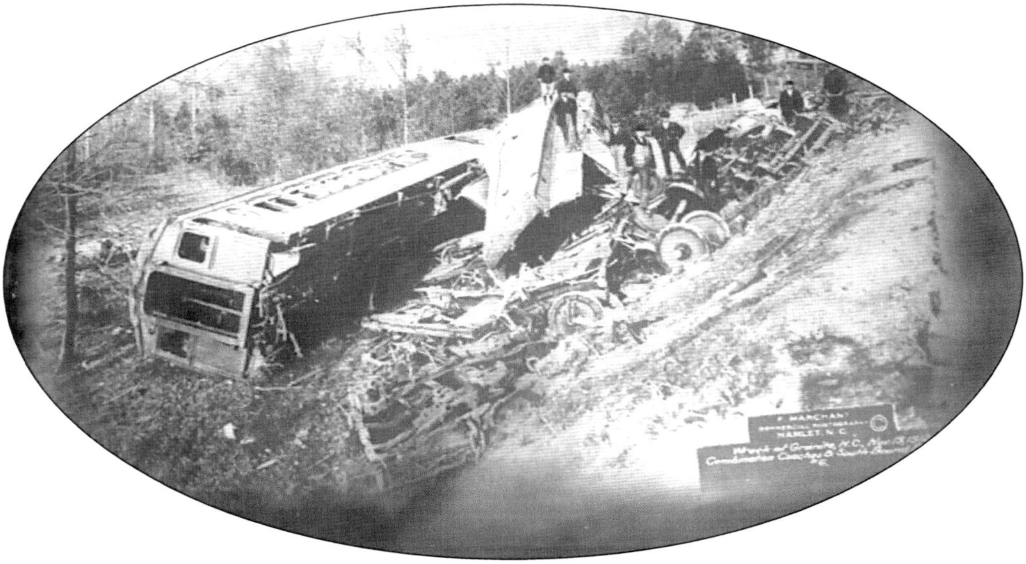

Reproduced here is a photograph of the wreckage of two Seaboard Air Line passenger through trains that collided head-on near Granite Station in northern Warren County on November 19, 1912. Men stand atop combination cars and the remains of south-bound Engine No. 6. North-bound train No. 84 and south-bound train No. 81 met at full speed just north of the station. Eight people were killed, including the two engineers Cornelius H. Beckham (born 1866) and William A. Faison (born *c.* 1861). (Courtesy T.T. Beckham.)

Five

Blewett Falls and Electric Power

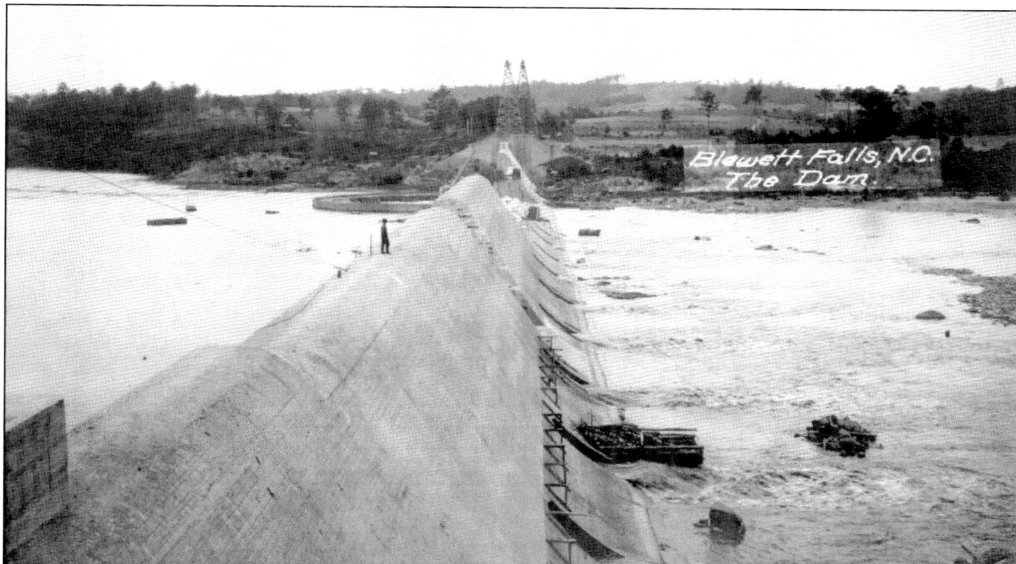

The Great Pee Dee Electric & Power Company began work on Blewett Falls Dam where the Pee Dee River separates Anson and Richmond Counties in 1905. Its purpose was to generate hydroelectric power to build and operate mills, power companies, transmission lines, railways, turnpikes, and telephone and telegraph systems. The company's name changed to Rockingham Power Company in 1906. Financial difficulties and construction problems ensued, and the Yadkin River Power Company was formed to complete the Blewett Falls project. The dam, located about nine miles northwest of Rockingham, was finished on December 15, 1911. The hydroelectric plant first produced power in February 1912. Here, a man stands atop the almost-completed dam about 1911. (Courtesy Durwood Barbour.)

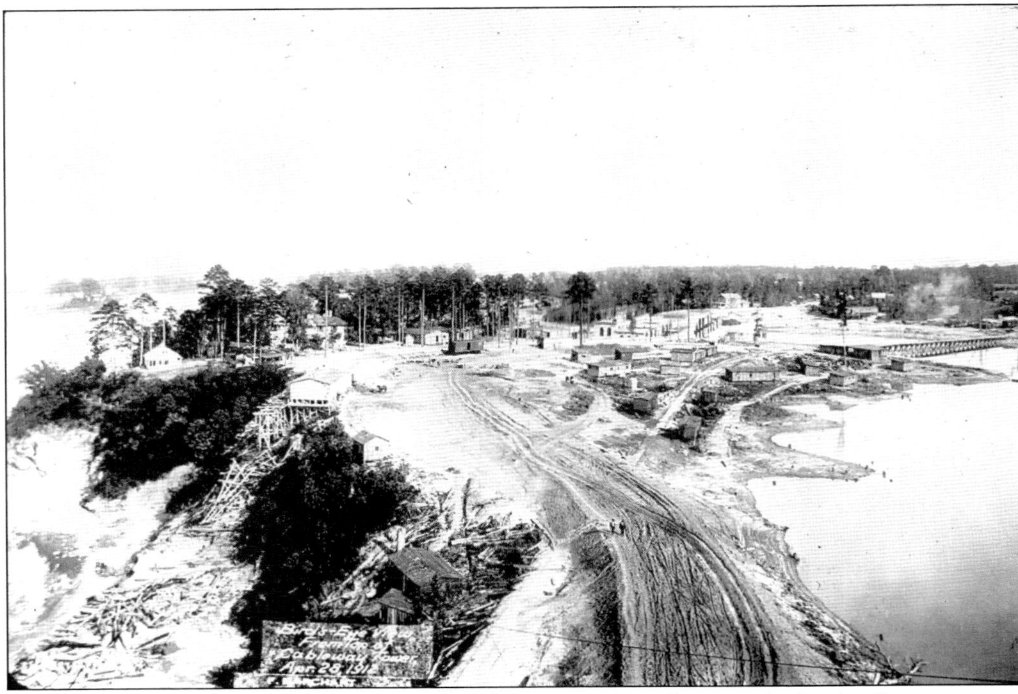

Marchant climbed to the summit of the cableway tower to photograph this bird's-eye view of the dam construction site on April 28, 1912. (Courtesy A&H.)

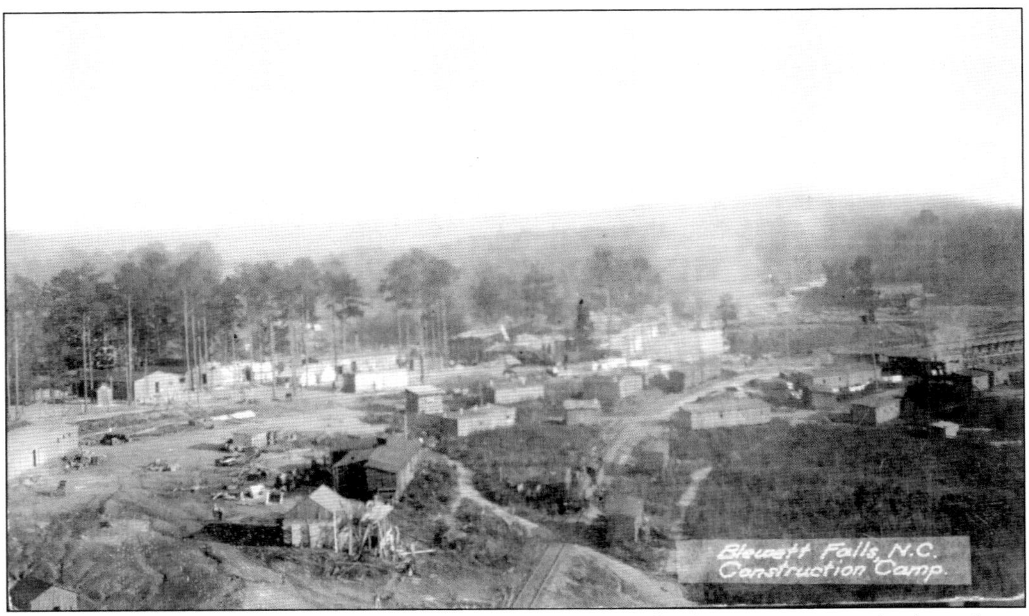

This elevated view of the construction camp at Blewett Falls about 1911 may also have been taken from the top of the cableway tower. (Courtesy Durwood Barbour.)

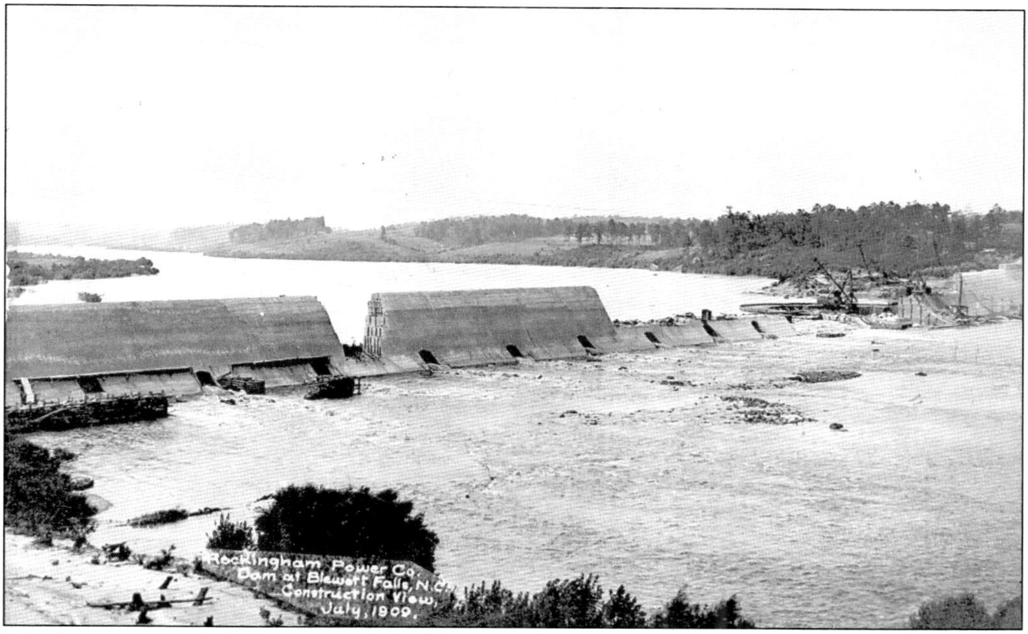

Marchant captured this distant view of the construction of the Rockingham Power Company (later Yadkin Power Company) dam in July 1909. (Courtesy A&H).

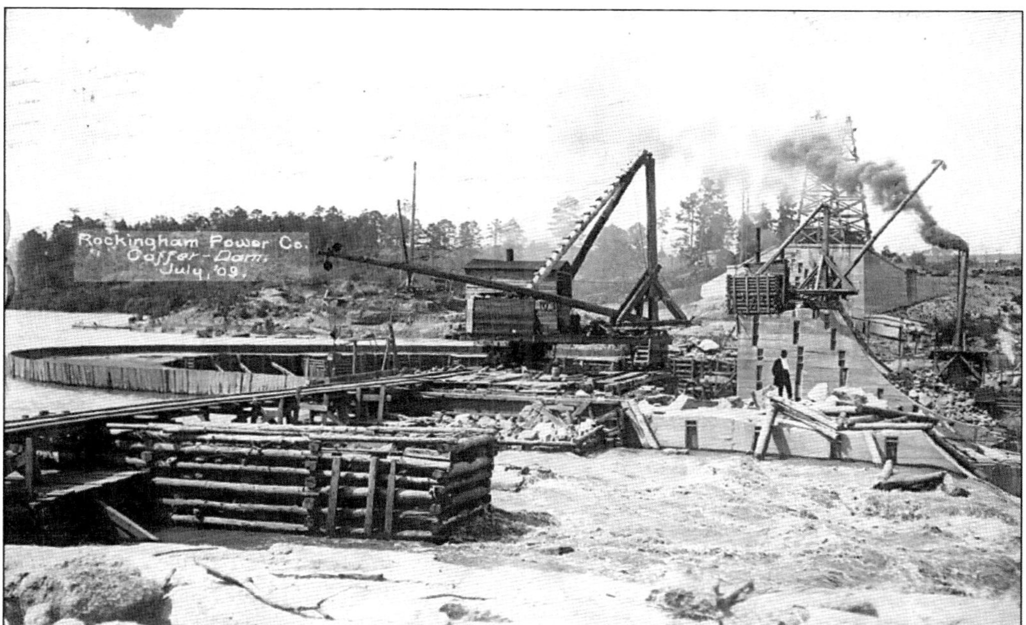

This July 1909 image features the building of a cofferdam, a temporary watertight enclosure that is pumped dry so that the remainder of the construction of the dam can be undertaken. (Courtesy Durwood Barbour.)

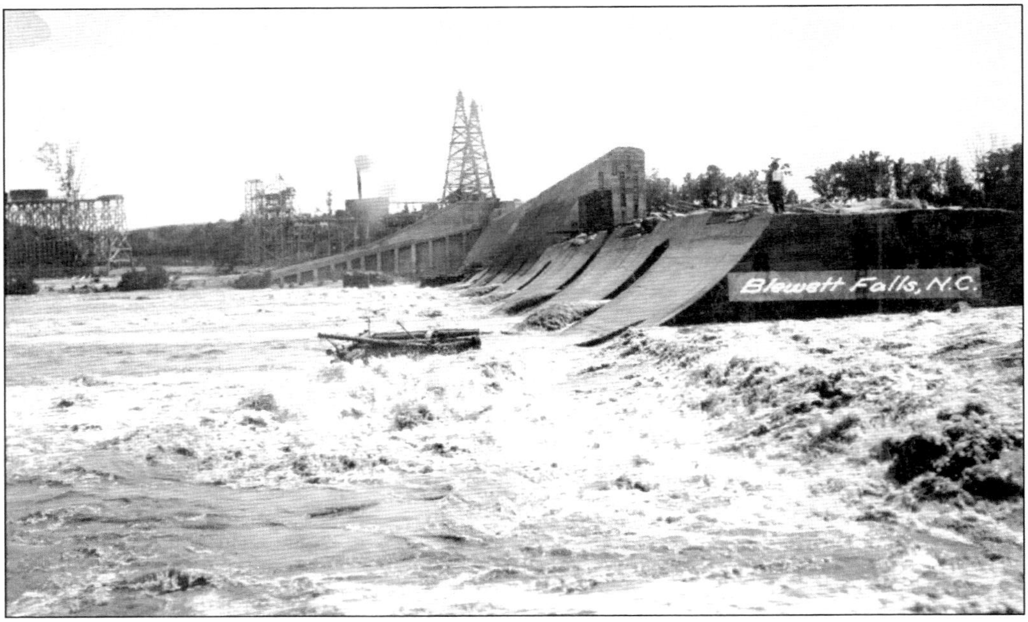

Pictured above and below on this page are two additional photographs showing the early stages of construction of the dam at Blewett Falls. (Above, courtesy C. Vernon Vallance; below, courtesy Wayne Chapman.)

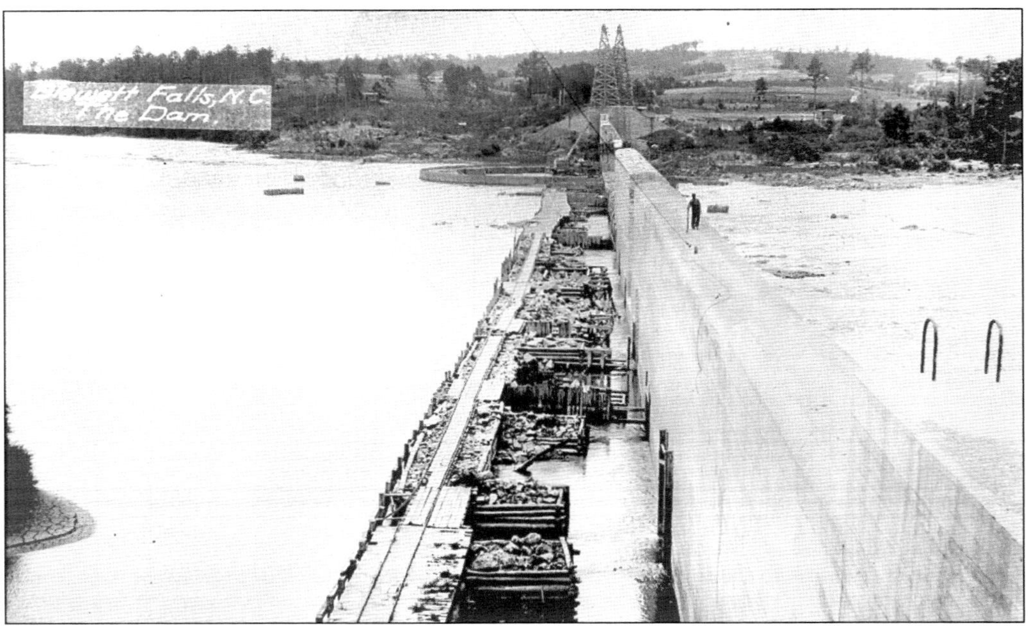

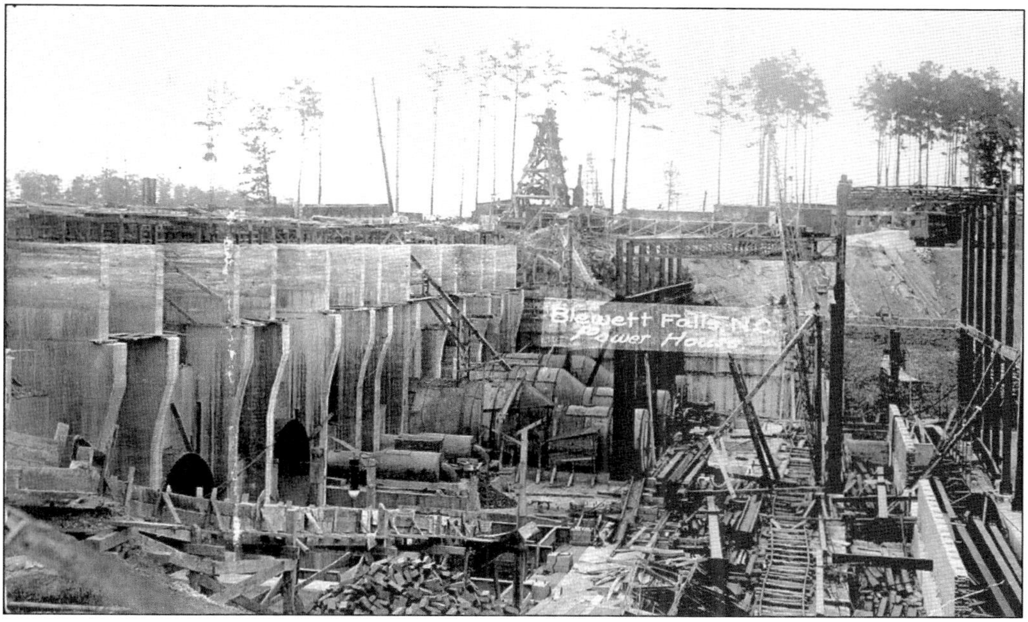

Both photographs reproduced on this page depict the beginning of the construction of the powerhouse at Blewett Falls in the autumn of 1911. (Courtesy C. Vernon Vallance.)

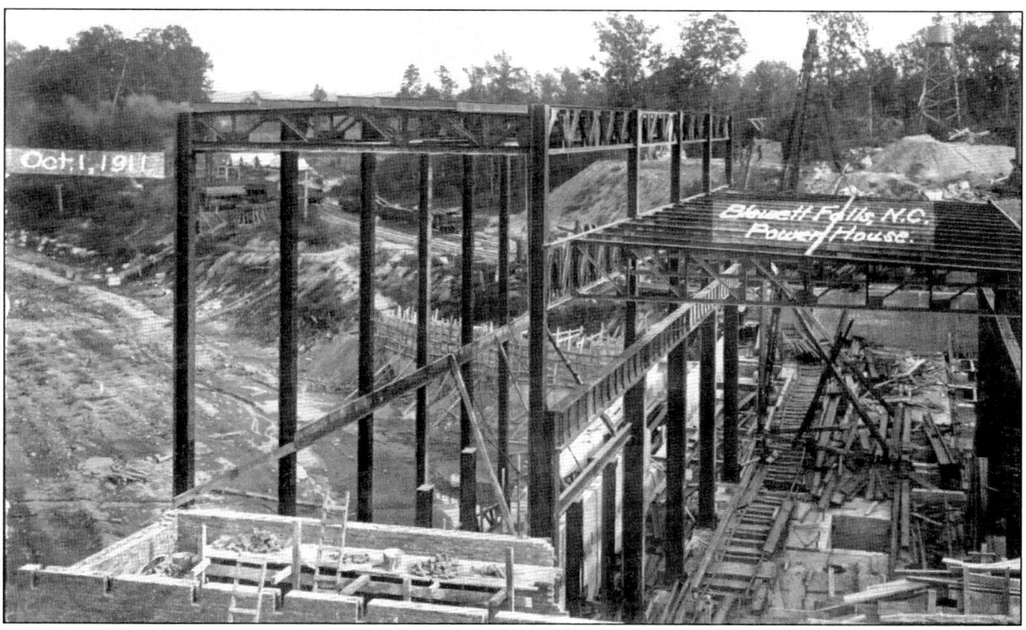

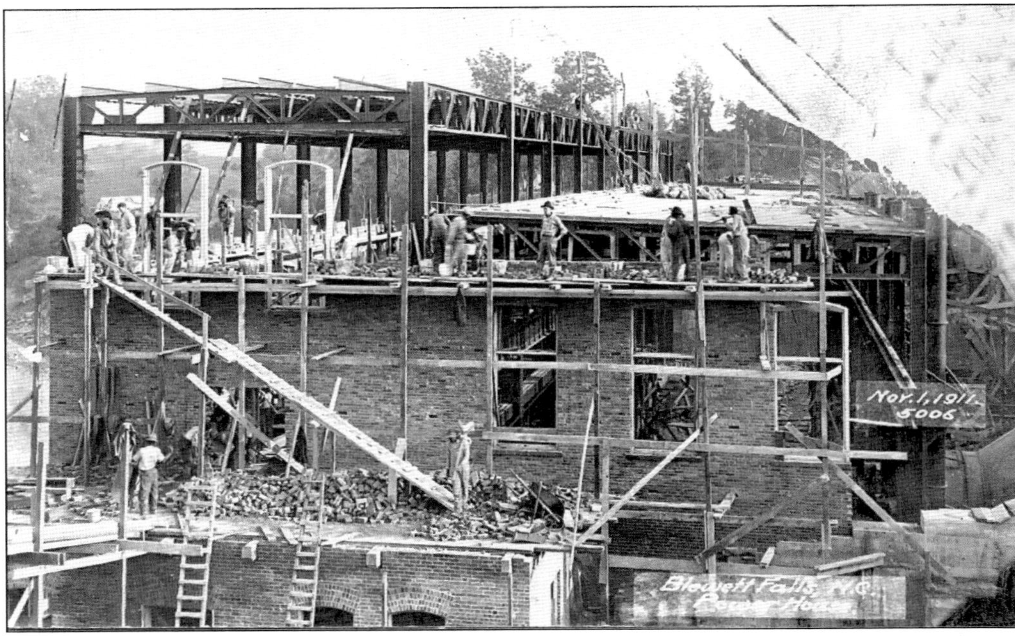

This photograph, dated November 1, 1911, shows laborers busily working at the powerhouse. (Courtesy Durwood Barbour.)

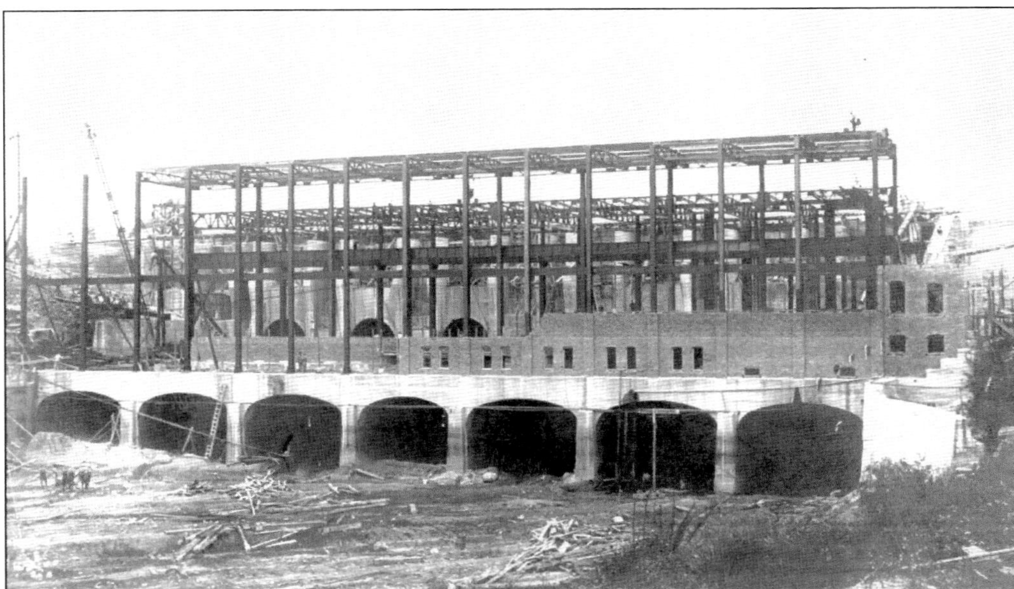

This frontal view of the powerhouse reveals the seven bays, through which water flowed to generate electric power. The date of the photograph is approximately December 1911. (Courtesy Durwood Barbour.)

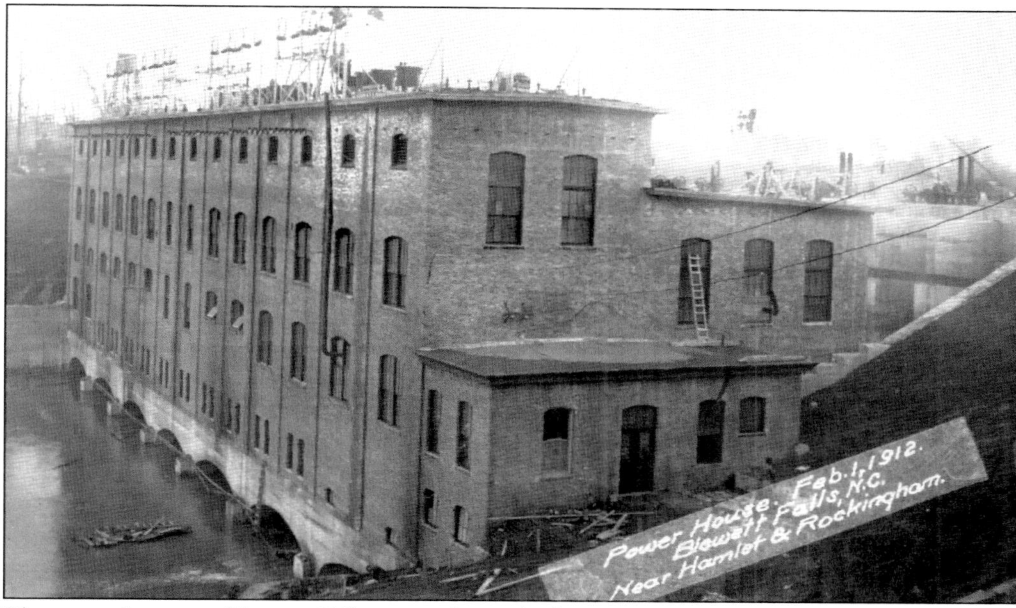

The powerhouse at Blewett Falls is nearly ready for service on February 1, 1912. (Courtesy Durwood Barbour.)

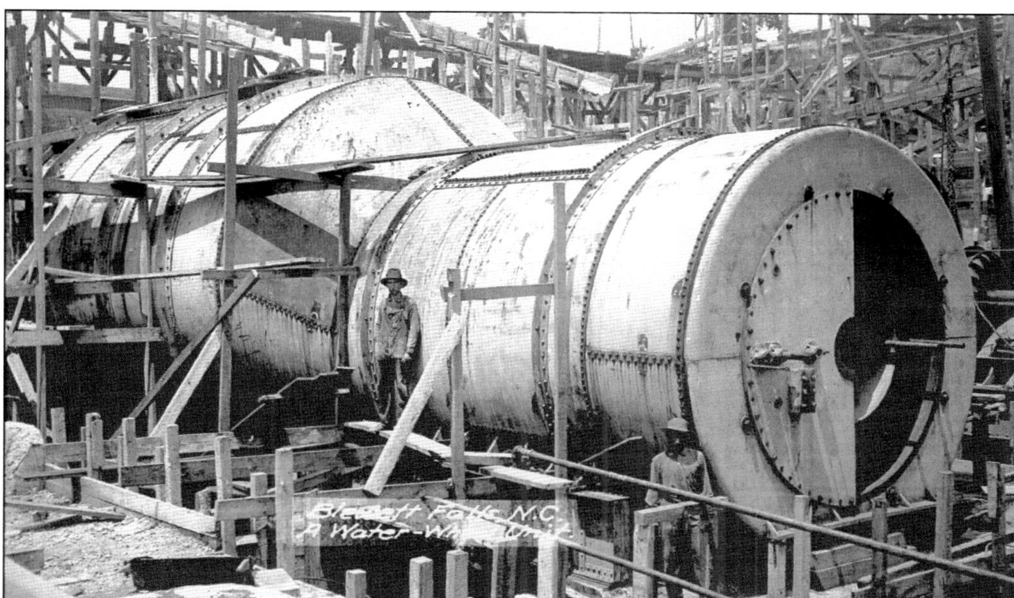

In this undated photograph, workers pose near two giant waterwheel units at the powerhouse. (Courtesy A&H.)

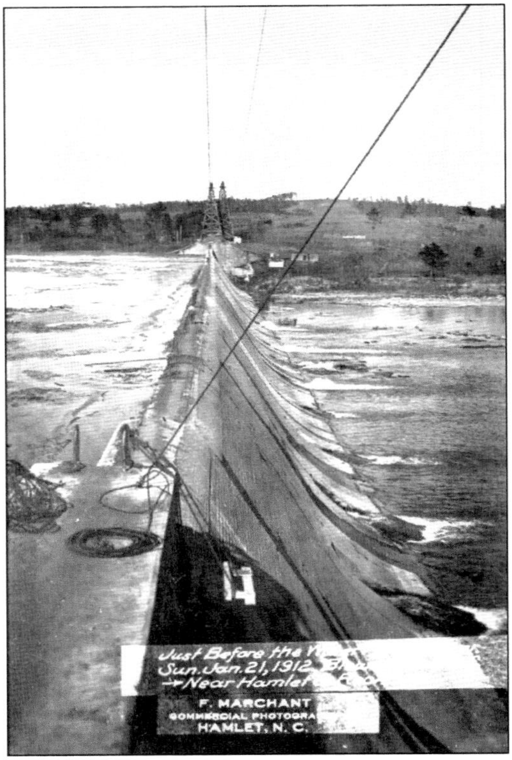

In early 1912, Marchant produced these two documentary before-and-after views of Blewett Falls Dam. The January 21 picture (at left) shows the dam just before water flowed over it; the February 1 photograph (below) is perhaps the first recorded image of the falls produced by the impounded waters of the Pee Dee River. (Courtesy Sarah M. Pope.)

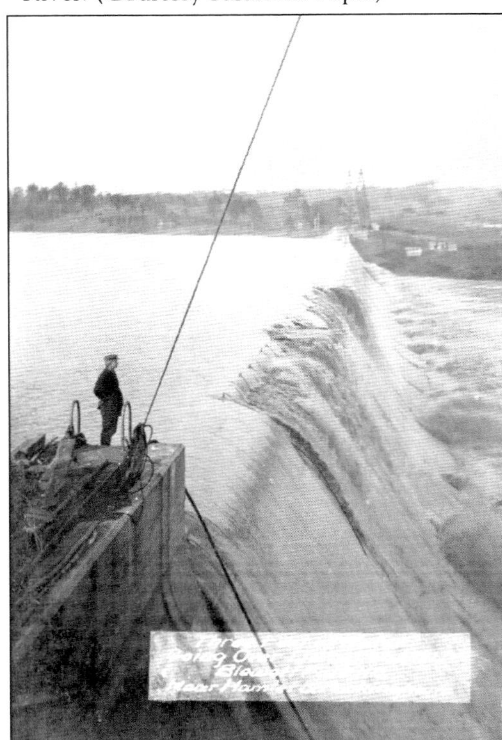

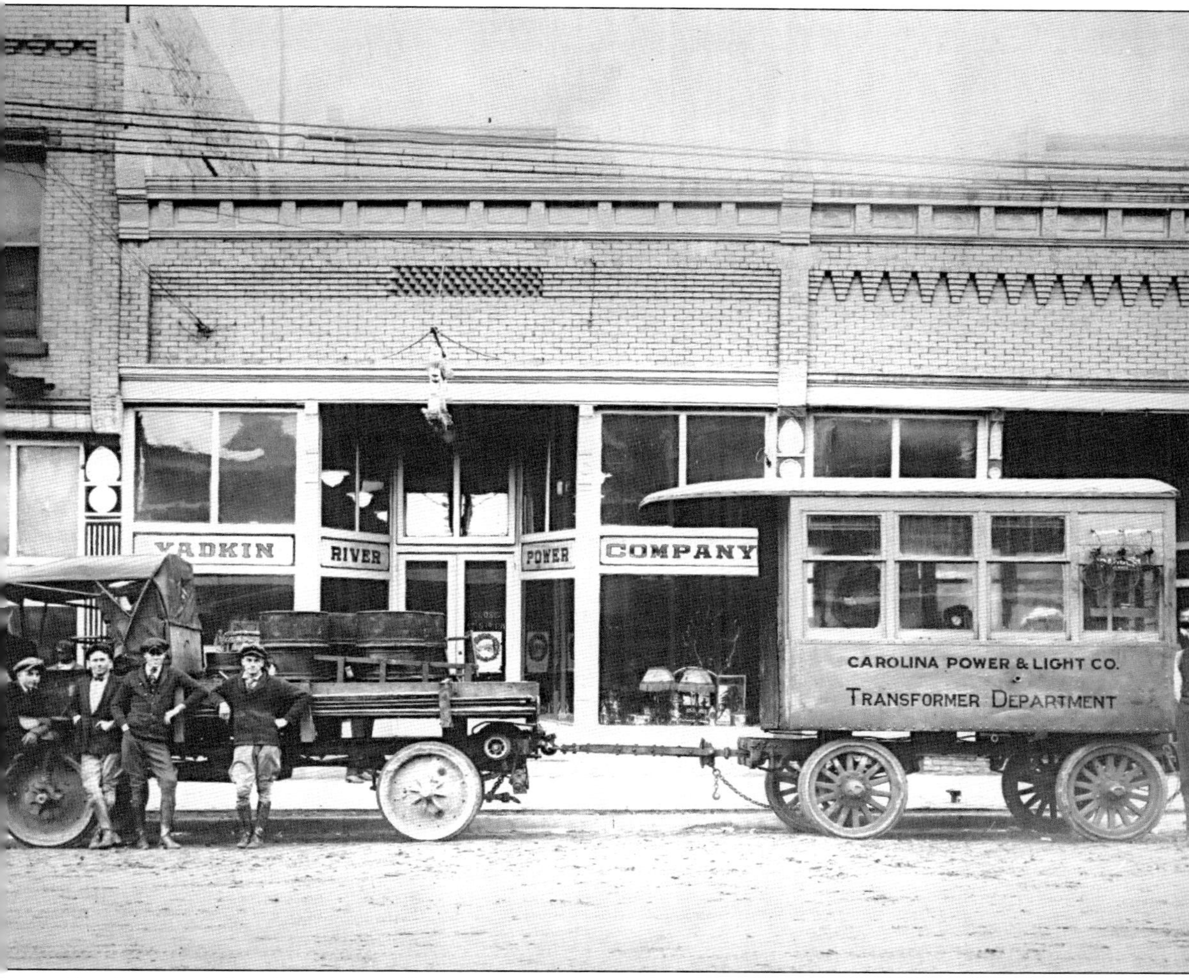

Employees of the Transformer Department of Carolina Power & Light Company pose here in front of the office of the Yadkin River Power Company at Hamlet in 1912. (Courtesy A&H.)

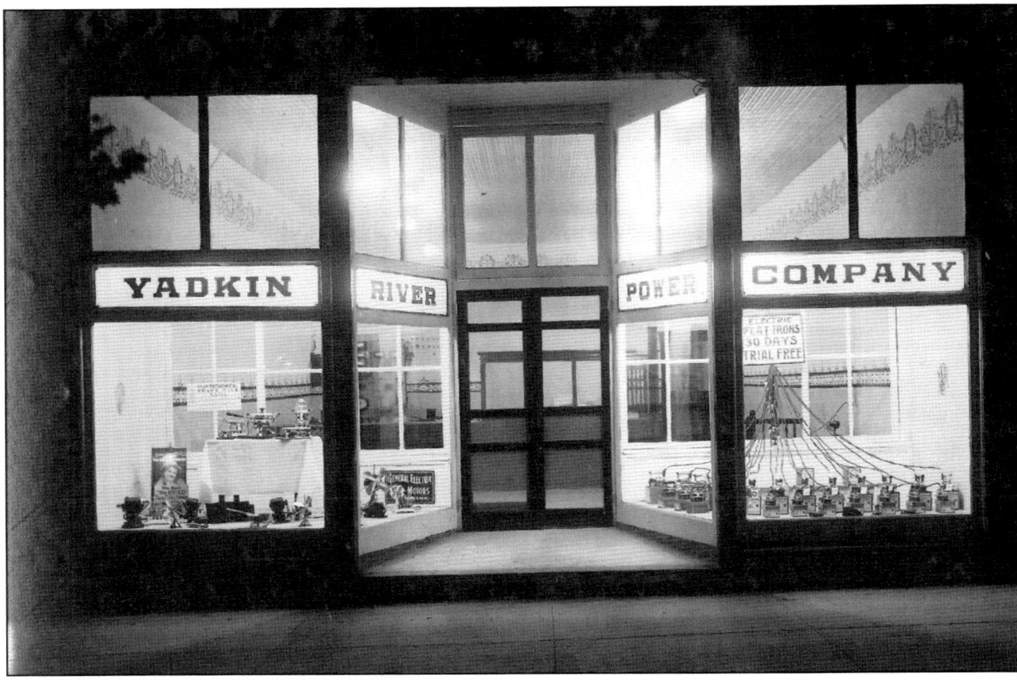

The offices of the Yadkin River Power Company in Hamlet (above) and Rockingham (below), as shown by these close-ups at night between 1910 and 1912, were almost identical. (Courtesy A&H.)

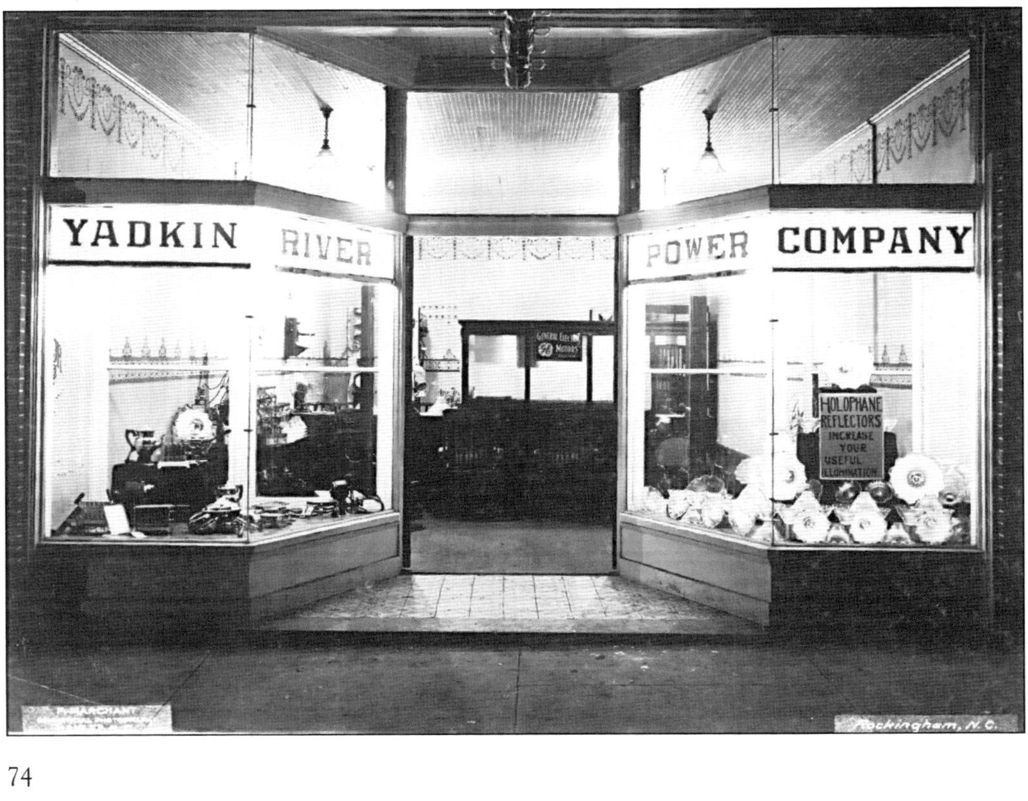

Six

Cotton and Textile Mills

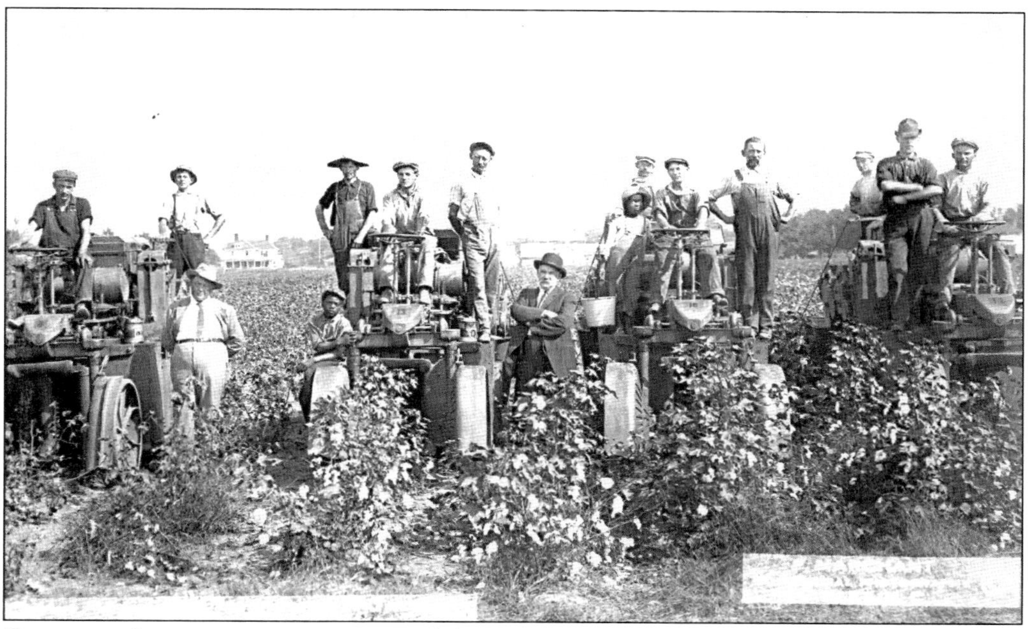

Cotton production was a major part of the economy in Richmond County during the early 20th century. Marchant photographed these workers and two company representatives near four Price-Campbell automatic cotton-picking machines in a cotton field at an unidentified location about 1913. The Campbell Cotton Picker Corporation manufactured the device, which could pick 2,000 pounds per hour. (Courtesy Durwood Barbour.)

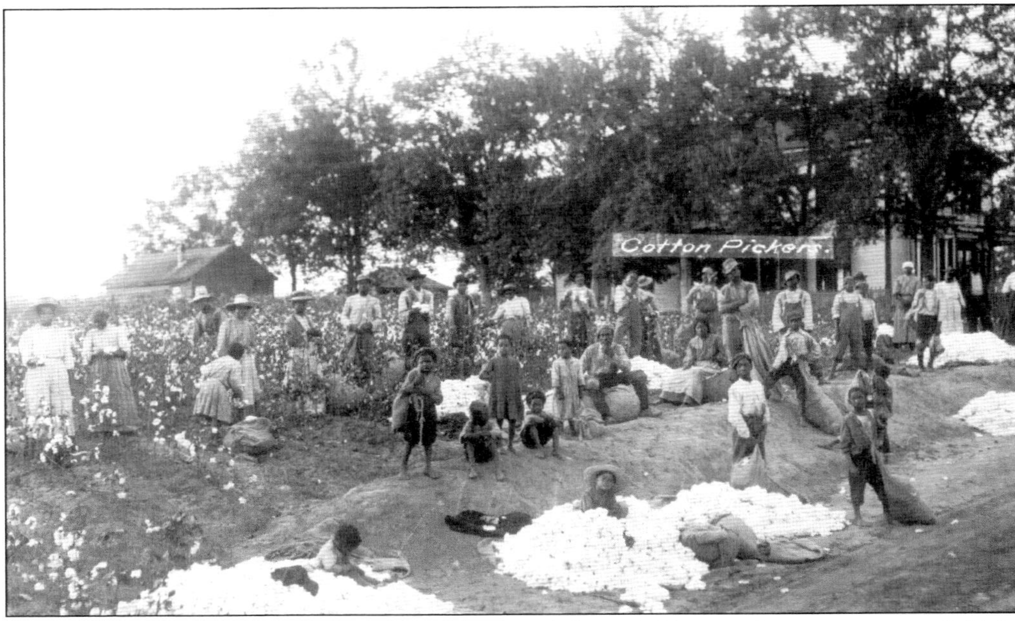

A group of African-American cotton pickers and their children gather in a cotton field for Marchant's camera at an unidentified location during the 1910s. (Courtesy Sarah M. Pope.)

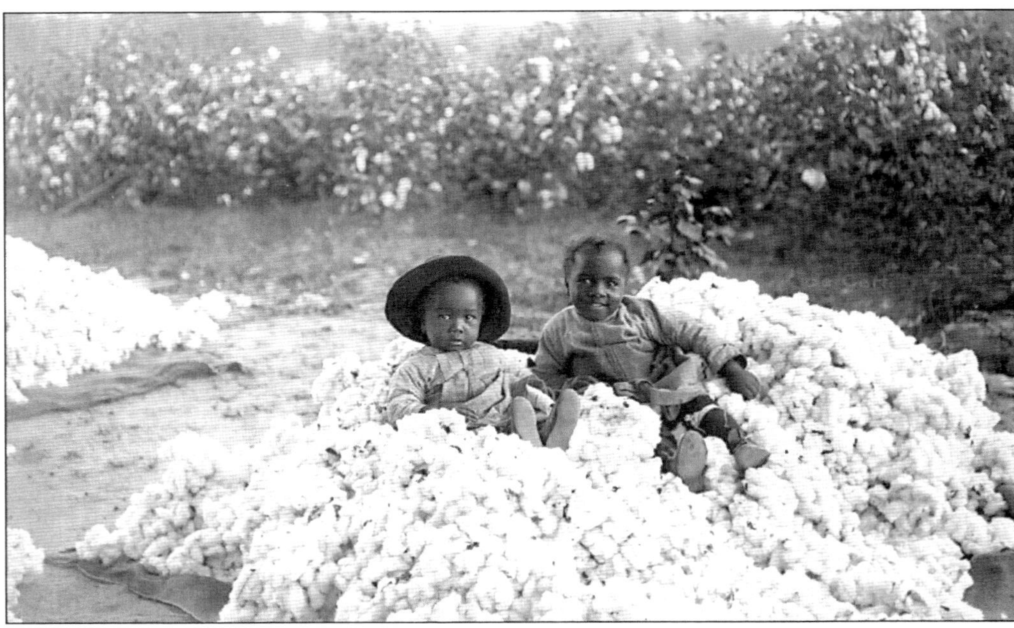

Photographers often placed African-American children in a pile of cotton balls to produce a stereotypical view or portrayal of the Old South. (Courtesy C. Vernon Vallance.)

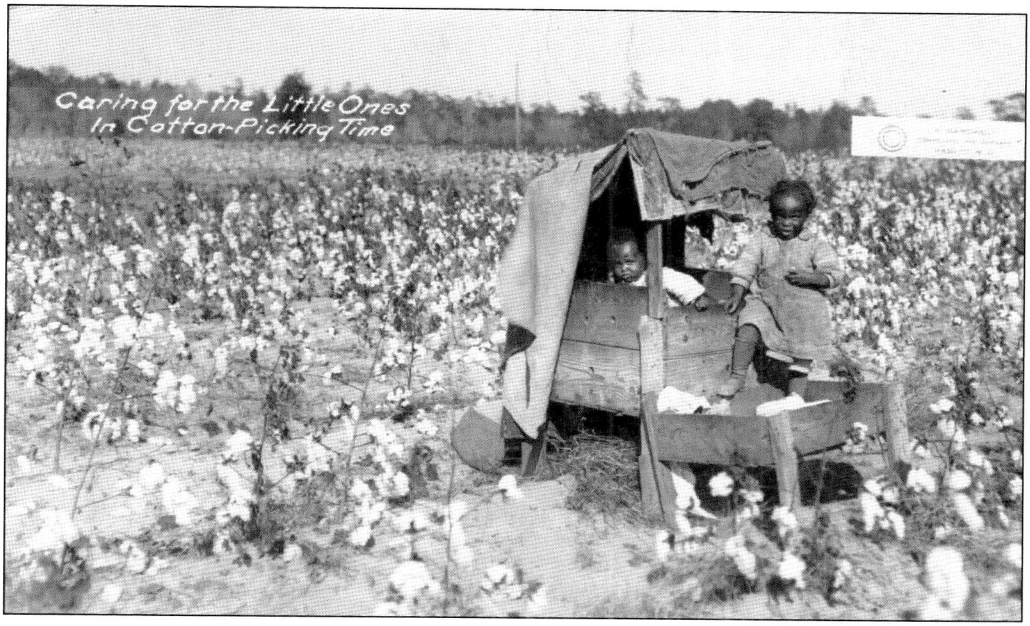

African-American field hands sometimes employed crudely constructed shelters to protect their little ones from the harsh outdoor elements. (Above, courtesy C. Vernon Vallance; below, courtesy Sarah M. Pope).

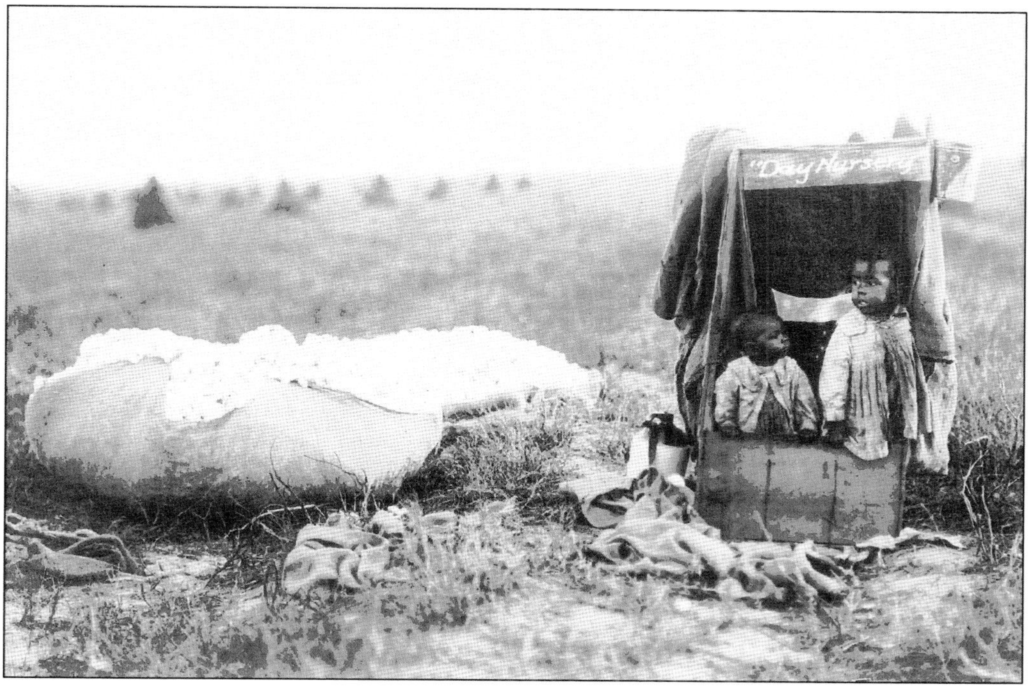

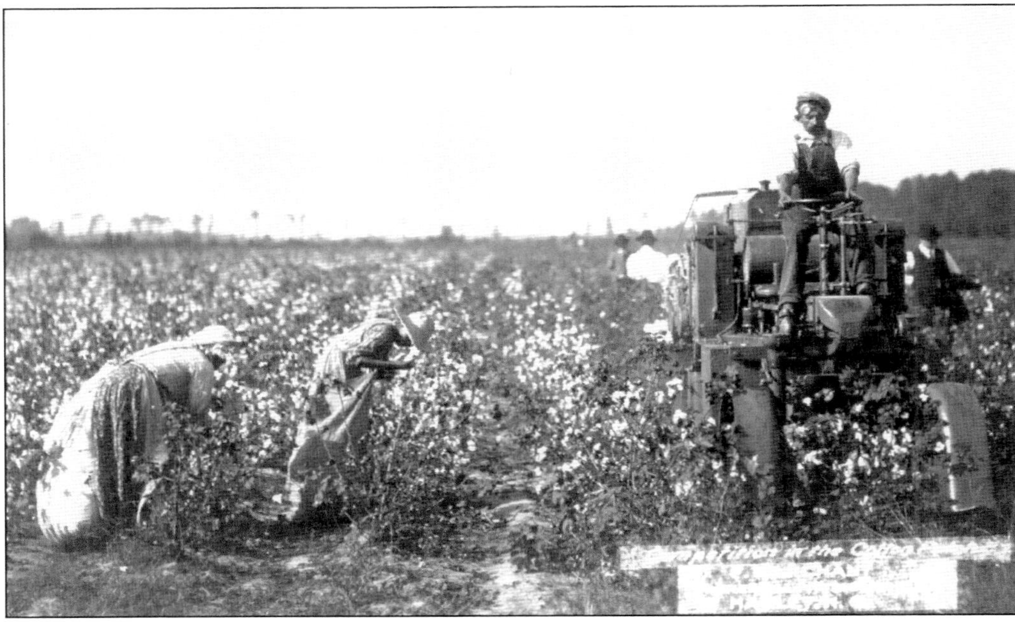

Machines increasingly began replacing workers in the cotton fields of Richmond County by 1913. Here, Marchant's photograph contrasts the old procedure (left) with the new method (right). (Courtesy C. Vernon Vallance.)

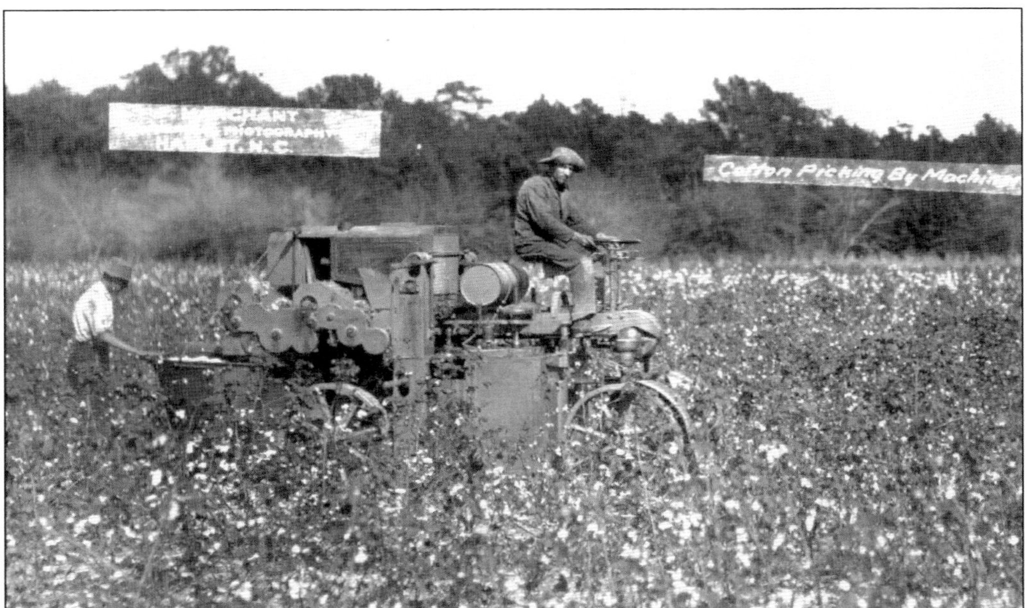

Shown here is a side view of a cotton-picking machine at an unidentified location about 1913. The driver maneuvers the device through the field as an attendant monitors the hopper. (Courtesy C. Vernon Vallance.)

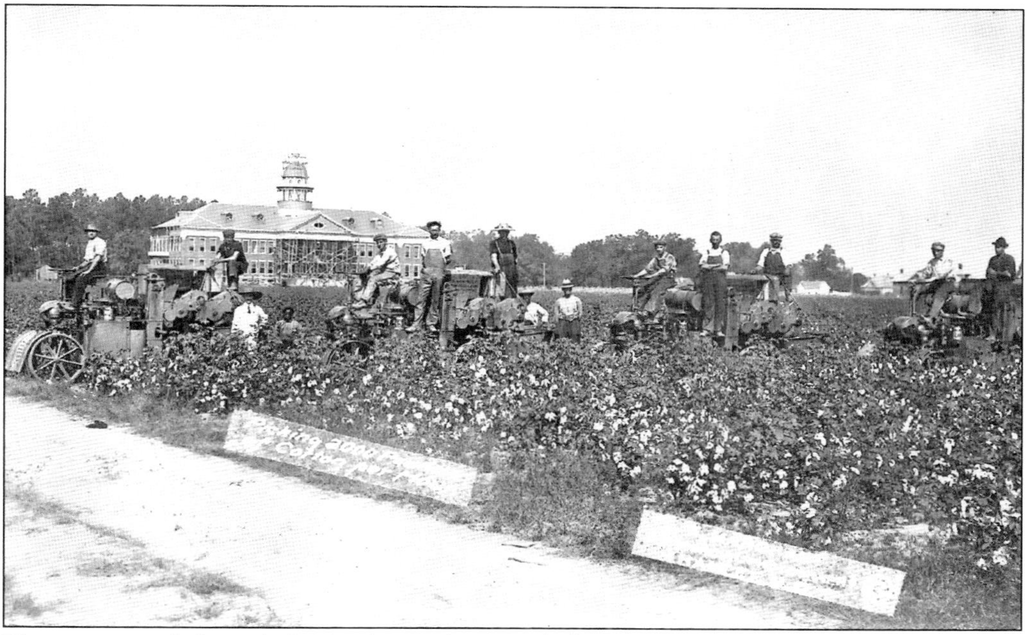

The caption of this 1913 Marchant photograph boasts that these machines are capable of "Picking 2000 Pounds of Cotton per Hour." The large building with the cupola in the background has not been identified. (Courtesy Wayne Chapman.)

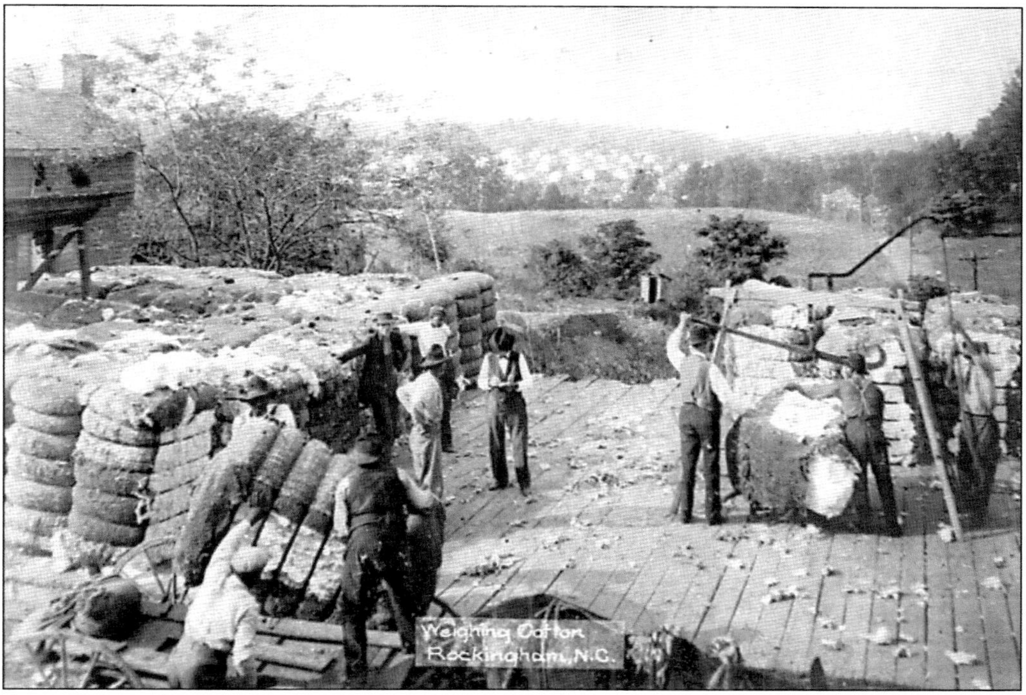

A cotton platform at Rockingham is the scene of laborers unloading wagons and weighing bales of the product with the large scales at right. The date of this photograph is unknown. (Courtesy A&H.)

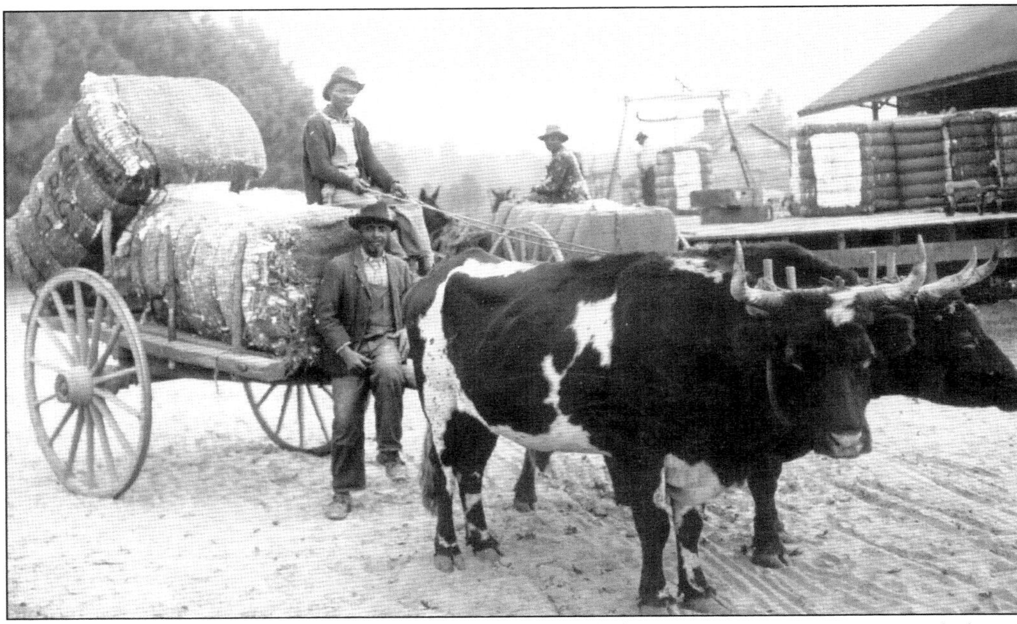

These African-American men are shown with a bull-drawn cart transporting two bales of cotton in 1910. A cotton platform and scales are visible in the right background. (Courtesy Sarah M. Pope.)

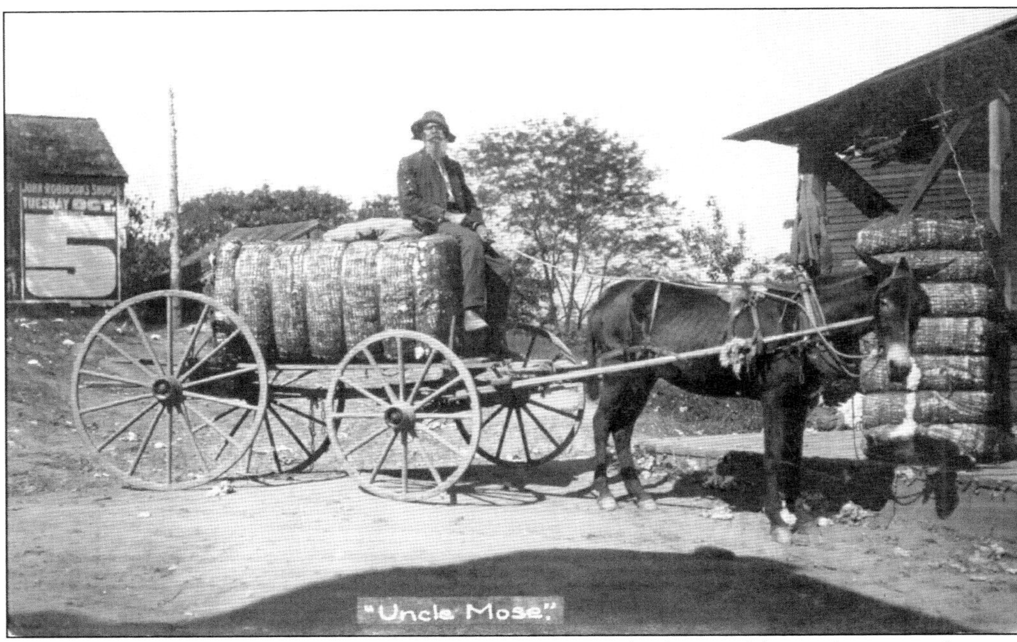

An African-American man identified as "Uncle Mose" is the driver of this mule-powered wagon filled with cotton. (Courtesy Durwood Barbour.)

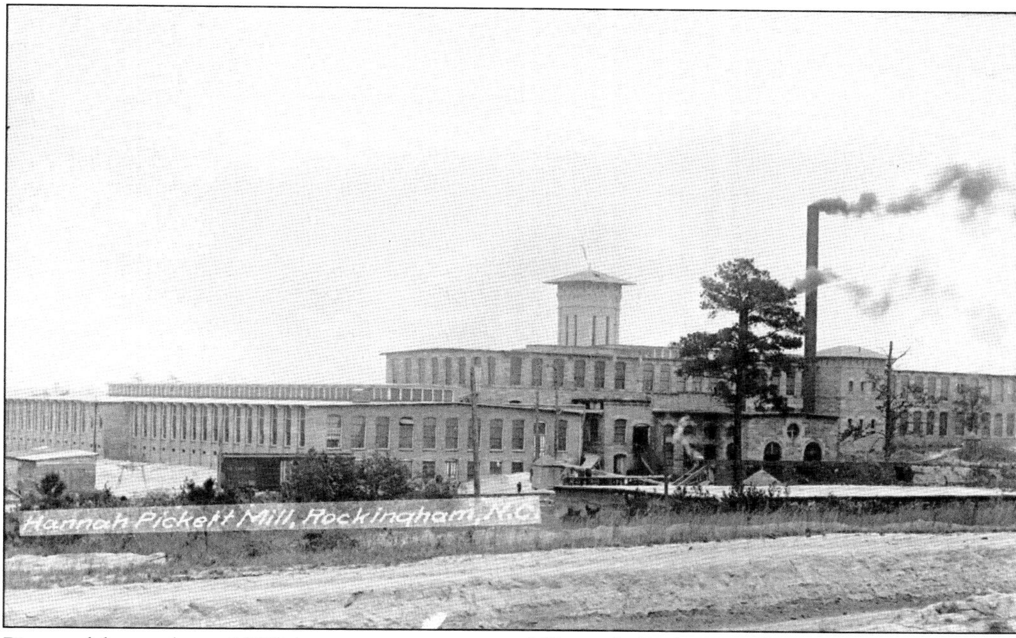

Pictured here about 1910 is an exterior view of Hannah Pickett Mill, one of several textile operations in the Rockingham area. Production at the mill commenced at the beginning of the 20th century in an area just east of the county seat. (Courtesy A&H.)

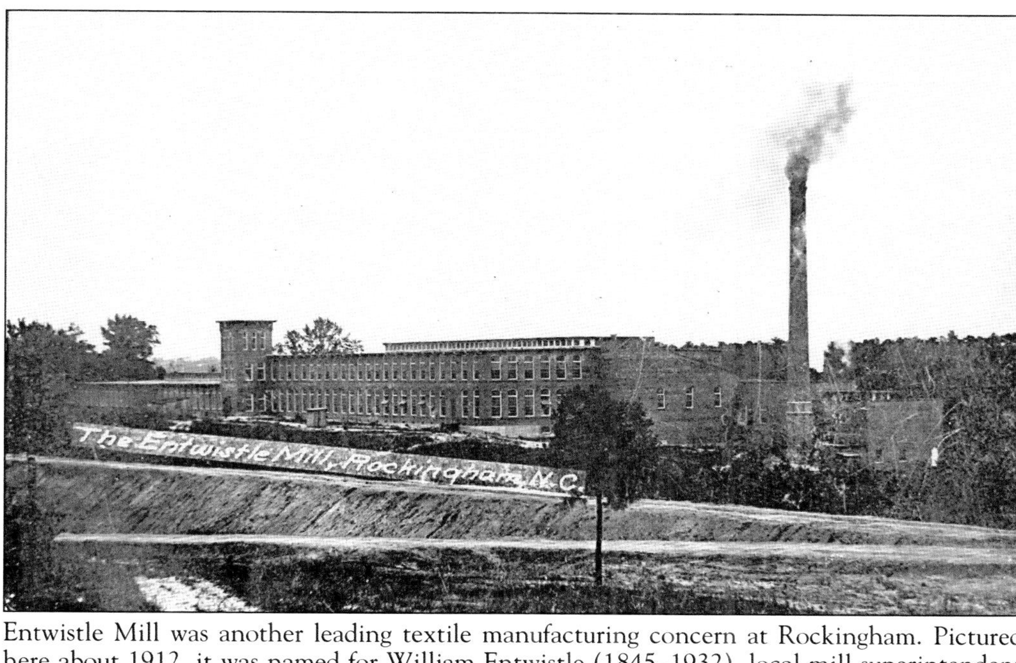

Entwistle Mill was another leading textile manufacturing concern at Rockingham. Pictured here about 1912, it was named for William Entwistle (1845–1932), local mill superintendent and owner. (Courtesy A&H.)

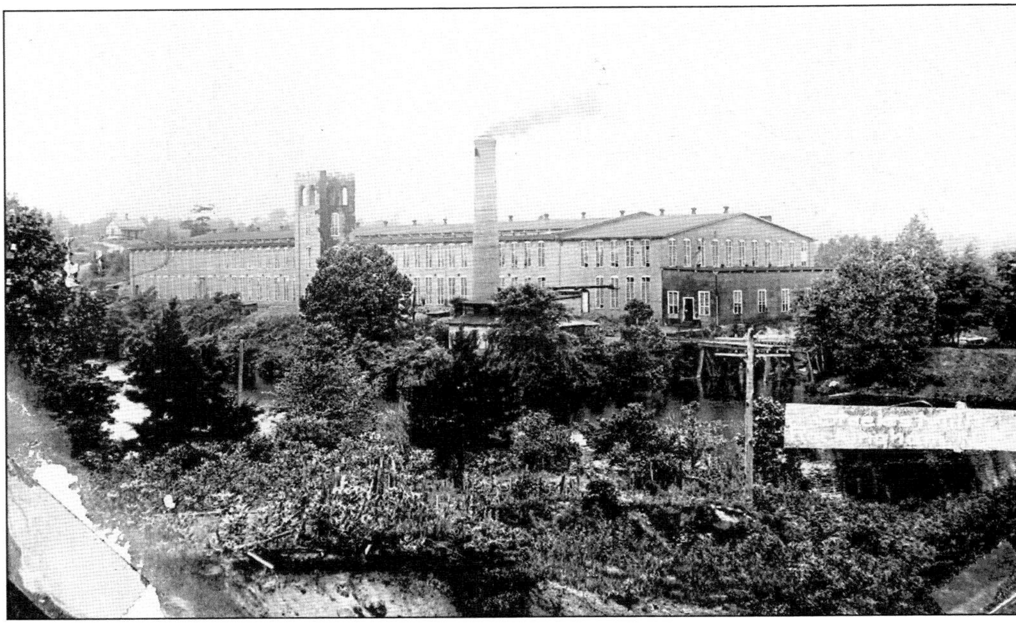

Shown on this page are two views of Steele's Mill, located about three and one-half miles southwest of Rockingham. The image above is a distant view taken about 1912, and the photograph below features the dam of the textile mill about 1911. The mill began operation in 1898 under the direction of Robert L. Steele. By 1911, the mill utilized more than 23,000 spindles and 600 looms for the manufacture of print cloths. (Above, courtesy A&H; below, courtesy Durwood Barbour.)

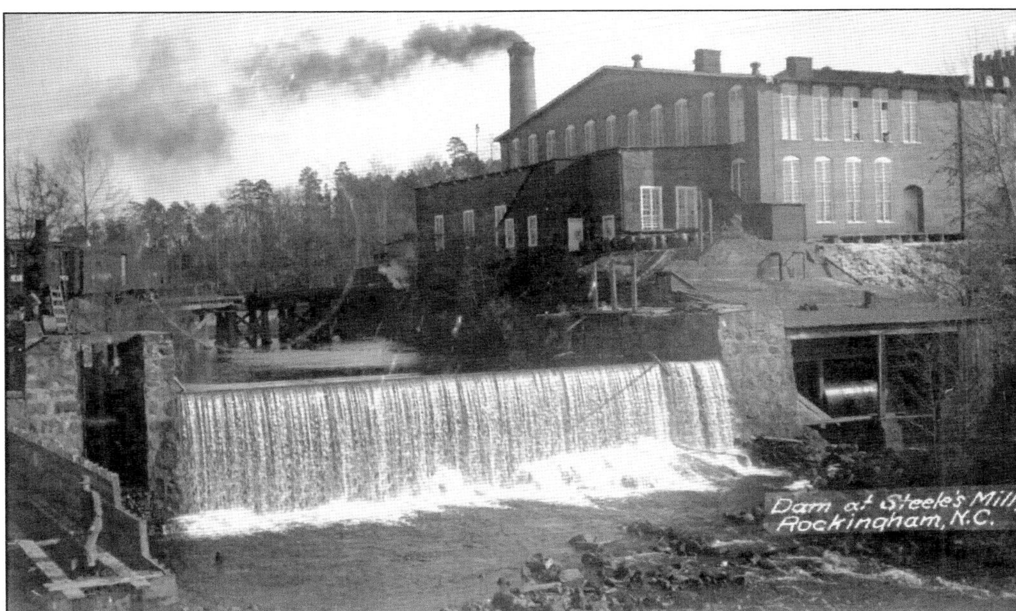

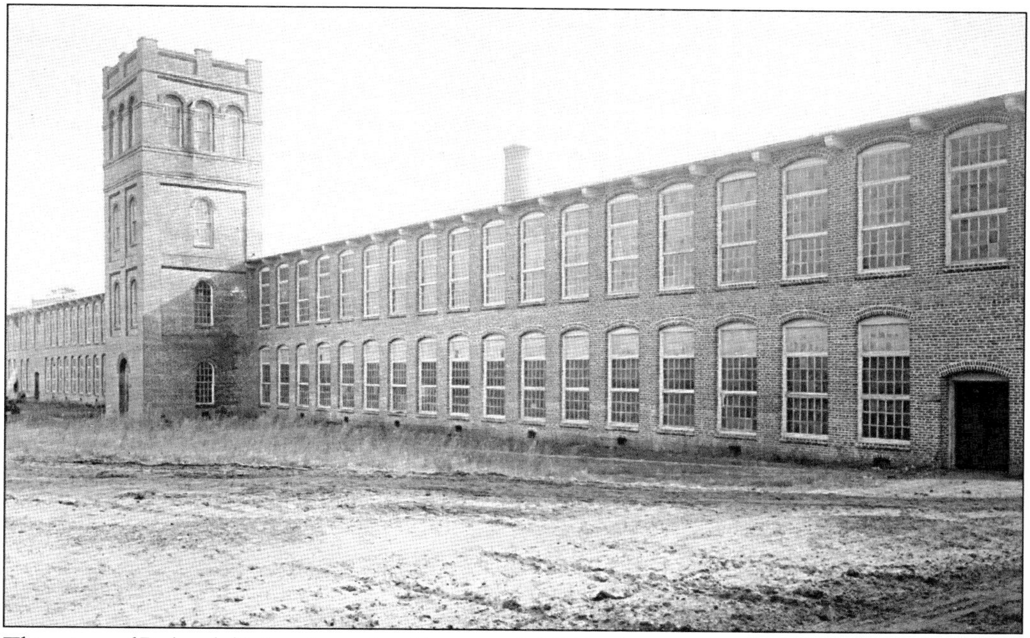

This view of Roberdel Manufacturing Company Mill No. 2 was taken in January 1913. The mill was located northeast of Rockingham and was named in honor of its founder, Robert L. Steele. (Courtesy A&H.)

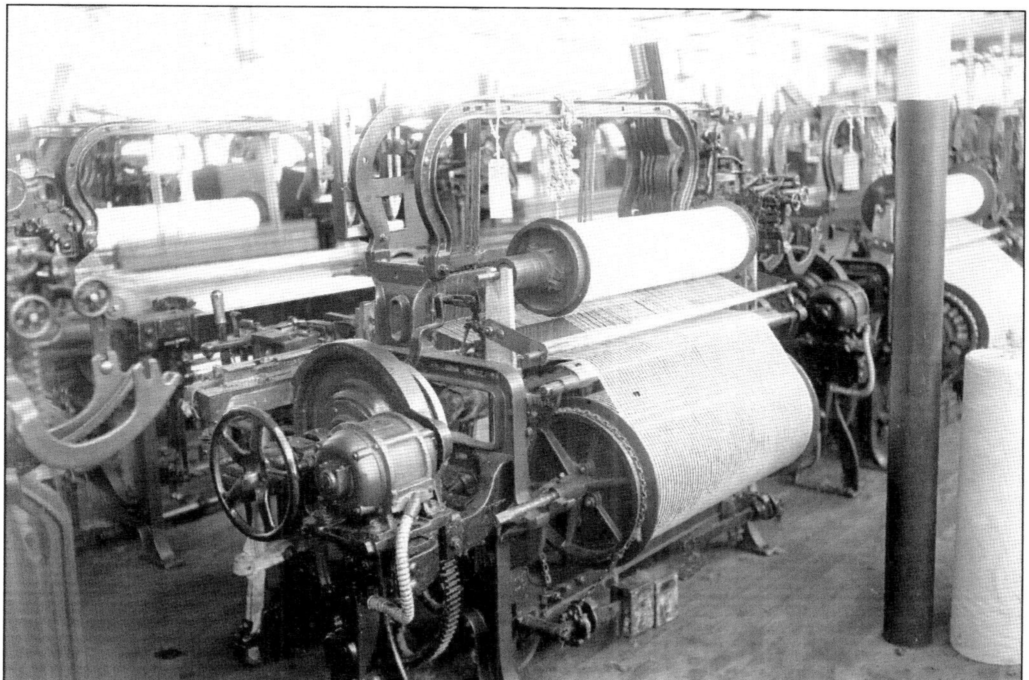

Shown here about 1912 is a rare interior view of an electric-powered loom at Roberdel Manufacturing Company Mill No. 2. The complex contained 500 looms by 1911. (Courtesy A&H.)

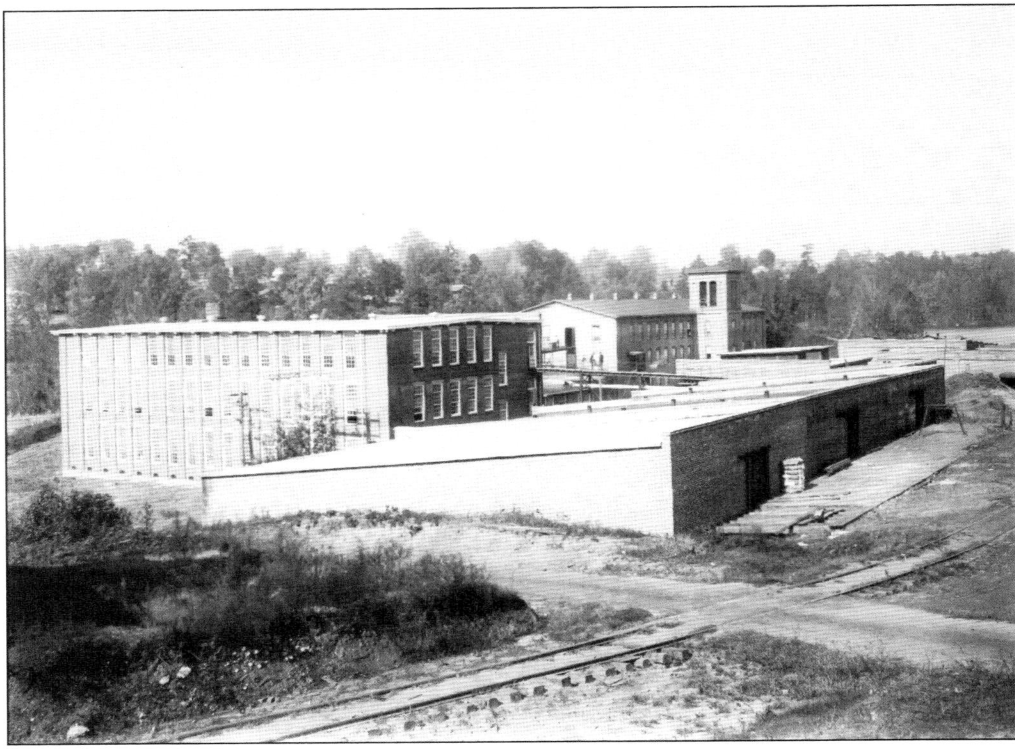

Robert L. Steele also opened Pee Dee Manufacturing Company Mill No. 1 near Rockingham. The facility, which contained 300 looms and 6,700 spindles in 1911, is pictured here at about that year. (Courtesy A&H.)

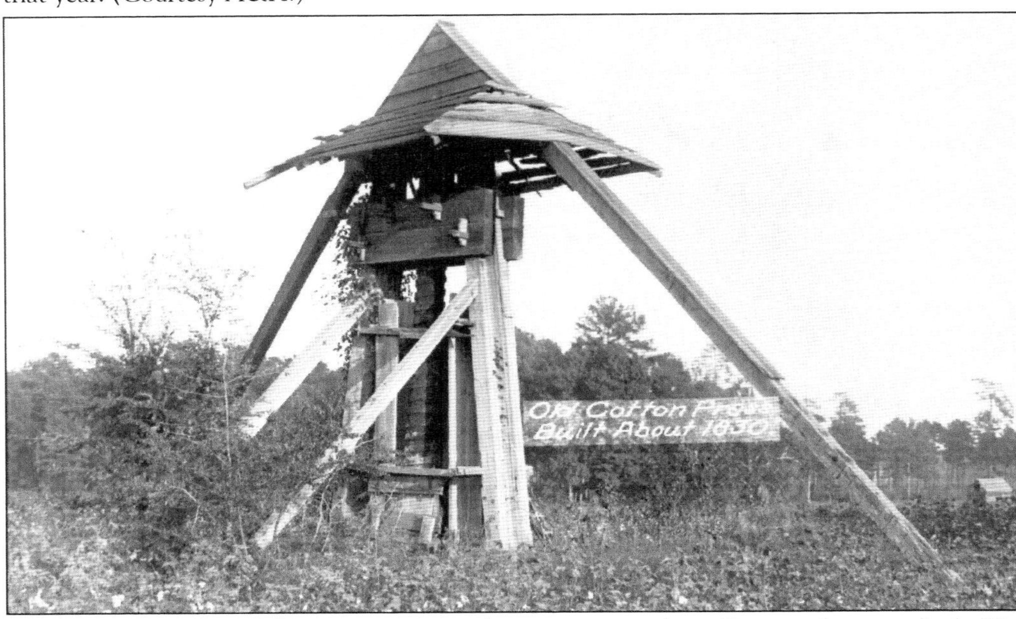

Marchant photographed this screw-type, wooden cotton press about 80 years after it was built. The press was used to compress cotton into bales at some unidentified location. (Courtesy A&H.)

Seven

Winter Pays a Brief Visit

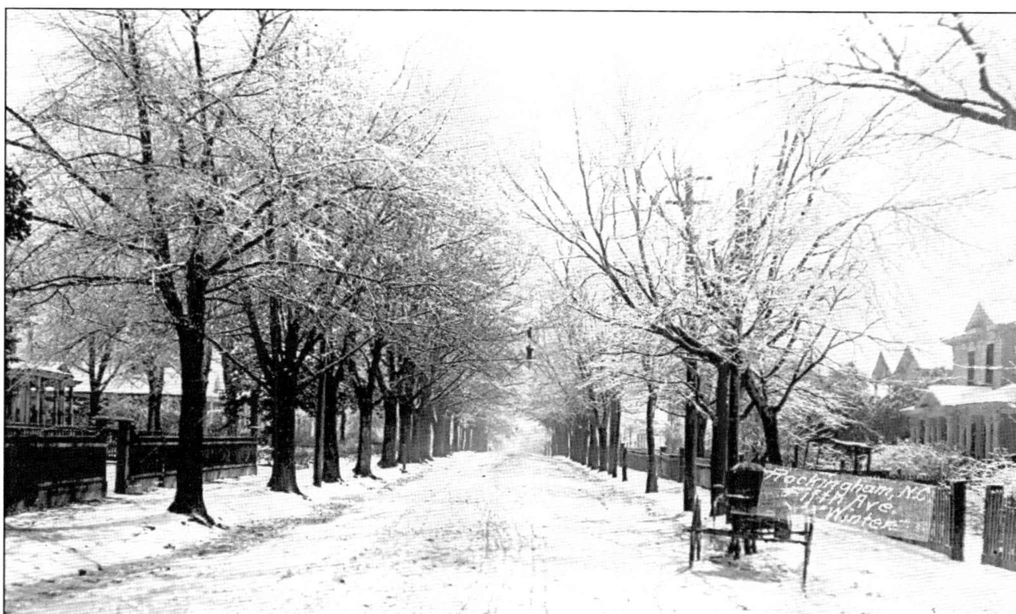

Reproduced here is a landscape of a residential section of Fifth Avenue (North Randolph Street) looking north in Rockingham following an ice storm in January 1910. (Courtesy Wayne Chapman.)

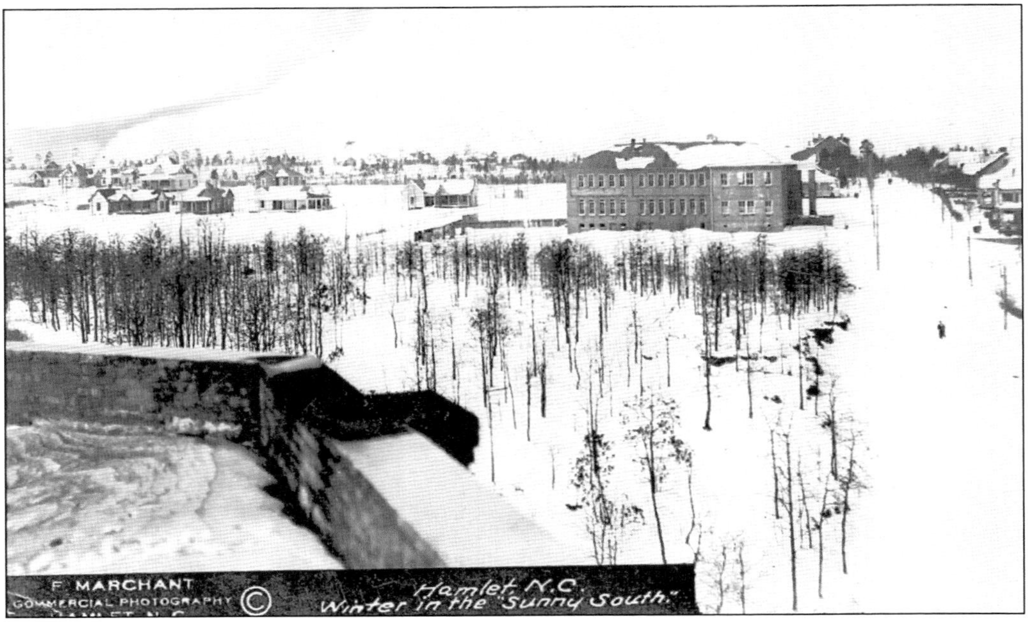

Marchant climbed to the top floor of an unidentified building to photograph this cold-weather scene, which he entitled "Hamlet, N.C. Winter in the Sunny South." (Courtesy A&H.)

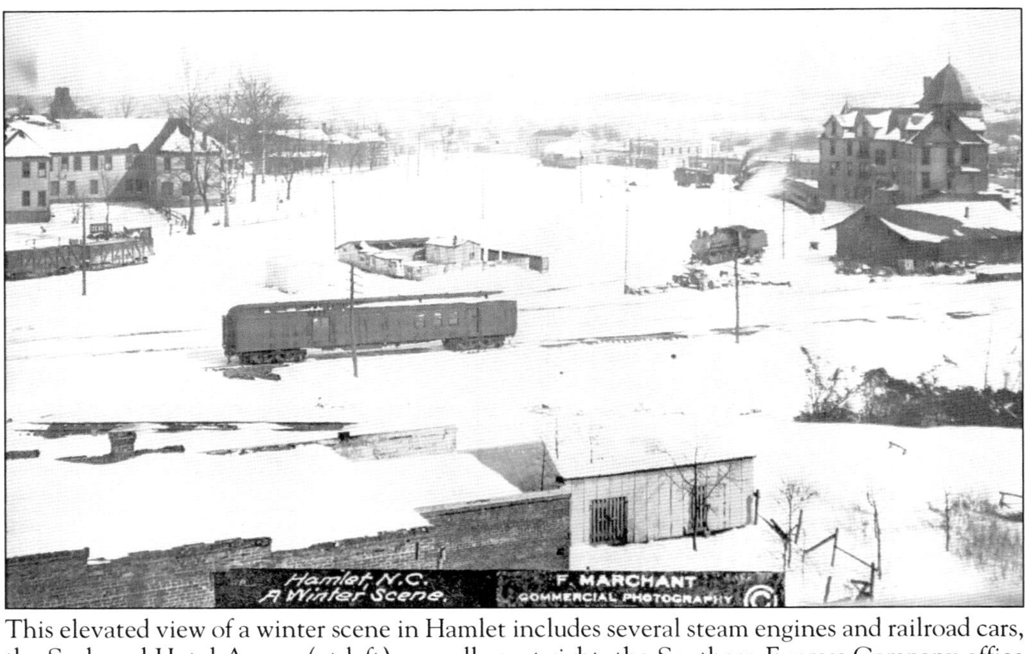

This elevated view of a winter scene in Hamlet includes several steam engines and railroad cars, the Seaboard Hotel Annex (at left), as well as, at right, the Southern Express Company office and the Seaboard Hotel. (Courtesy A&H.)

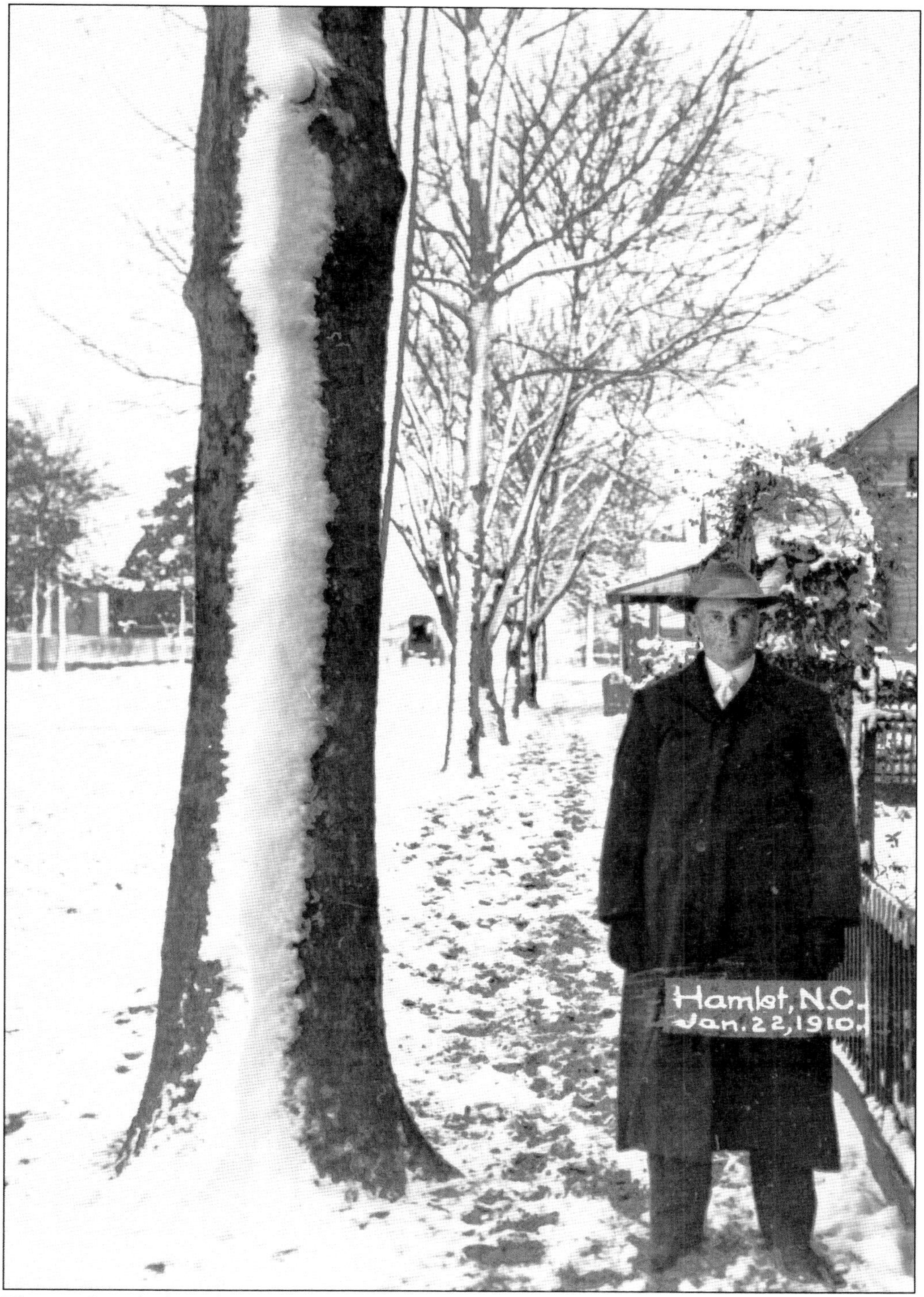

This unidentified gentleman pauses briefly for Marchant beside a tree on a snowy day in Hamlet on January 22, 1910. (Courtesy A&H.)

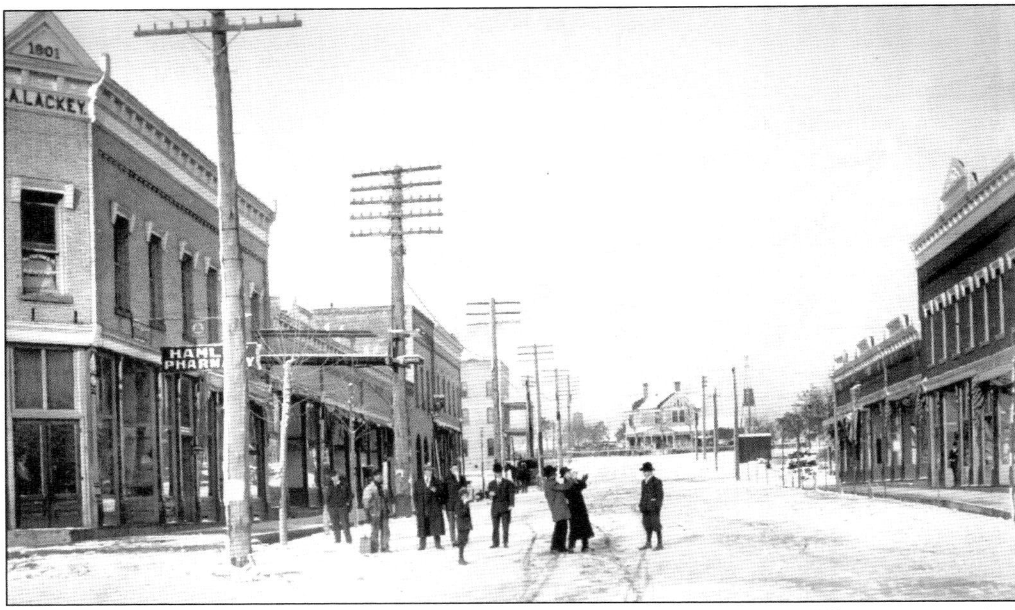

Main Street in Hamlet is the setting of this photograph taken after a snowfall in January 1910. A group has gathered in the street in front of Hamlet Pharmacy, located in the E.A. Lackey Building. (Courtesy Durwood Barbour.)

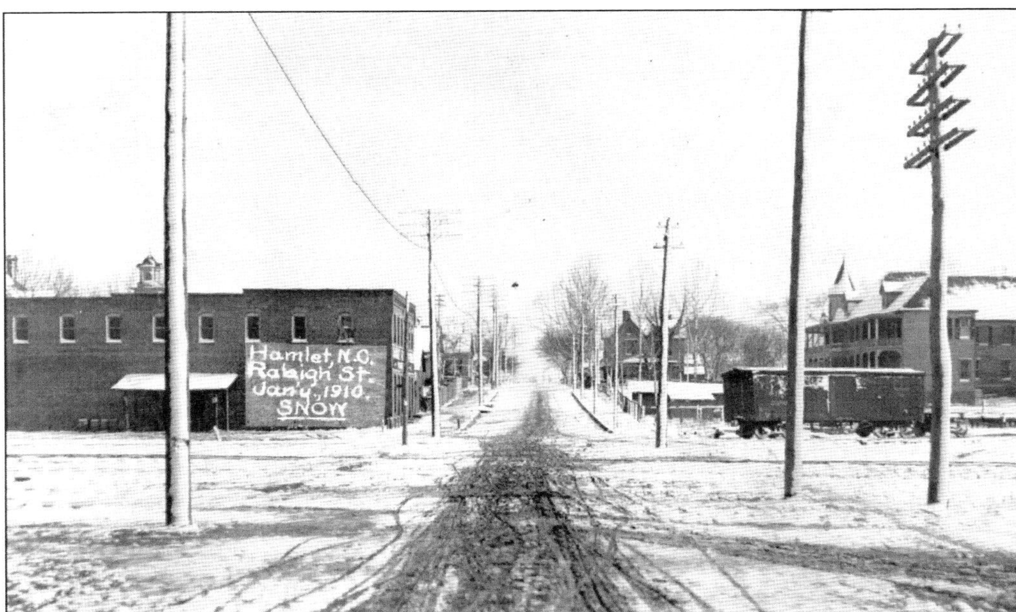

Marchant placed his camera in the center of Raleigh Street, looking north, in Hamlet to capture this view after a snowfall in January 1910. The building at left is occupied by O.T. Goodwin's wholesale grocery, and the structure partially hidden by the boxcar is the Seaboard Hotel Annex. (Courtesy Wayne Chapman.)

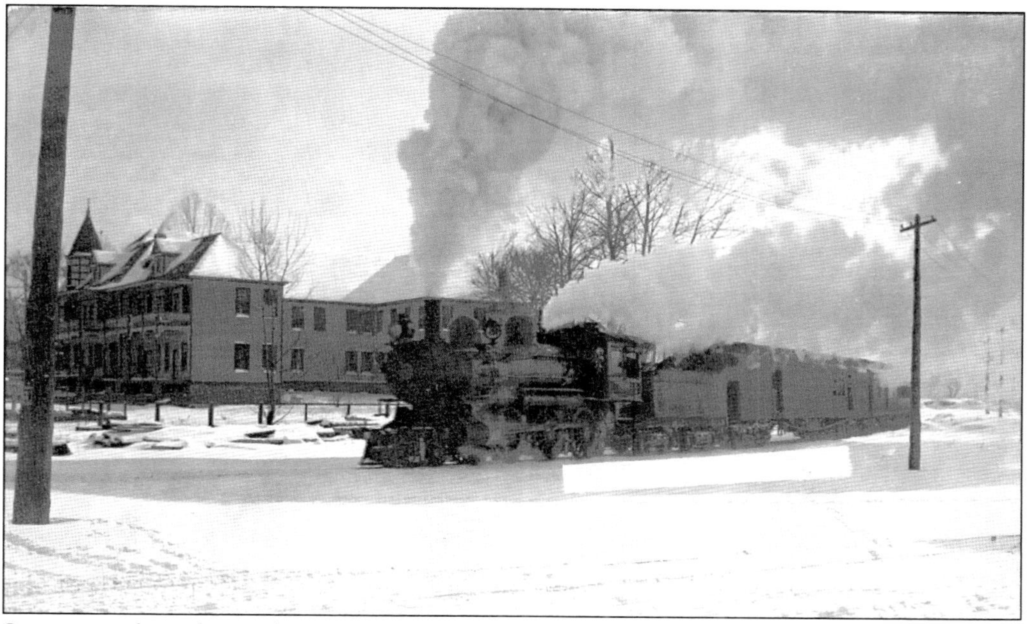

Steam rises from the smokestack of this train as it nears the Seaboard Hotel Annex at Hamlet on February 11, 1912. (Courtesy A&H.)

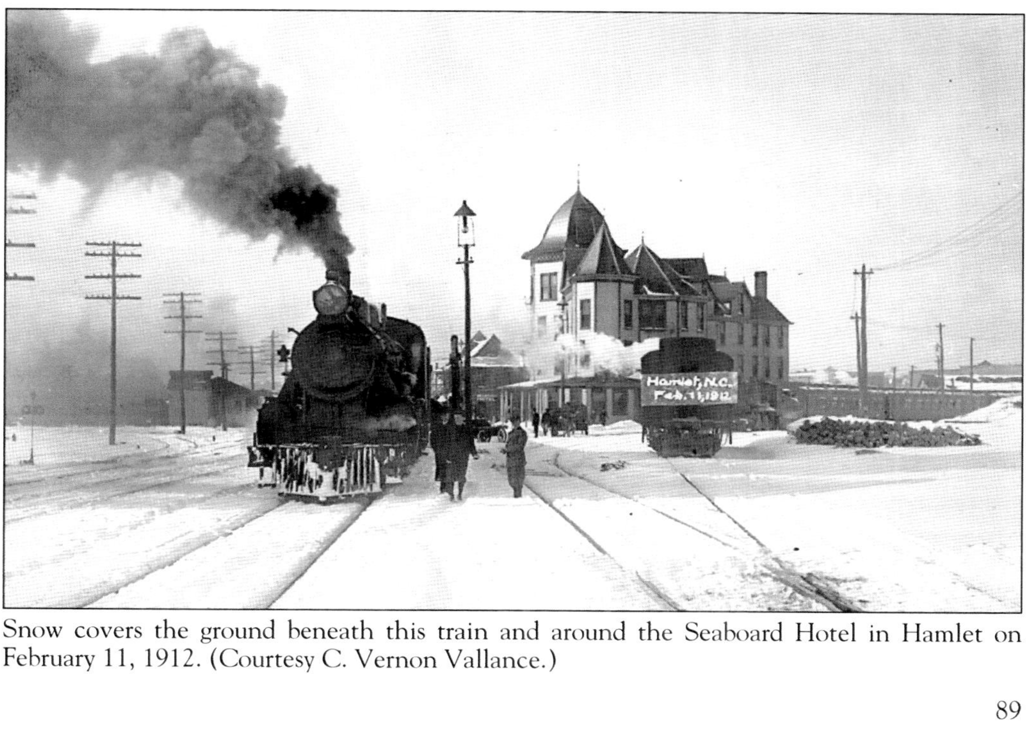

Snow covers the ground beneath this train and around the Seaboard Hotel in Hamlet on February 11, 1912. (Courtesy C. Vernon Vallance.)

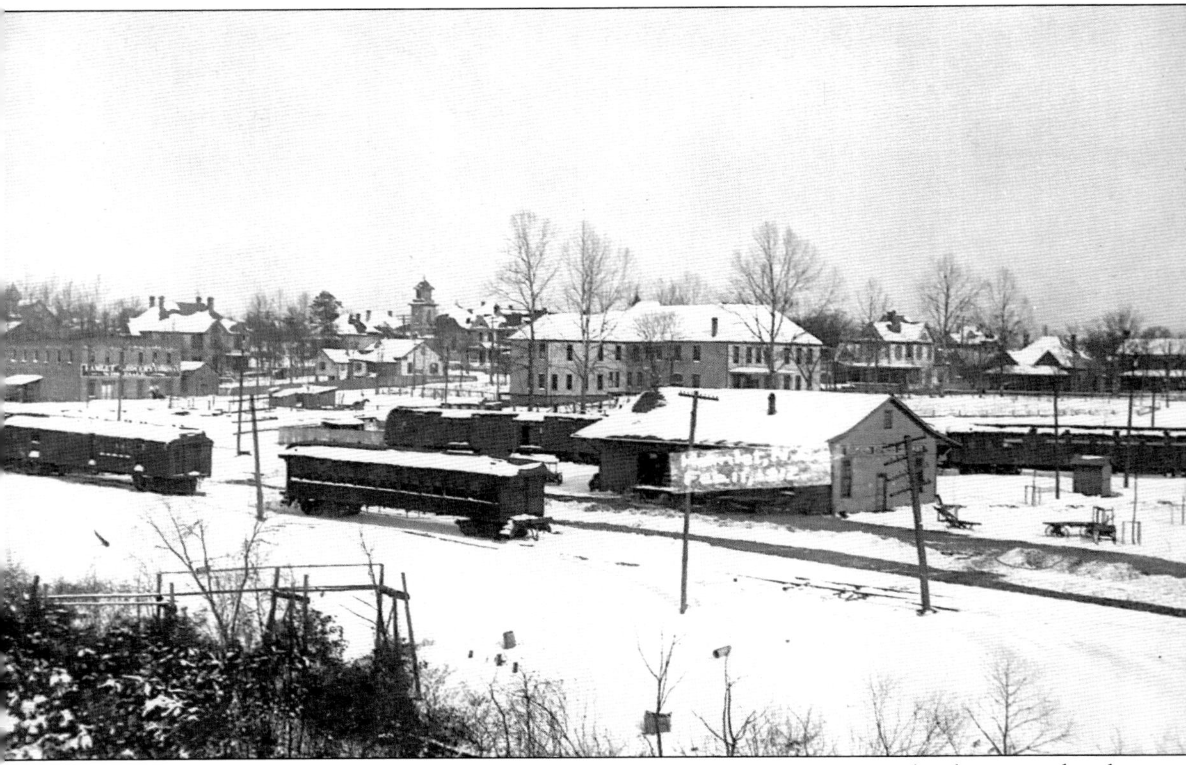

Here is still another photograph of the snowstorm of February 11, 1912. The distant and wide view encompasses Hamlet Grocery Company (at left) and passenger cars near the office of the Southern Express Company. (Courtesy Aubrey T. Haddock.)

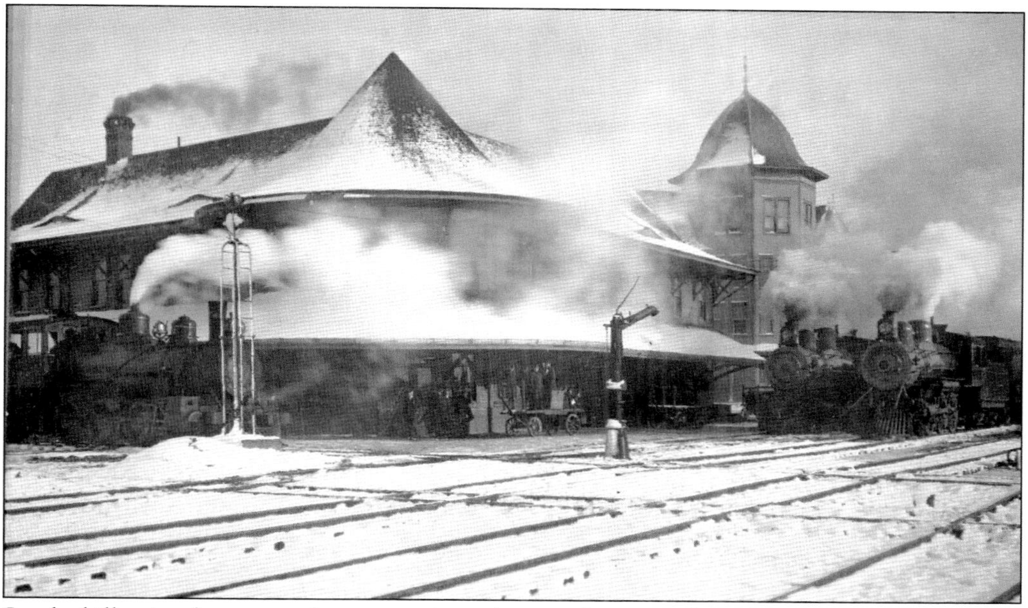

Smoke billowing from several steam engines obscures the view of the depot and Seaboard Hotel at Hamlet on this winter day in 1912. (Courtesy Durwood Barbour.)

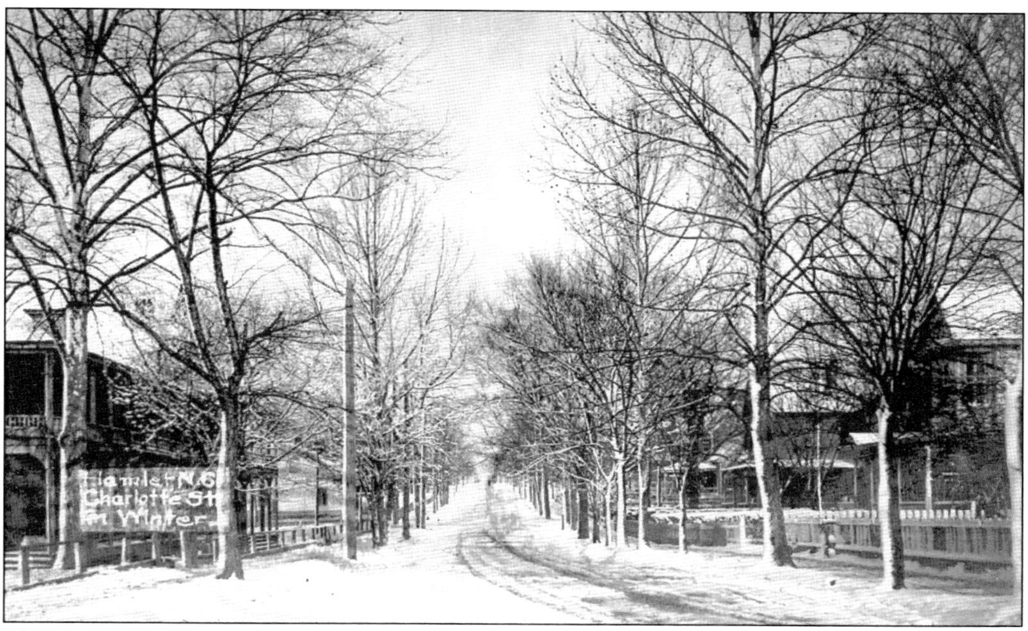

This wintertime view shows Charlotte Street in a residential neighborhood in Hamlet. The building on the left is the Seaboard Hotel Annex. Marchant resided with his mother on this street at the time of this snowfall, about 1912. (Courtesy A&H.)

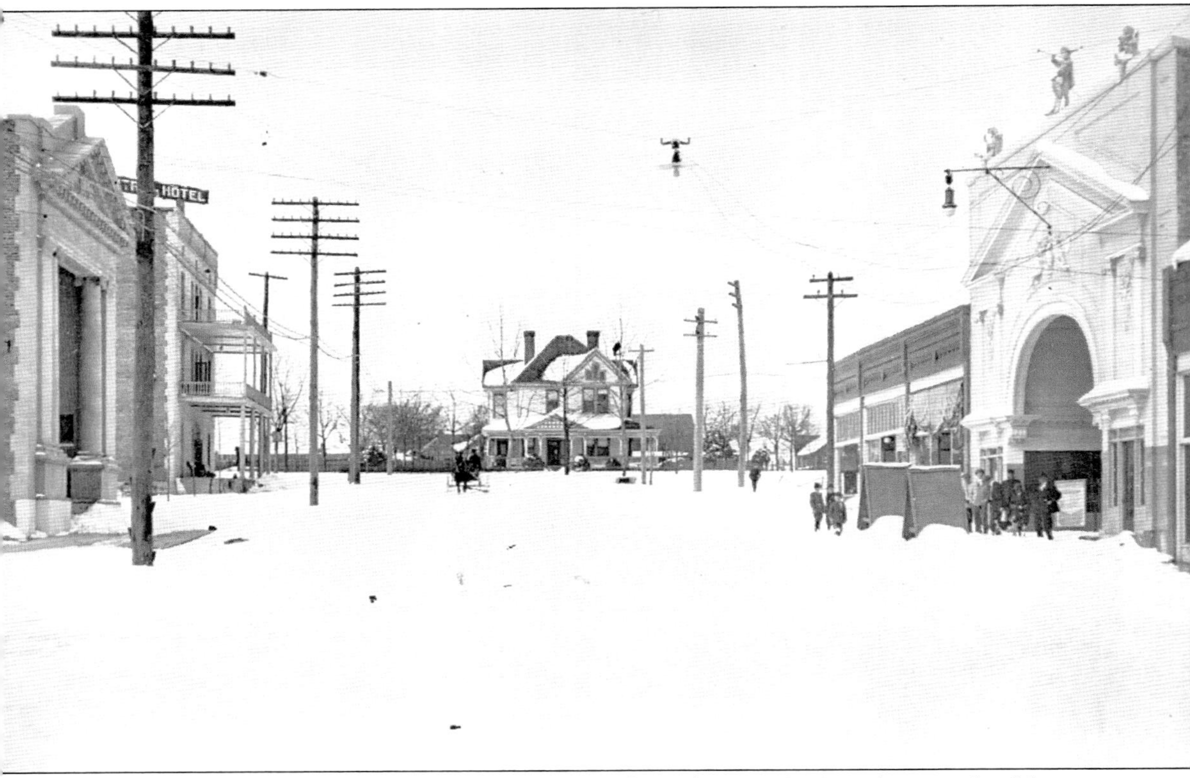

There is an absence of footprints in the snow in this February 26, 1914 photograph of the upper portion of Main Street in Hamlet. The two buildings at left are the Bank of Hamlet and the Central Hotel; the ornate structure on the right is the opera house. The snow-covered residence in the center is the Lackey House. (Courtesy Wayne Chapman.)

Eight

PEOPLE, POSSUMS, AND PECULIARITIES

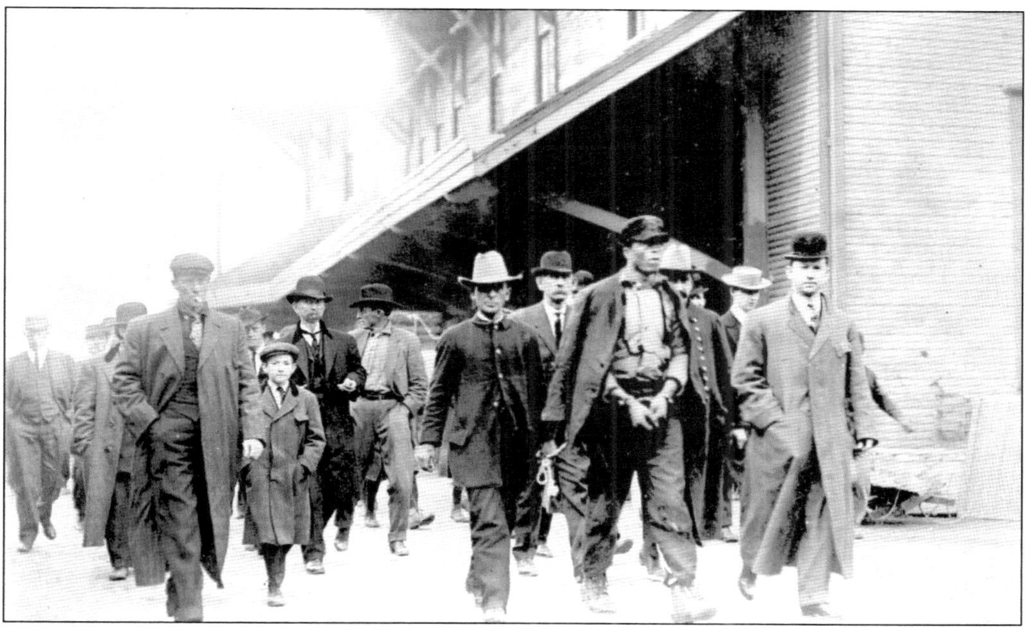

Law-enforcement officers are shown here in February 1911 escorting Lewis West (in handcuffs) past the railroad depot in Hamlet to a waiting train that will transport him to Central Prison in Raleigh. See chapter nine for additional details about the West case. (Courtesy A&H.)

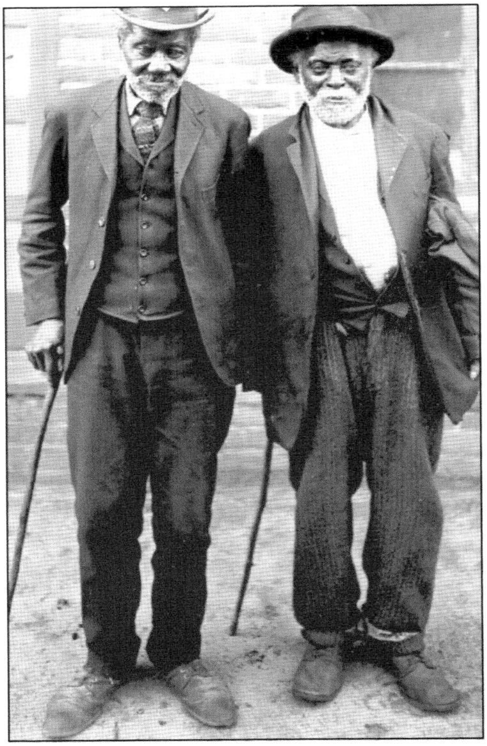

An unidentified pair of elderly African-American men pose here for Marchant. The date and location are unknown. (Courtesy A&H.)

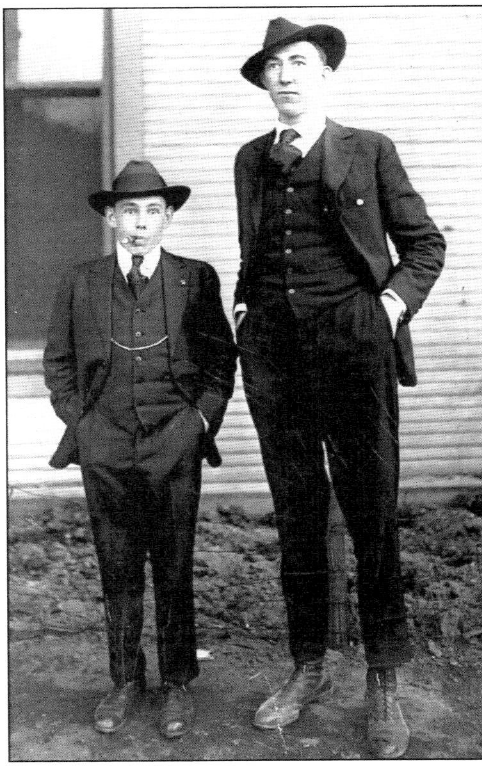

Marchant may have photographed this unusually well-dressed pair of gentlemen in Hamlet, but the date of the picture is unknown. The men are identified as "Squat" Porter and "Slim" Lawson. (Courtesy A&H.)

Reproduced here is an outdoor portrait of an unidentified mother and children, date unknown. (Courtesy A&H.)

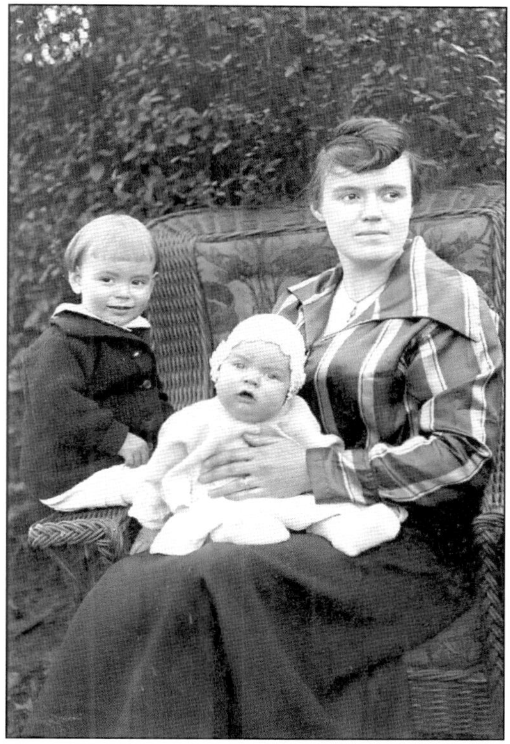

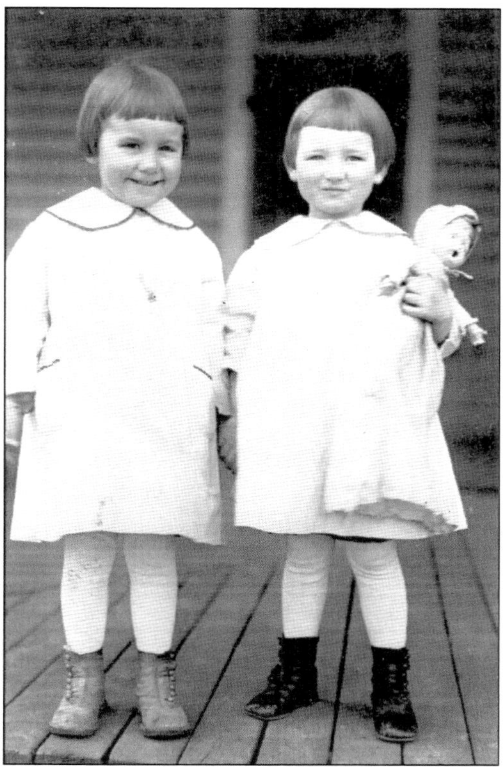

Just prior to taking their photograph, Marchant elicited laughter from these two little girls, who are standing on the porch of an unidentified residence in Hamlet, date unknown. The girl on the left is Alice Kirkland, who later married Edgar L. Robinson. (Courtesy A&H.)

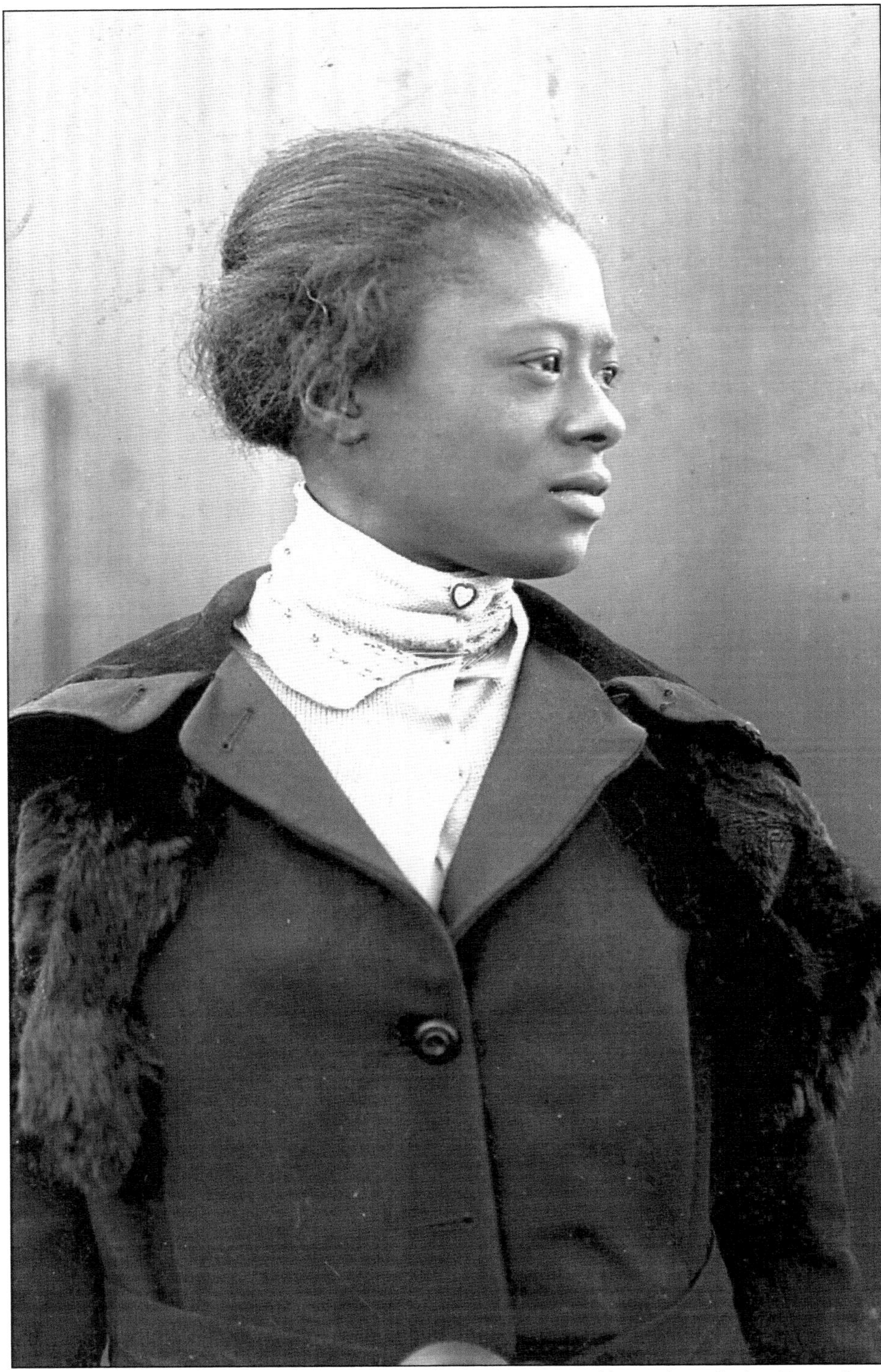

The attractive African-American woman pictured here in profile is identified as Rosa Crockett. Marchant took the photograph on February 24, 1919. (Courtesy A&H.)

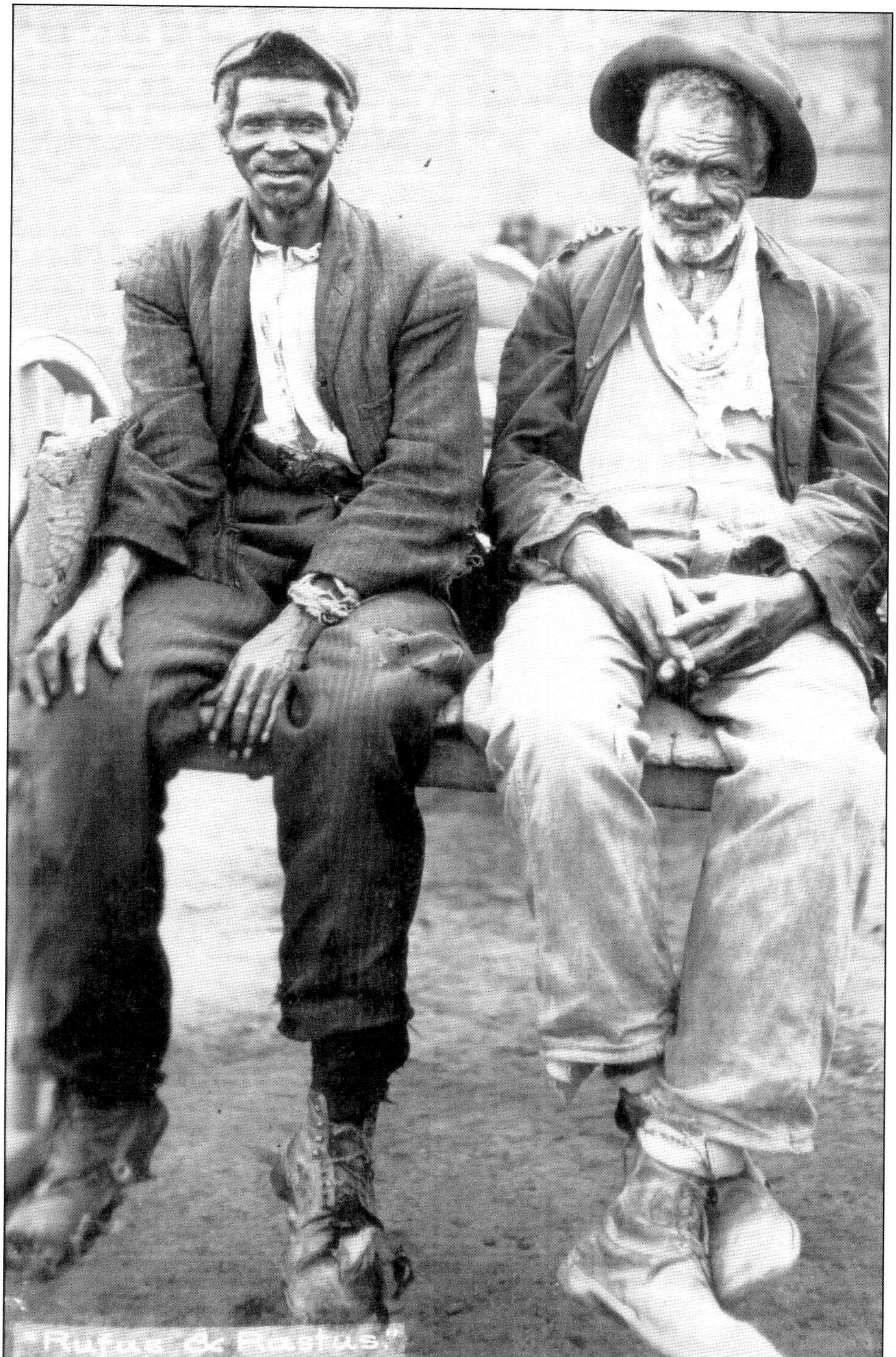

It appears that these two African-American men are seated on the back of a wagon or cart. The Hamlet photographer produced this postcard view about 1915. (Courtesy Sarah M. Pope.)

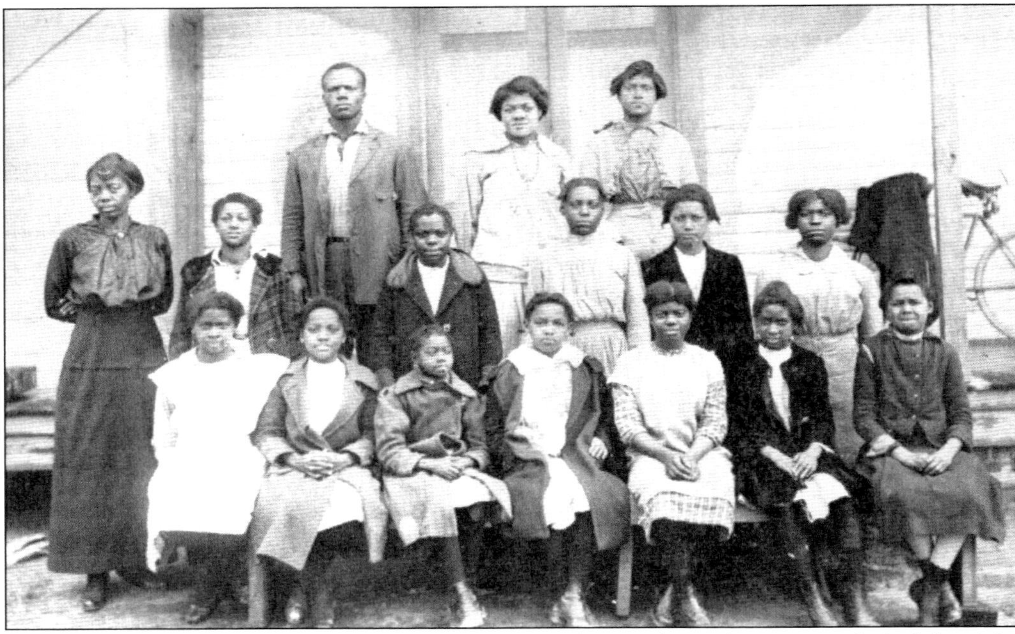

Faculty and students at the Pee Dee Institute in Hamlet are shown here in 1916. At left is Miss Dora Jane Portervine, a teacher at the institution. The Baptist-affiliated school was located in the present Dobbins Heights community. (Courtesy James E. and Ida C. Honeycutt, *A History of Richmond County*, Raleigh: Edwards & Broughton Company, 1976, p. 307.)

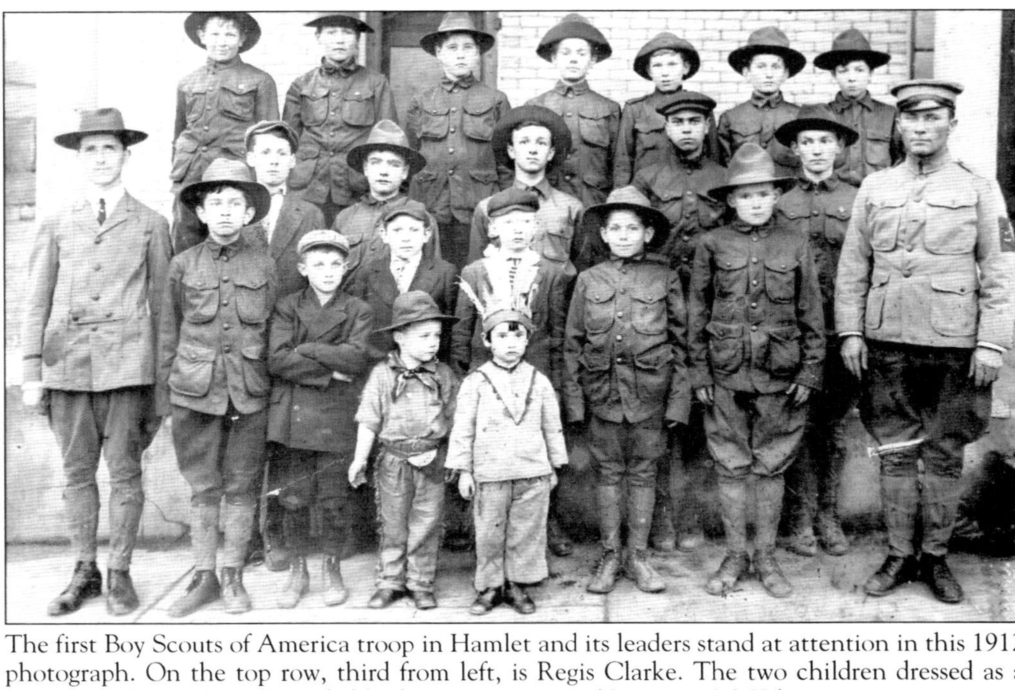

The first Boy Scouts of America troop in Hamlet and its leaders stand at attention in this 1912 photograph. On the top row, third from left, is Regis Clarke. The two children dressed as a cowboy and an Indian are probably the scout mascots. (Courtesy A&H.)

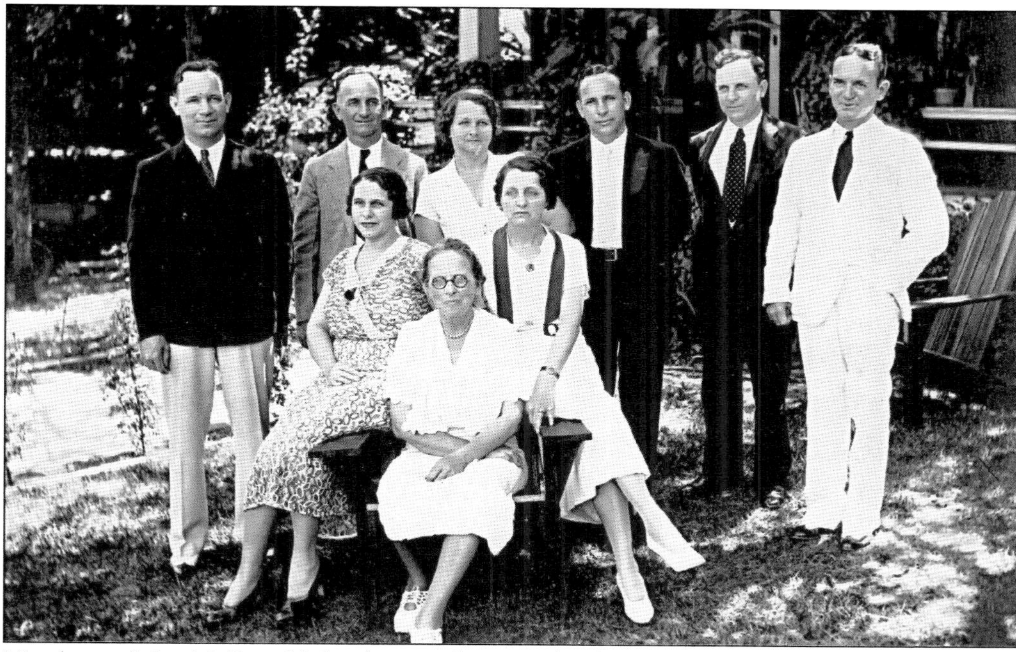

Members of the McDonald family pose here in the front yard at the residence of Murphy McDonald (standing second from left) in Hamlet about 1930. The family persuaded Marchant to make this family portrait during the twilight of his career, when he was not as active in the profession. The people pictured here are the children of Lydia Bynum (Mrs. Malcolm) McDonald, the woman seated in the chair. (Courtesy A&H.)

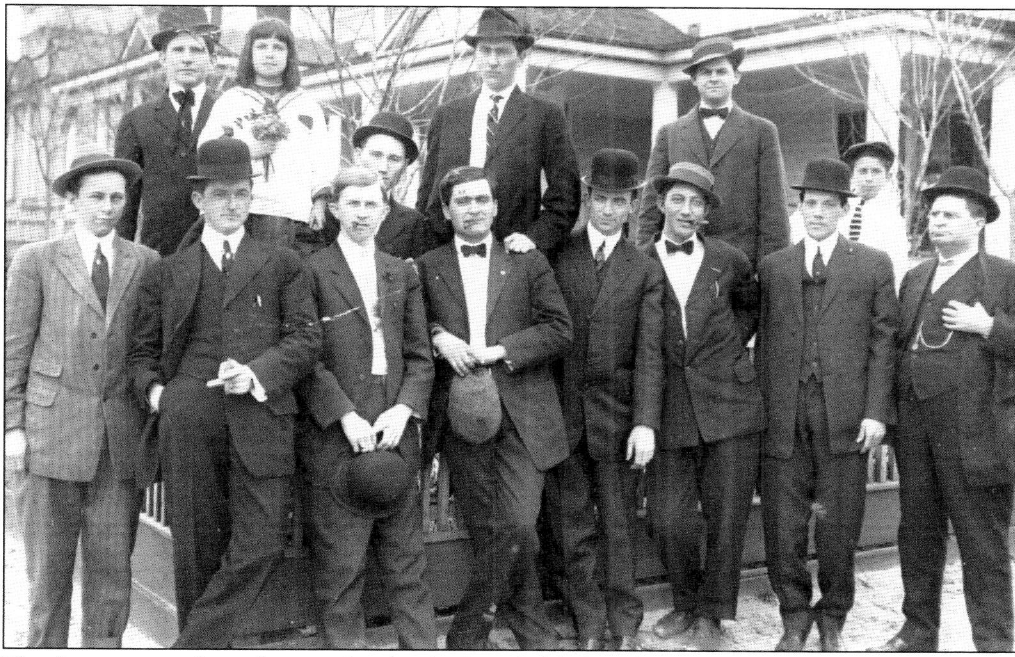

This large group of nattily attired individuals probably hired Marchant to take their photograph, perhaps in Hamlet (date unknown). (Courtesy A&H.)

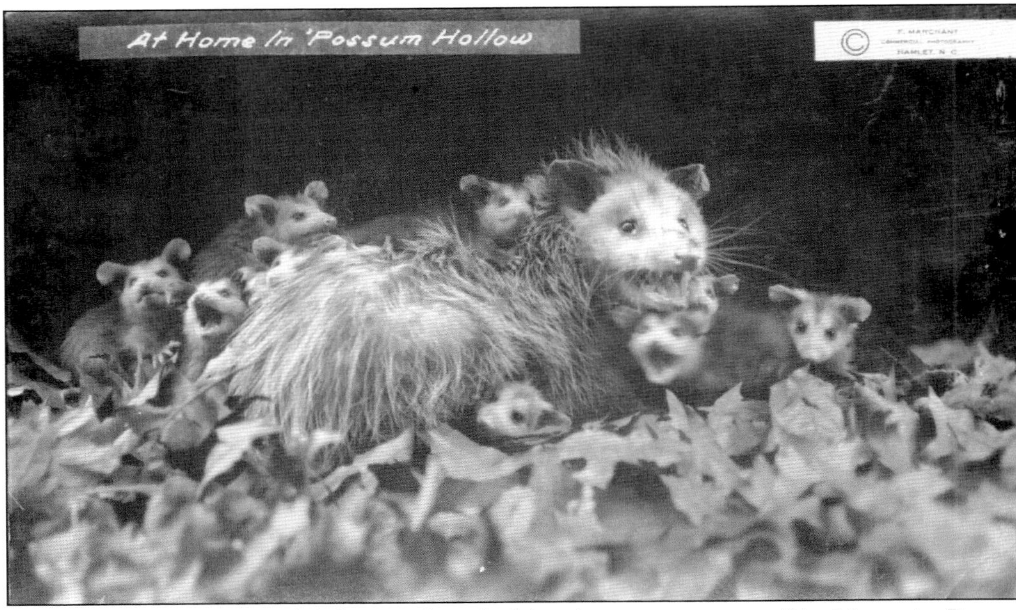

This mother opossum and baby are described by the cameraman as "At Home in Possum Hollow." (Courtesy Durwood Barbour.)

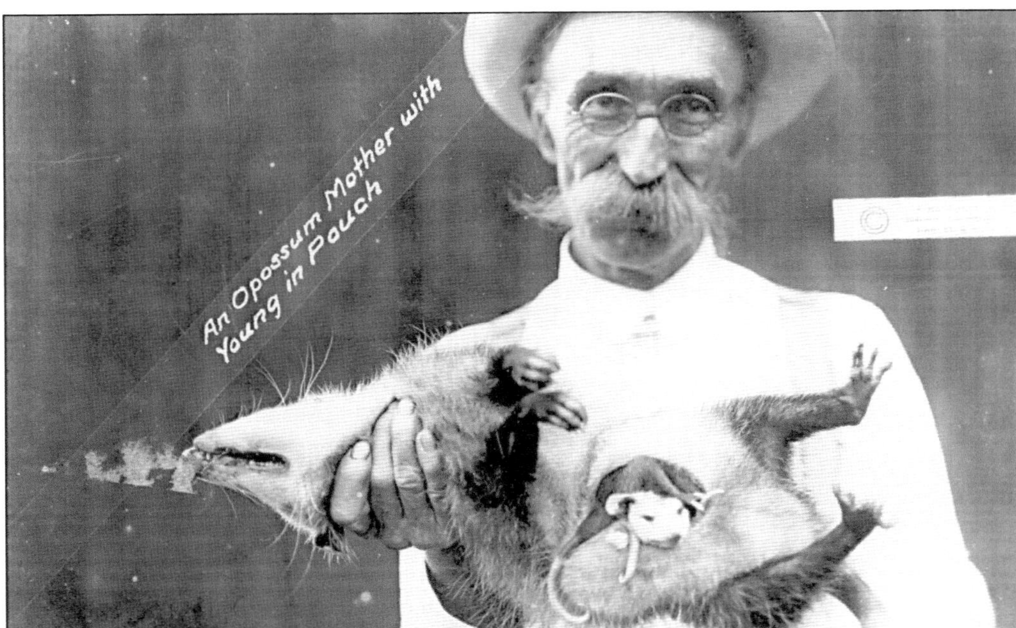

An unidentified bespectacled man is shown here holding a female opossum with a young "possum" peeking from her pouch. (Courtesy Wayne Chapman.)

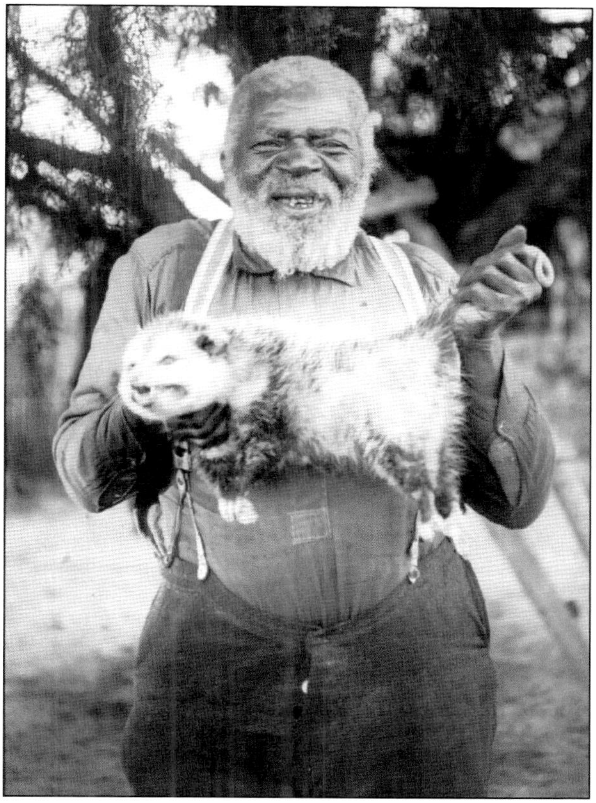

The African-American man shown in both photographs proudly displays opossums that he caught during hunts for the marsupials. (At right, courtesy C. Vernon Vallance; below, courtesy Stephen E. Massengill.)

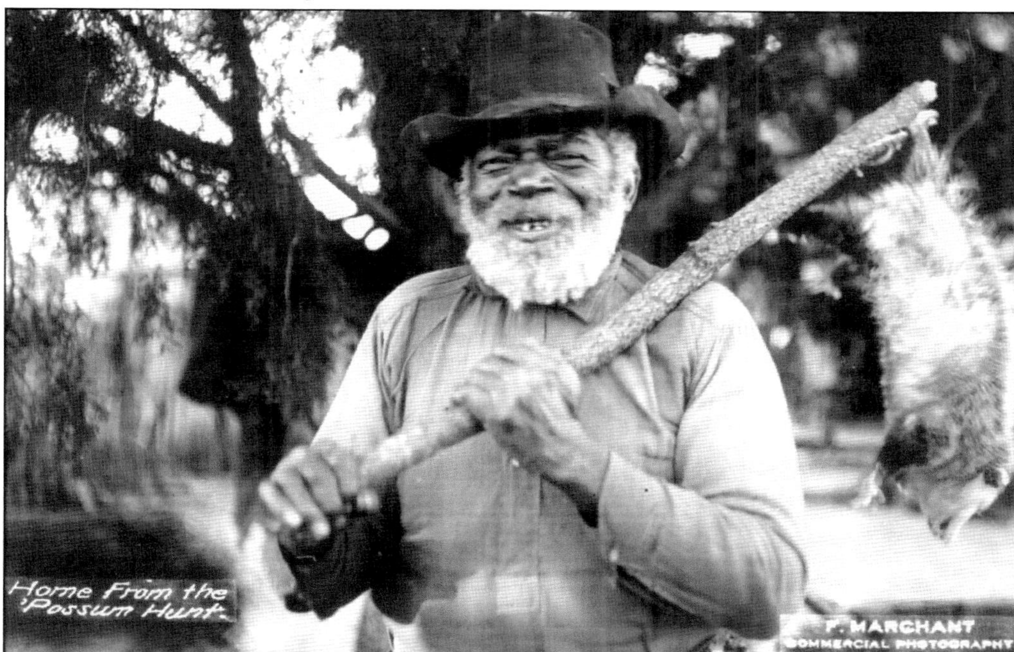

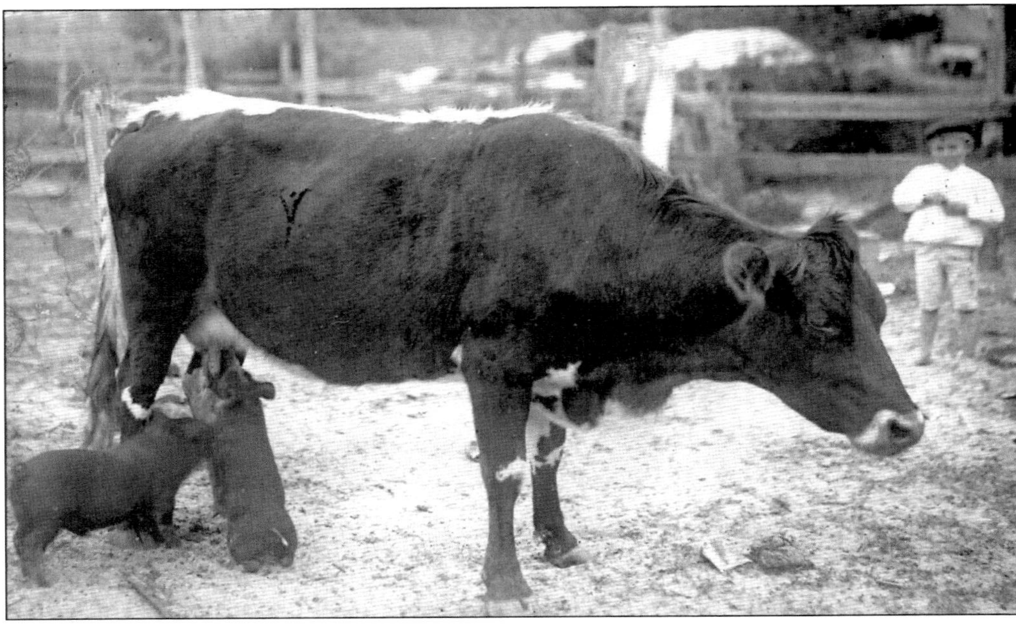

The photographs on this page show piglets suckling a cow (above) and a sow (below). Marchant humorously described the unusual images as "A Meal Station" and "A Private Boarding House." (Above, courtesy Wayne Chapman; below, courtesy Durwood Barbour.)

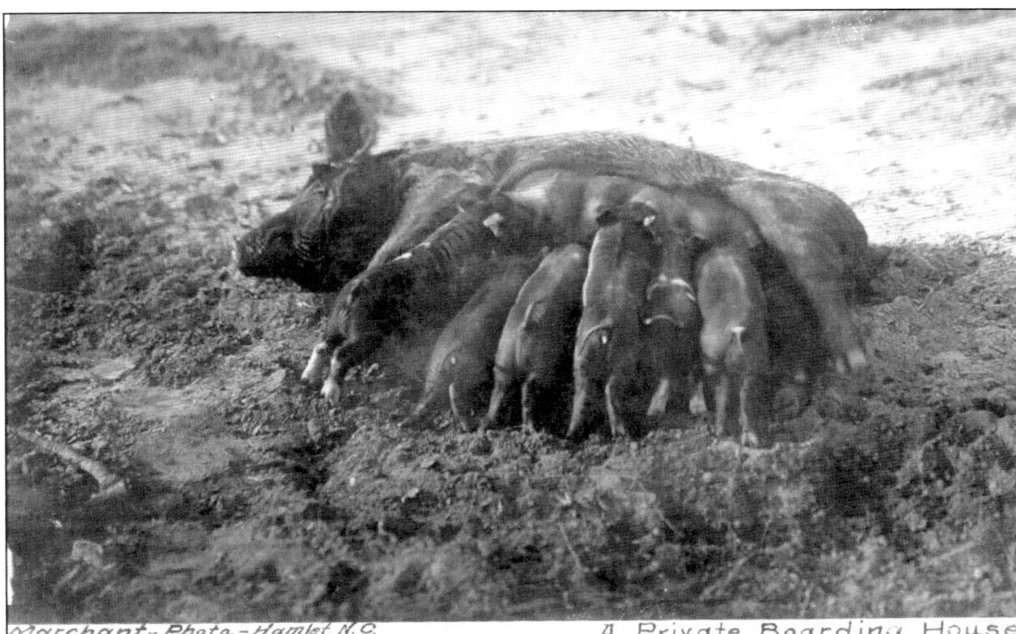

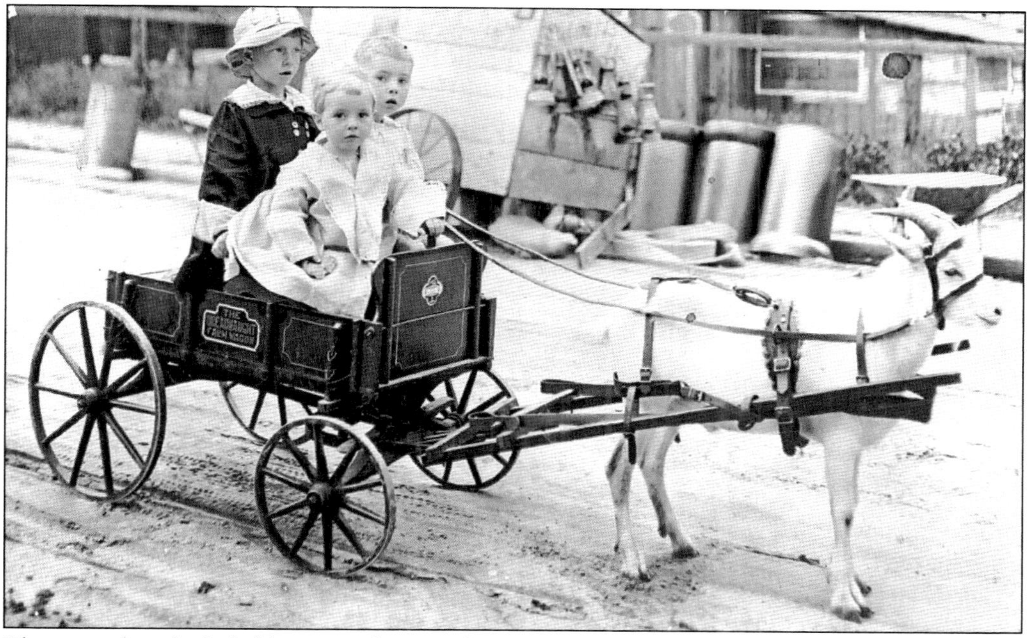

These unidentified children are shown taking a ride in a goat-powered conveyance dubbed "The Dreadnaught Farm Wagon." The place and date of the photograph are not known. (Courtesy A&H.)

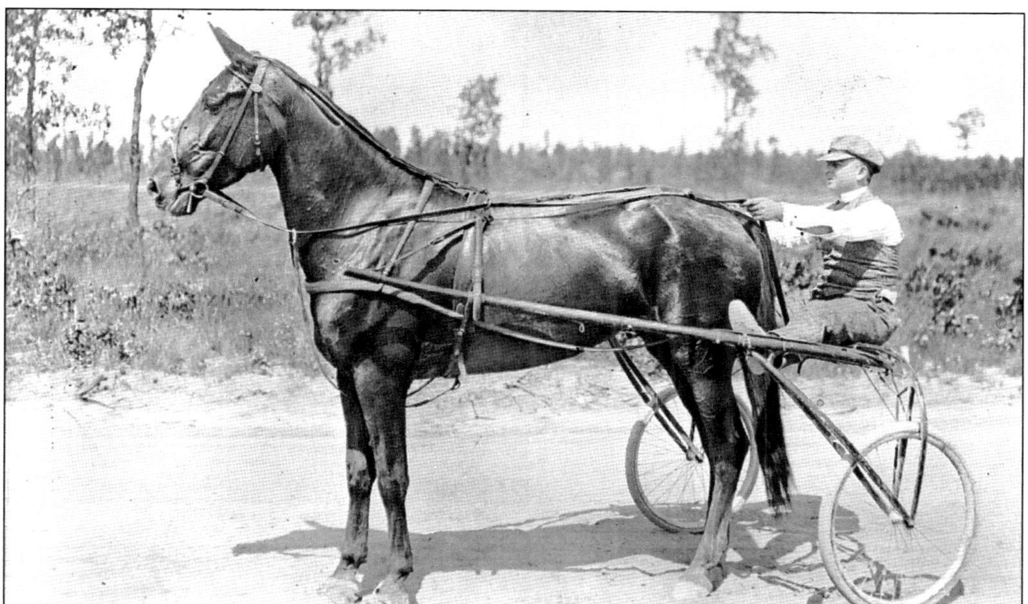

Marchant probably traveled to the site of a race to photograph this horse-drawn sulky and rider. The place could have been Southern Pines, but the date is unknown. (Courtesy A&H.)

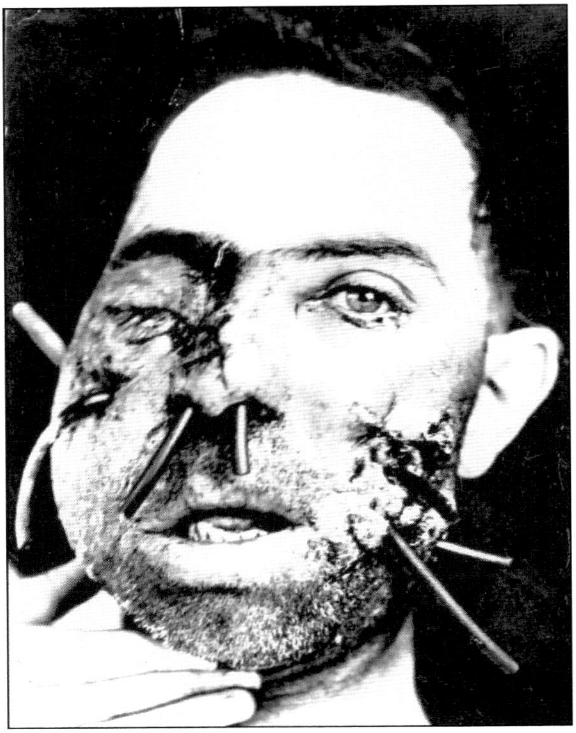

Displayed above is a dramatic portrait of Richmond County deputy sheriff James Branson Reynolds (1881–1958) taken at Hamlet Hospital in 1917. Reynolds received severe gunshot wounds to the face from a man named Lee Covington, who subsequently was convicted of secret assault and sentenced to a term of 20 years at the state prison in Raleigh. Physicians at the hospital treated Reynolds's wounds with the Carrel-Dakin antiseptic solution, an effective remedy developed during World War I. The picture at right shows Reynolds seven weeks after undergoing the treatment. The injuries have healed, but his face is scarred and deformed. (Courtesy Wayne Chapman.)

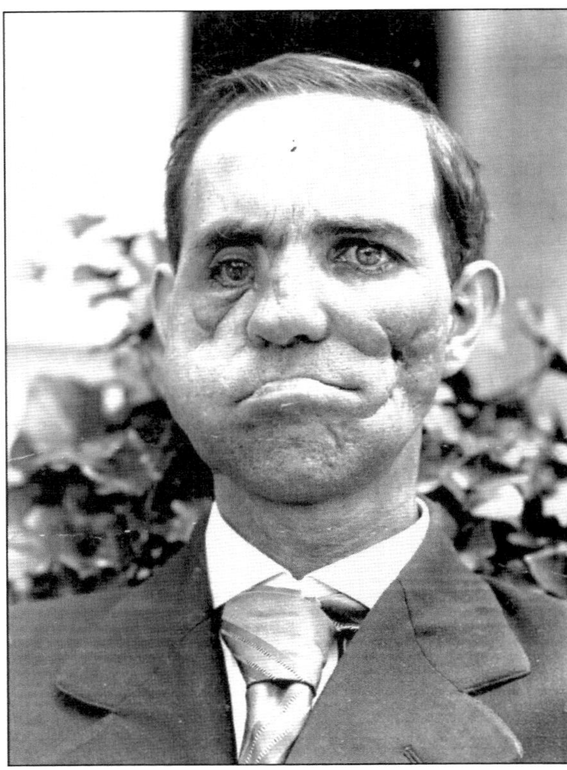

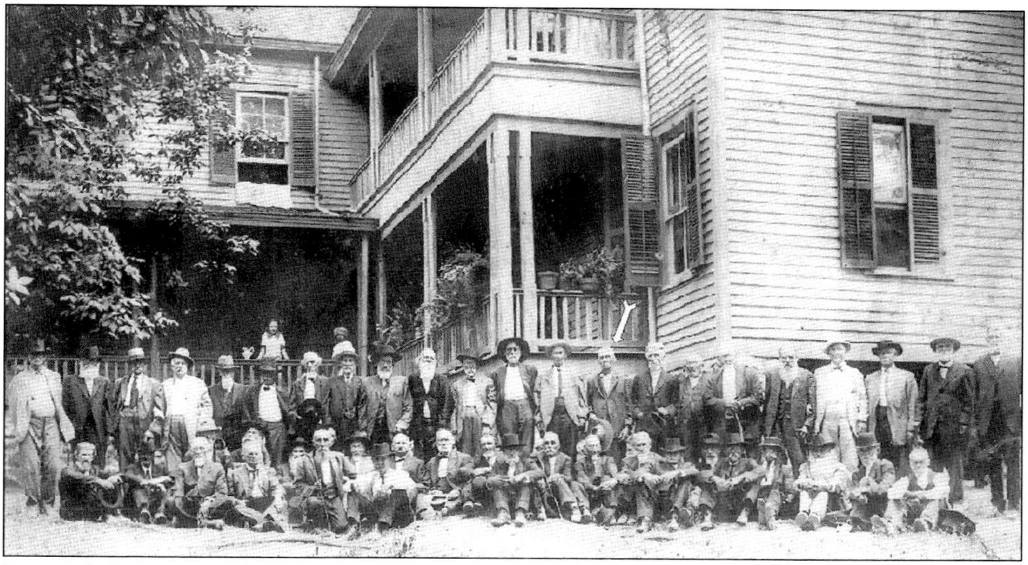

Pictured above is a gathering of Richmond County Confederate veterans at the Ellerbe Springs Hotel about 1910. Identified people are (seated) Starling McDonald (4th from left), R.C. Meacham (to right of man kneeling with cane), and Elisha Chappel (far right); (standing) Claude Dockery (4th from left), Solomon Ford (7th from left), Wilkes Pankey (10th from left), John Bowden (12th from left), Solomon McLean (14th from left), William Johnson McLeod (15th from left), Hadd Shepard (18th from left), Walter Thomas (19th from left), James Covington (20th from left), W.T. Covington (21st from left), and Capt. W.I. Everett (far right.) The maker of this photograph is unknown, but it was likely Marchant or Rockingham photographer J.E. Spencer. (Courtesy John Hamer.)

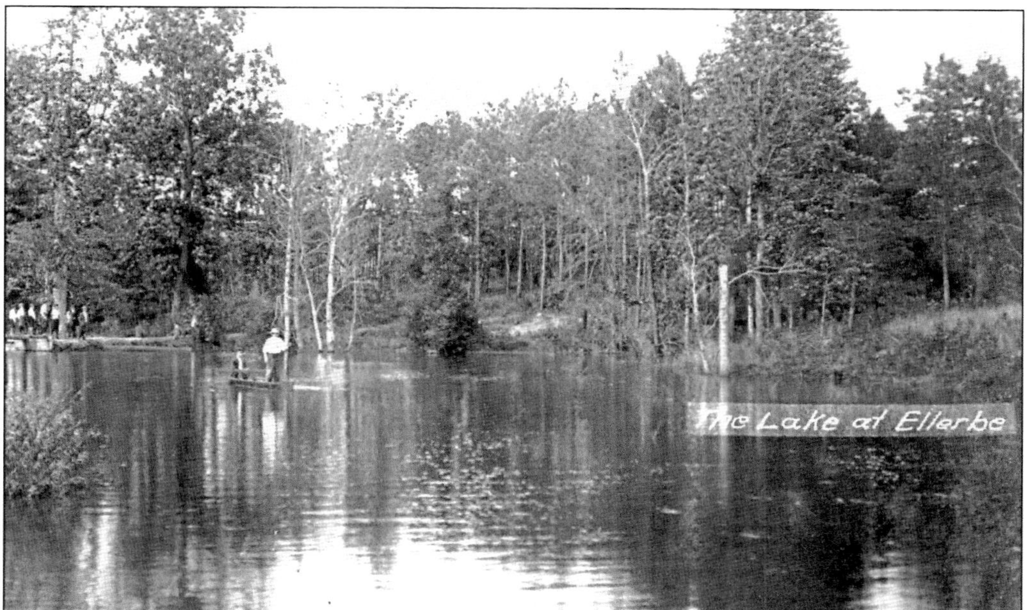

The waters of the lake at Ellerbe Springs are so placid that the man in the bow of the boat is able to stand as the vessel approaches the camera. (Courtesy J. Neal Cadieu Jr.)

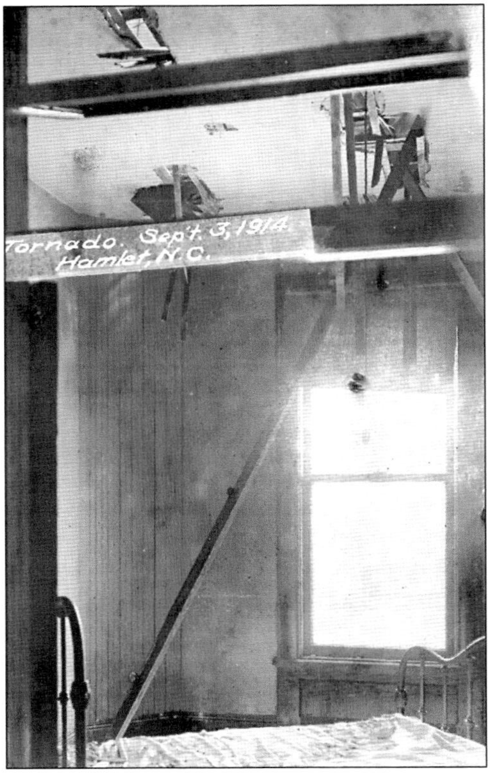

Damage to the ceiling and wall of this unidentified room is evidence of the passage of a tornado through the Hamlet area on September 3, 1914. (Courtesy Stephen E. Massengill.)

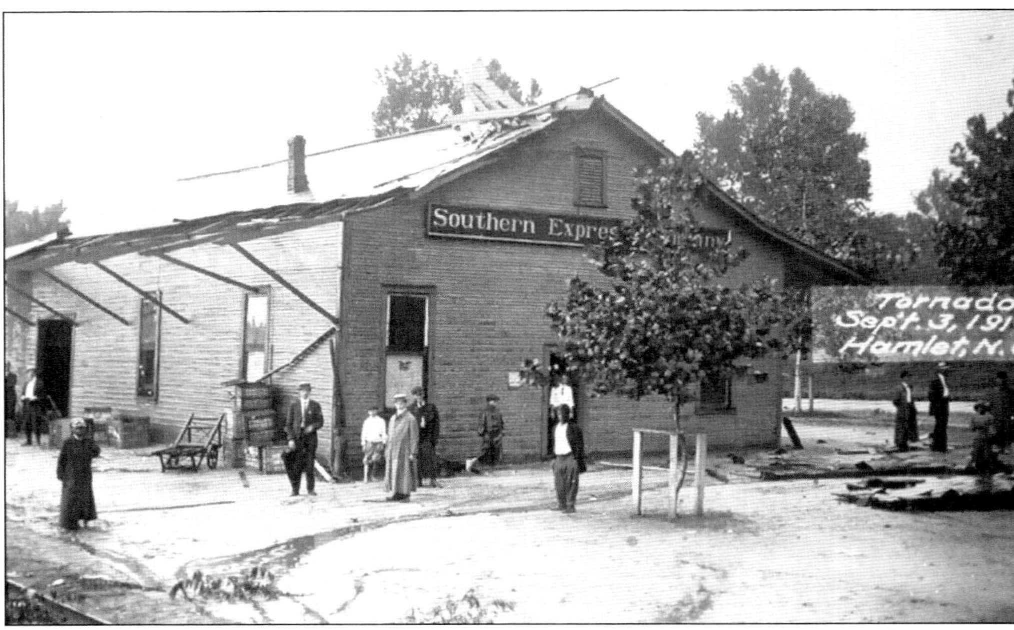

The storm of September 1914 also damaged the roof of the building that housed the Southern Express Company in Hamlet. Townspeople stand outside of the structure following the heavy wind and rain generated by the cyclone. (Courtesy of Hamlet Public Library.)

Nine

BEYOND THE COUNTY LINE

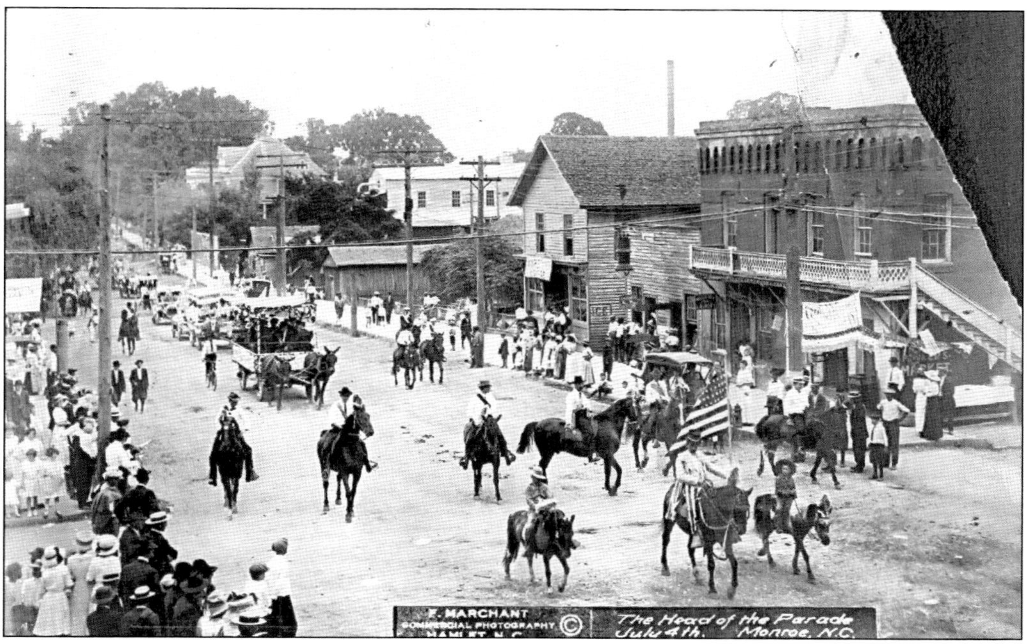

Pictured here is an elevated view of the beginning of a Fourth of July parade on an unpaved street in Monroe (Union County), North Carolina, about 1909. (Courtesy A&H.)

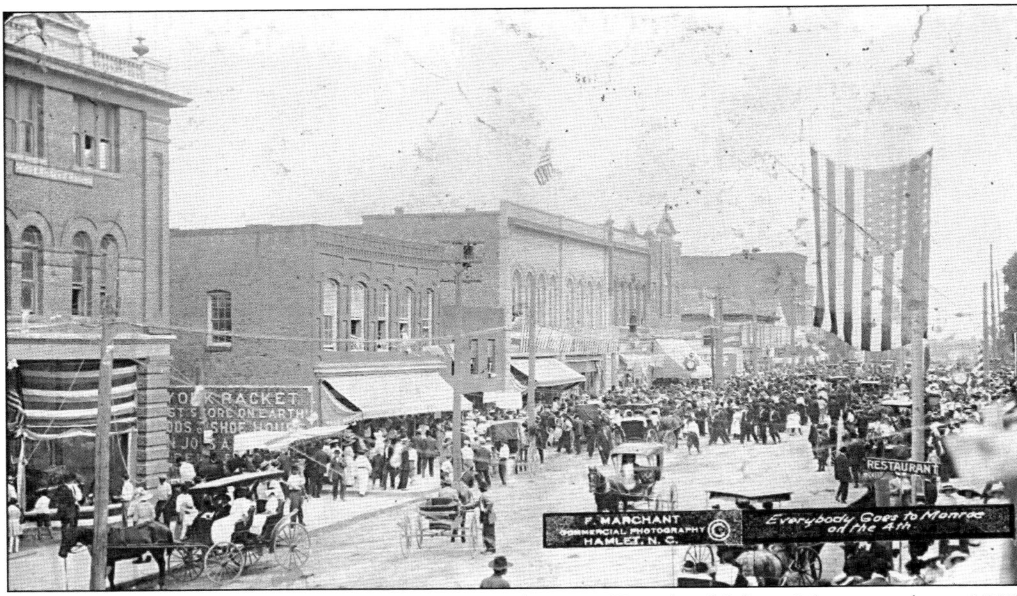

Crowds fill one of the main streets in Monroe during a Fourth of July celebration about 1909. (Courtesy A&H.)

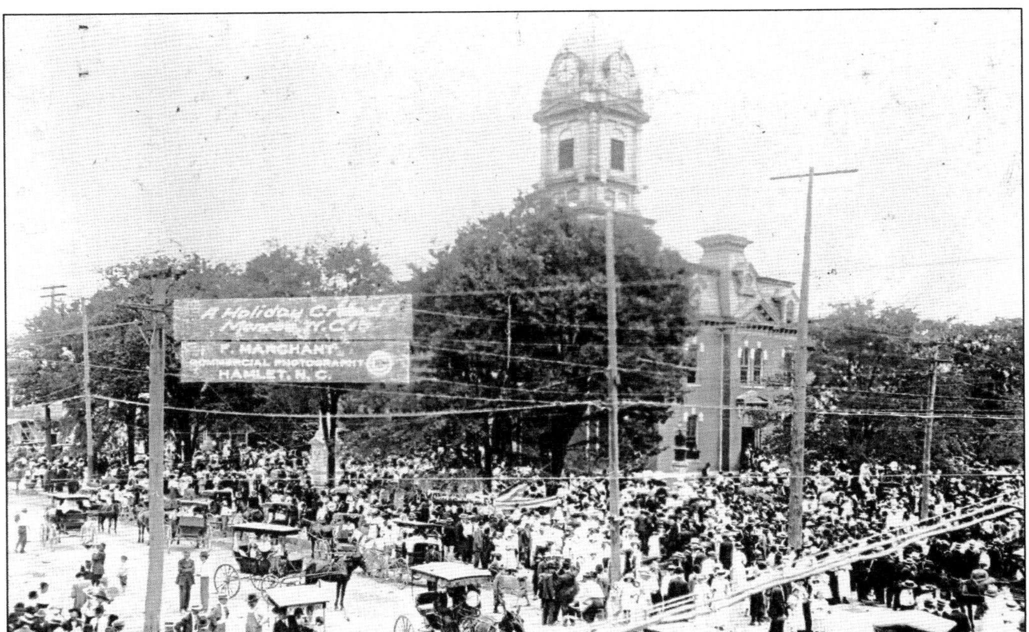

A throng of celebrants mingles on the grounds of the Union County Courthouse in Monroe during this July fourth gathering about 1909. The courthouse was bounded by Lafayette (later Main), Jefferson, Hayne, and Franklin Streets. (Courtesy A&H.)

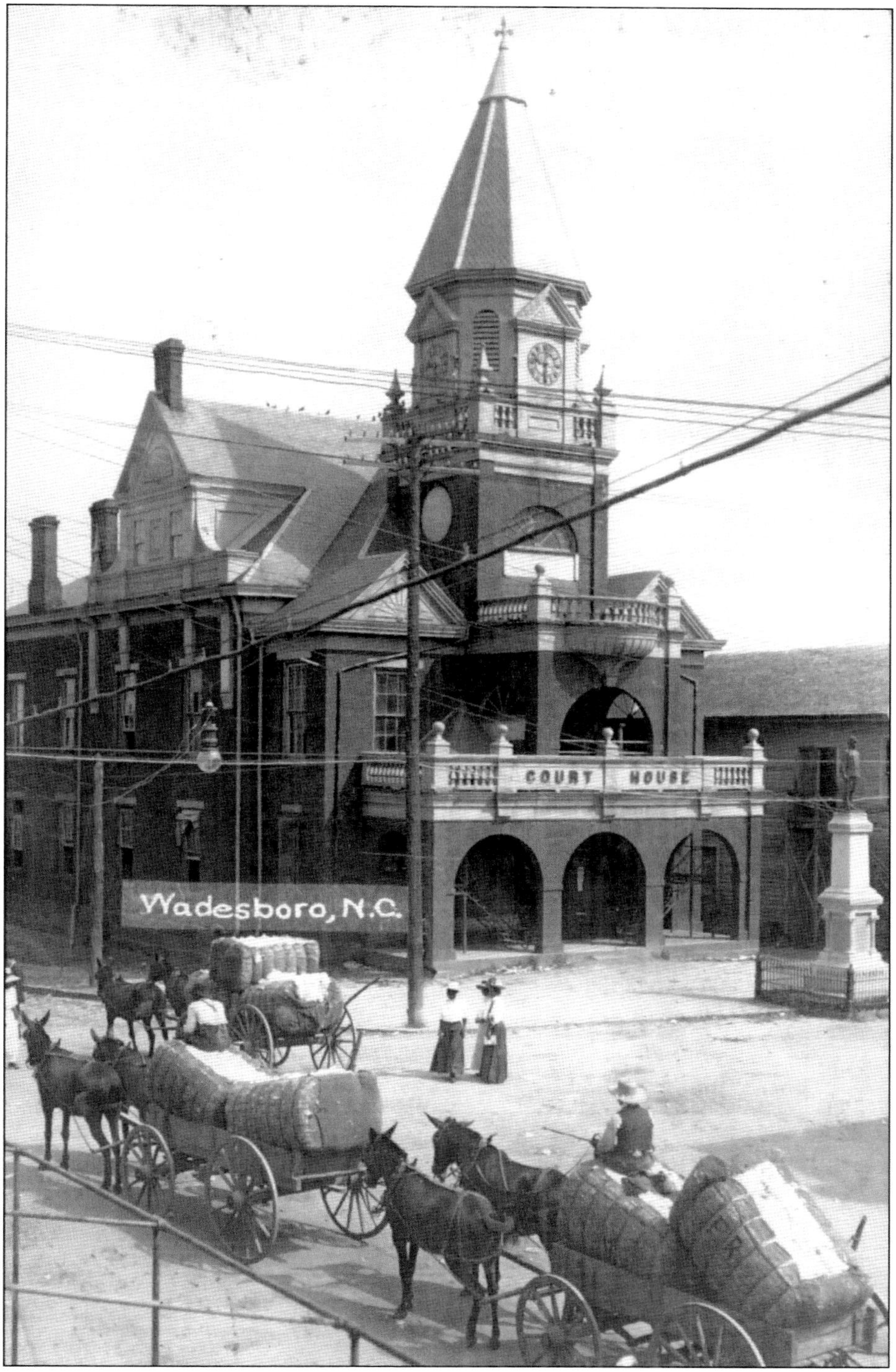

Wagons filled with cotton are parked near the Anson County Courthouse in Wadesboro about 1910. The structure, situated at the corner of Wade and Greene Streets, was constructed about 1870 and remodeled in 1891. (Courtesy Stephen E. Massengill.)

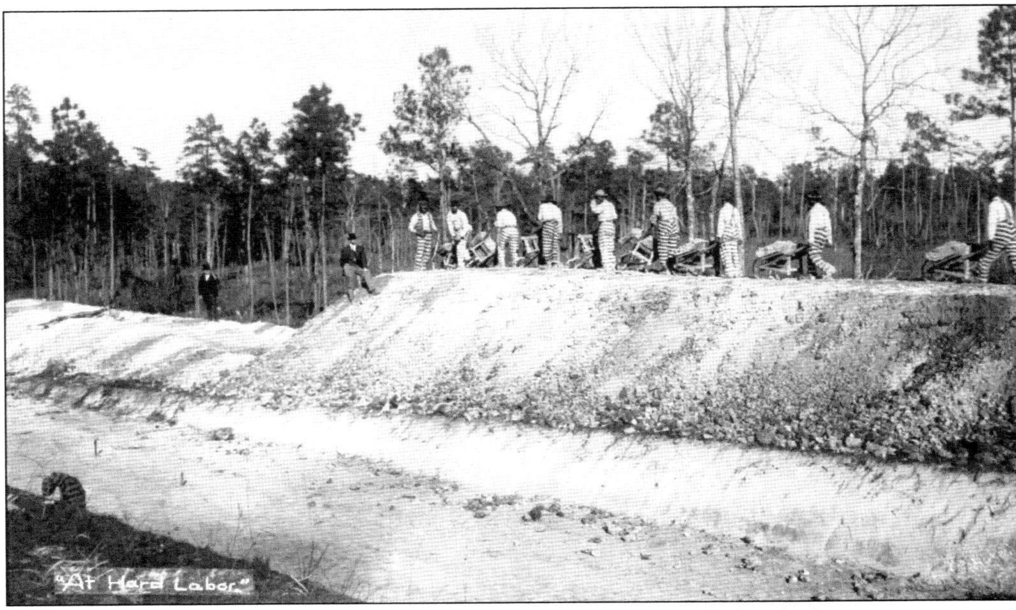

African-American convicts are shown unloading wheelbarrows filled with dirt at a construction site of the Laurinburg & Southern Railroad about 1911. Able-bodied, as well as long- and life-term, men at Central Prison in Raleigh were often sent to perform "hard labor" on the state's railroads. North Carolina leased convicts to companies and corporations as a form of cheap labor and to gain revenue for the state. (Courtesy Durwood Barbour.)

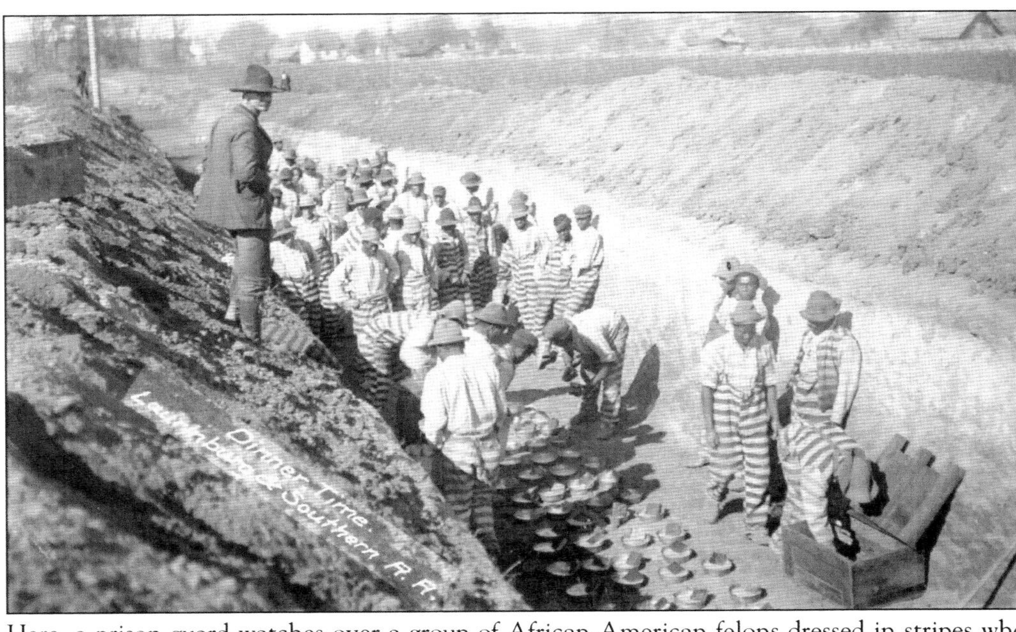

Here, a prison guard watches over a group of African-American felons dressed in stripes who gather in a ditch for a lunch break. The prisoners are working on the Laurinburg & Southern Railroad about 1911. This short-line railway operated in Scotland County from Johns through Laurinburg to Wagram. (Courtesy Durwood Barbour.)

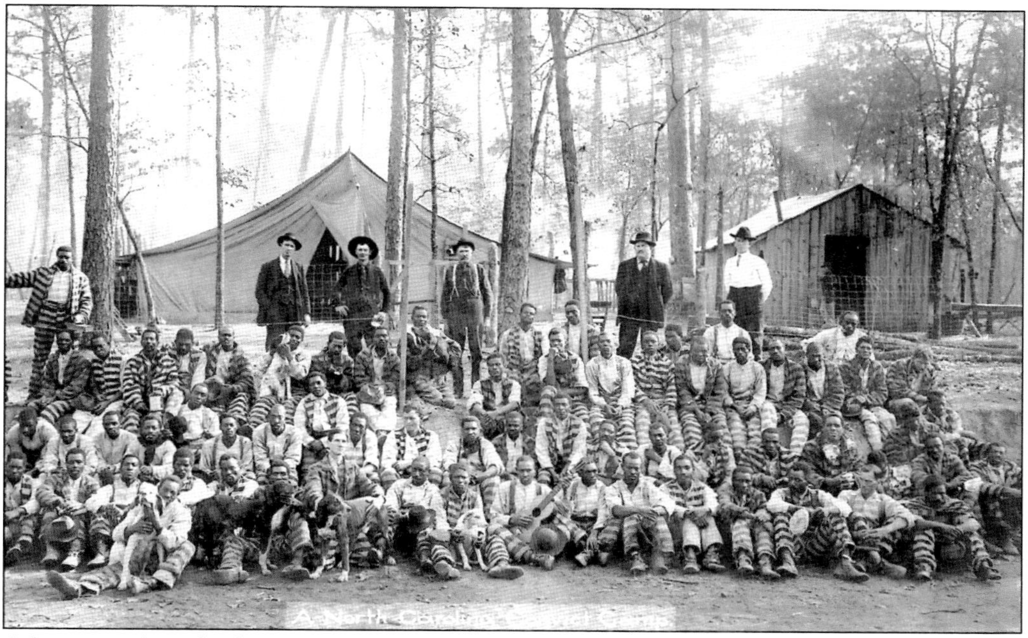

A large number of African-American prisoners are shown at a convict railroad camp, perhaps located near a construction site on the Laurinburg & Southern Railroad in 1911. In the front row, two felons are holding dogs, and one has a guitar. A total of 528 African-American male prisoners were incarcerated by the state in 1911. (Courtesy Wayne Chapman.)

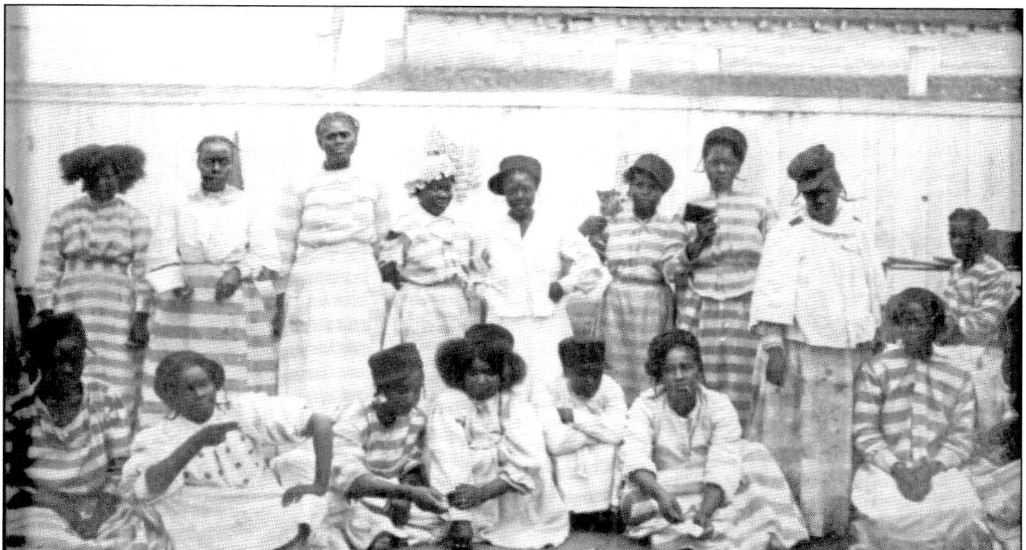

Photographed here is an undated, rare view of African-American women prisoners clothed in striped dresses at the North Carolina State Prison Farm, known as Caledonia, in eastern Halifax County. The state leased the farm and provided roughly constructed board houses for the felons. Prisoners with physical disabilities and female convicts were sent to the farm, where they helped raise cotton, corn, peanuts, and other crops. The state realized thousands of dollars from the sale and consumption of these agricultural products. (Courtesy Durwood Barbour.)

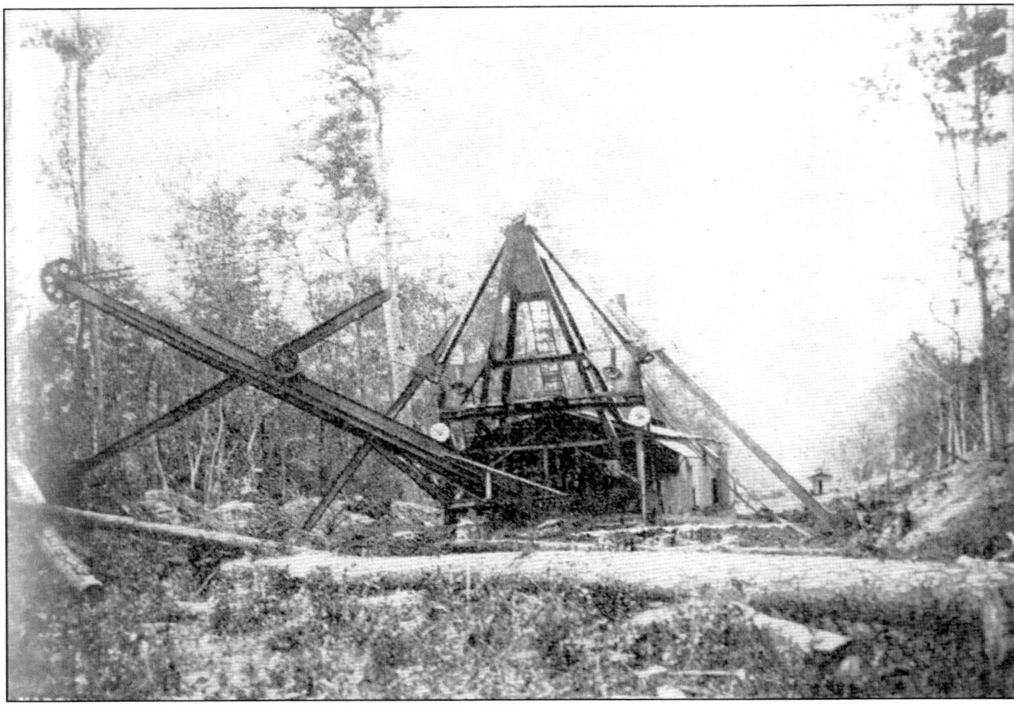

These two views show equipment involved in the expensive project of draining swamplands in Robeson County in about 1913. Reclaiming farmland in that portion of North Carolina may have cost the state as much as $130,000. (Courtesy A&H.)

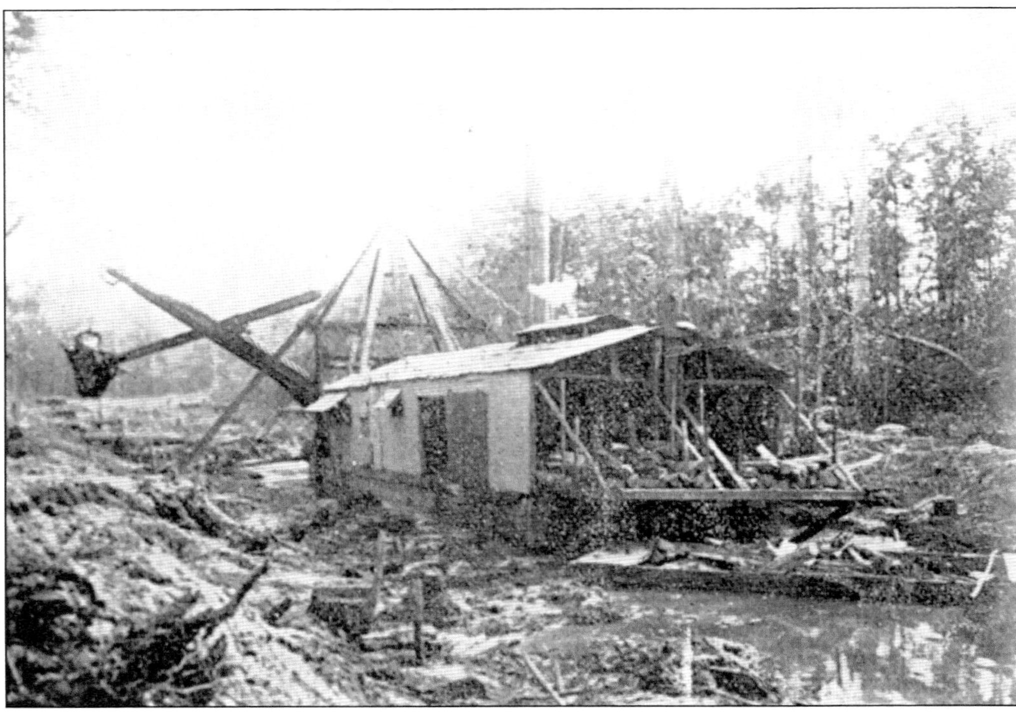

This handsome, two-story building with a bell tower housed the graded school of Aberdeen in Moore County during the early 20th century. (Courtesy Stephen E. Massengill.)

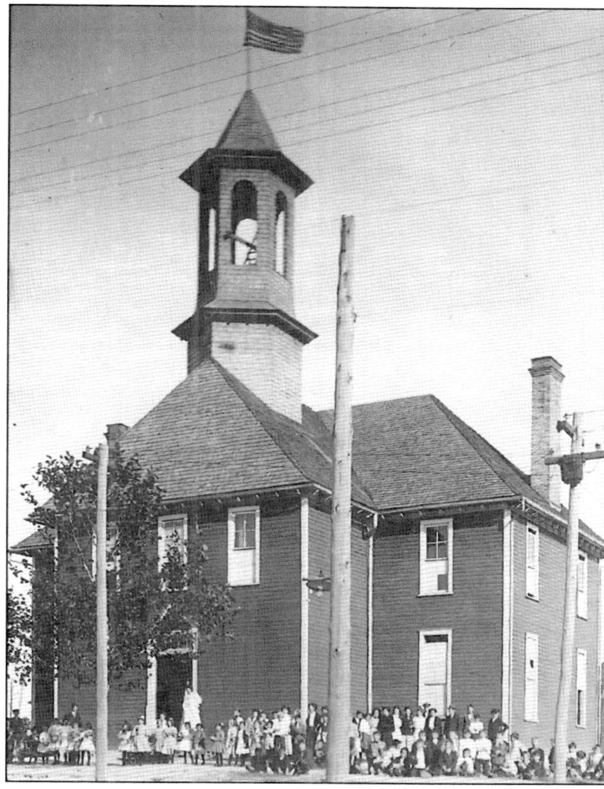

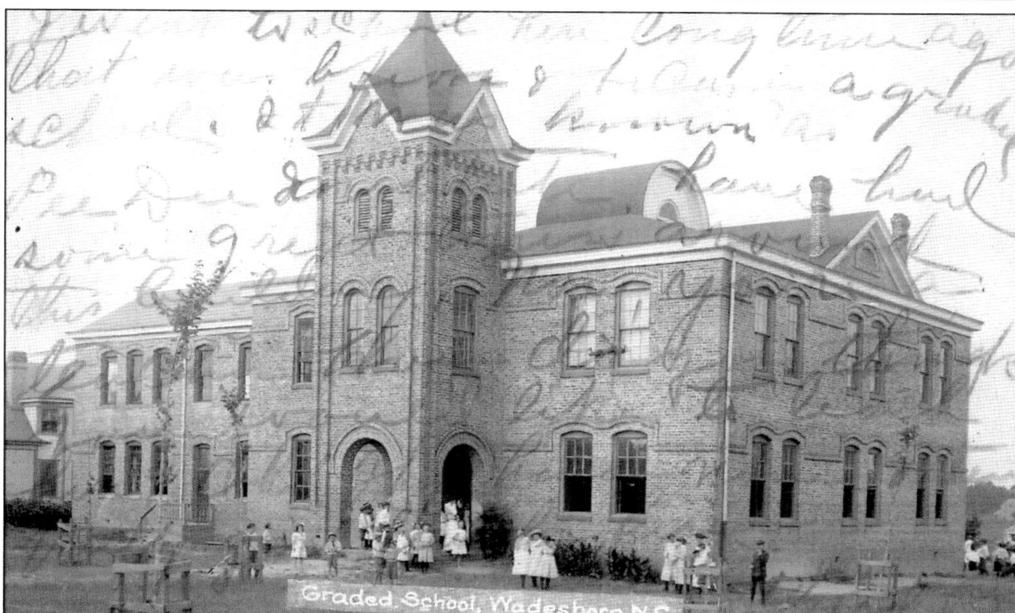

The handwritten message on the front of this postcard view indicates that this brick building in Wadesboro (Anson County) was once known as Pee Dee Institute. By 1910, it was home to a graded school. (Courtesy Wayne Chapman.)

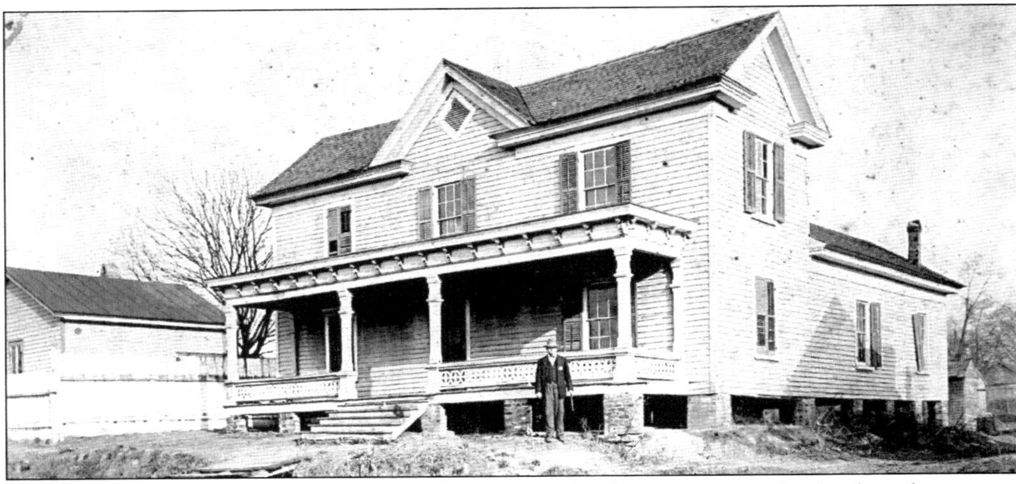

Lewis West (1887–1911), a criminal from Cumberland County, was the leader of a gang of thieves and plunderers who terrorized eastern North Carolina in the winter of 1911. The desperadoes began their stealing rampage in Fayetteville and went to Dunn in Harnett County. Several armed gang members made their way to Wilson. Cumberland County law enforcement officials warned authorities in Wilson County; Wilson chief of police O.A. Glover and county deputy sheriff George Mumford attempted to arrest West at the home of Mary Young in Wilson on February 3. West shot and killed Mumford and severely wounded Glover. Here, Wilson County sheriff W.D.P. Sharp points to the spot where Deputy Sheriff George Mumford was killed. (Courtesy A&H.)

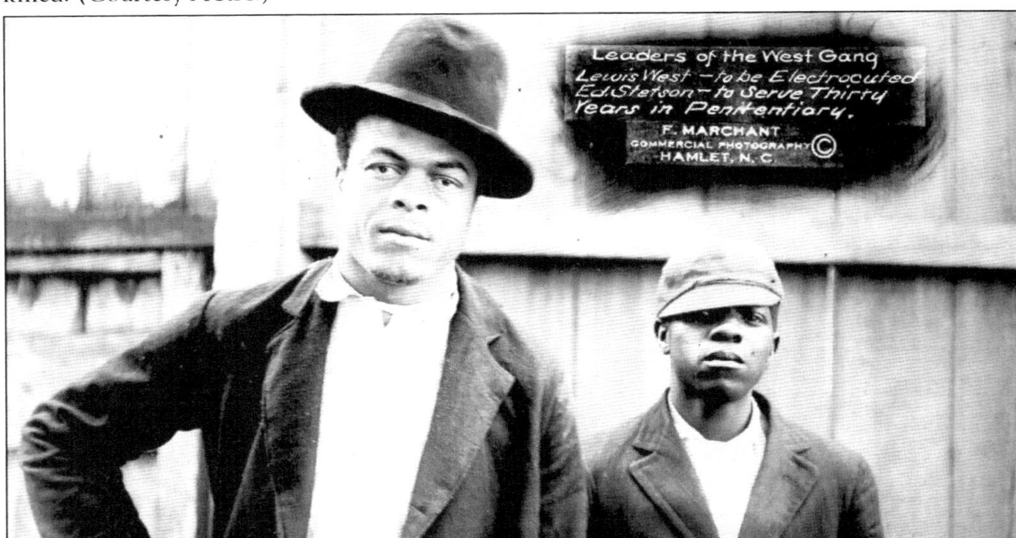

The gang left Wilson and separated, and West hid in Robeson County swamps for about a week. Sam H. "Jake" Dunlap, chief of police of Maxton, captured West at a Maxton diner on February 11. Dunlap and officers from Cumberland and Wilson Counties escorted West to Hamlet, where they boarded a train to Raleigh's Central Prison, the state penitentiary. A special session of the Wilson County Superior Court was called on March 13, 1911, to try West and his accomplices. Marchant took this unusual photograph of Lewis West and Ed Stallings (alias Stetson), the leaders of the "West Gang," at the time of their trial. (Courtesy A&H.)

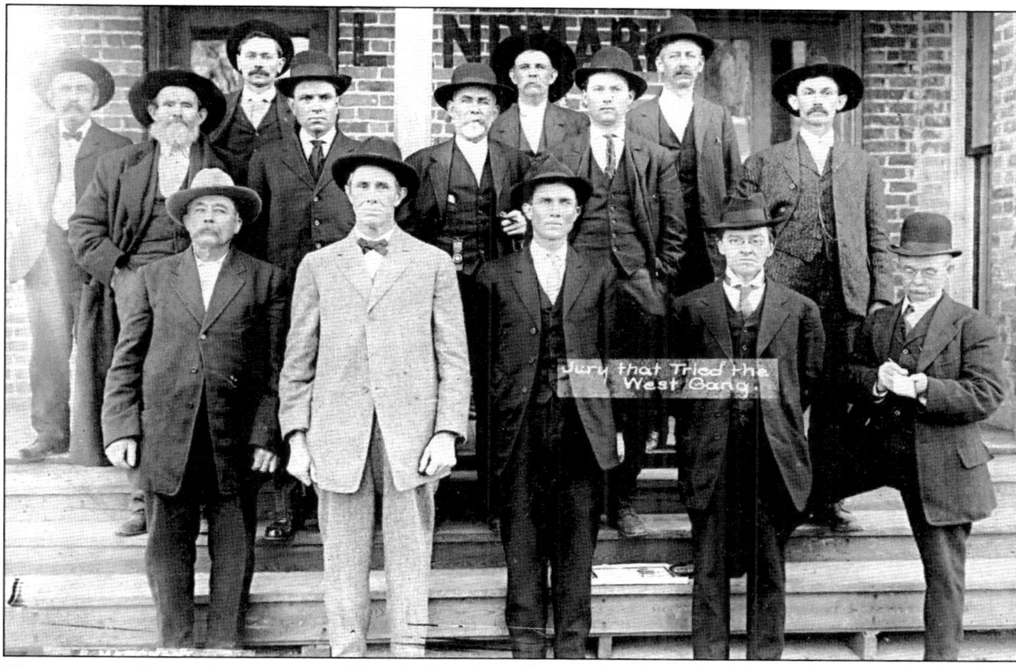

Newspapers throughout eastern North Carolina devoted a great deal of attention to the murder and trial. West was convicted of first-degree murder on March 17 and sentenced to die in the electric chair at Central Prison in Raleigh. The sentence was carried out on May 5, 1911. Here, members of the jury that heard the West case in Wilson pose for Marchant in March 1911. (Courtesy A&H.)

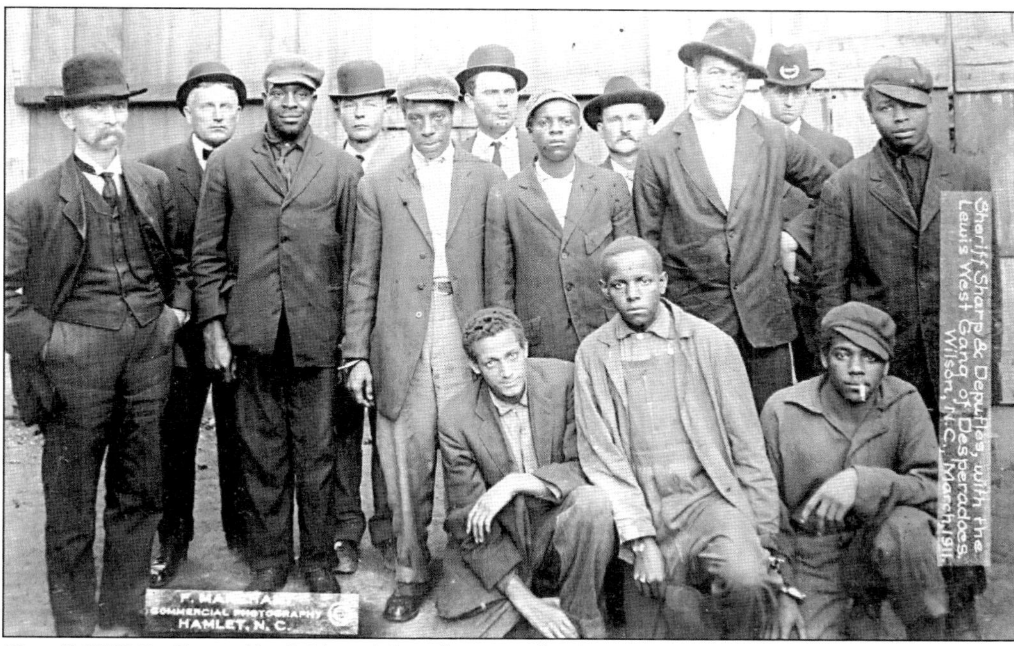

Sheriff W.D.P. Sharp (far left) and five deputies (back row) stand with West and six members of his band at Wilson during the time of the trial in 1911. (Courtesy A&H.)

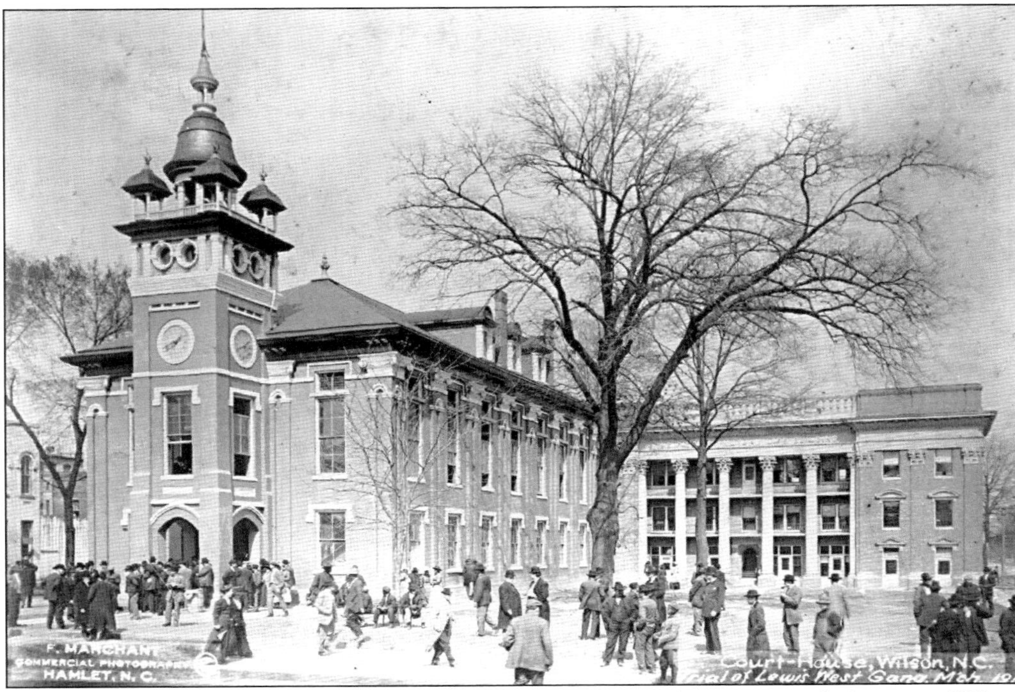

A crowd of interested spectators fills the grounds of the courthouse on Nash Street in Wilson during the litigation of Lewis West and his men in March 1911. (Courtesy A&H.)

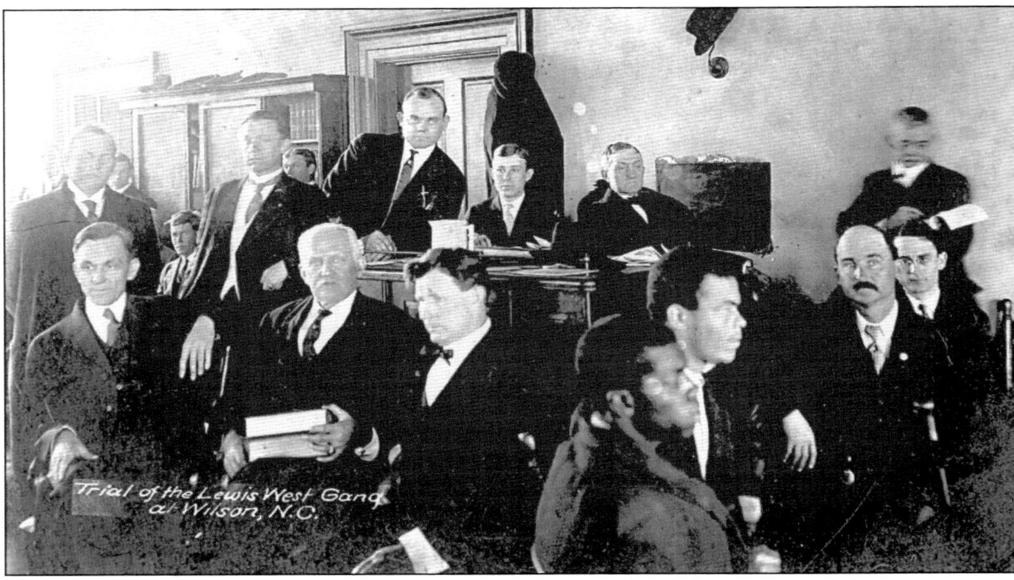

The Hamlet photographer also took this staged photograph of the interior of the courtroom at the time of the proceedings in 1911. The two leaders of the gang—Ed Stallings (alias Stetson) and Lewis West—are shown in profile in the right foreground surrounded by attorneys and other court personnel. The older man seated on the bench is almost certainly presiding judge Joseph S. Adams. Probably also present are defense attorneys W.A. Lucas and E.J. Barnes and solicitor R.G. Allsbrook. (Courtesy A&H.)

Marchant traveled to Raleigh and entered the Central Prison to photograph the infamous electric chair in 1911. Lewis West was the fourth man in North Carolina to be put to death in this chair. (Courtesy C. Vernon Vallance.)

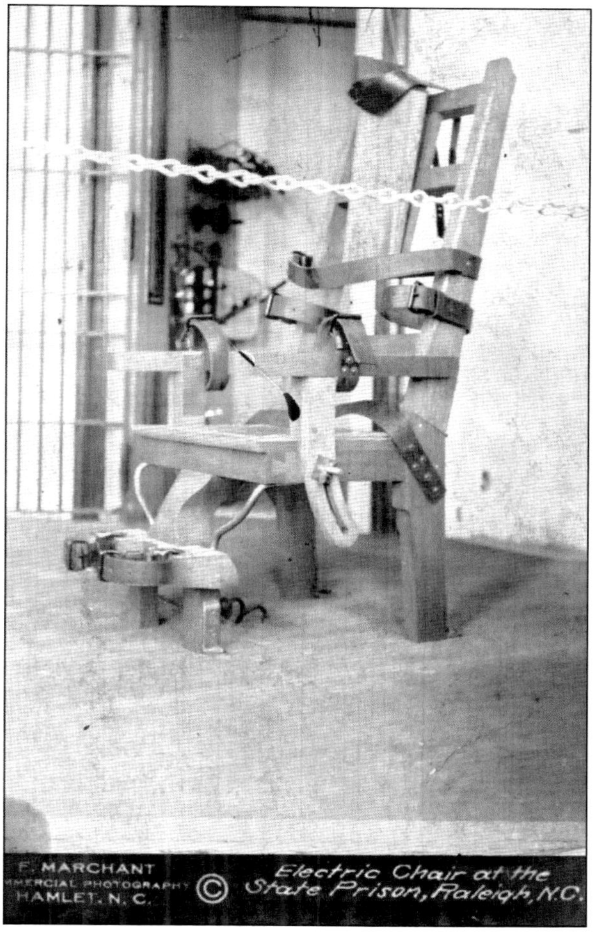

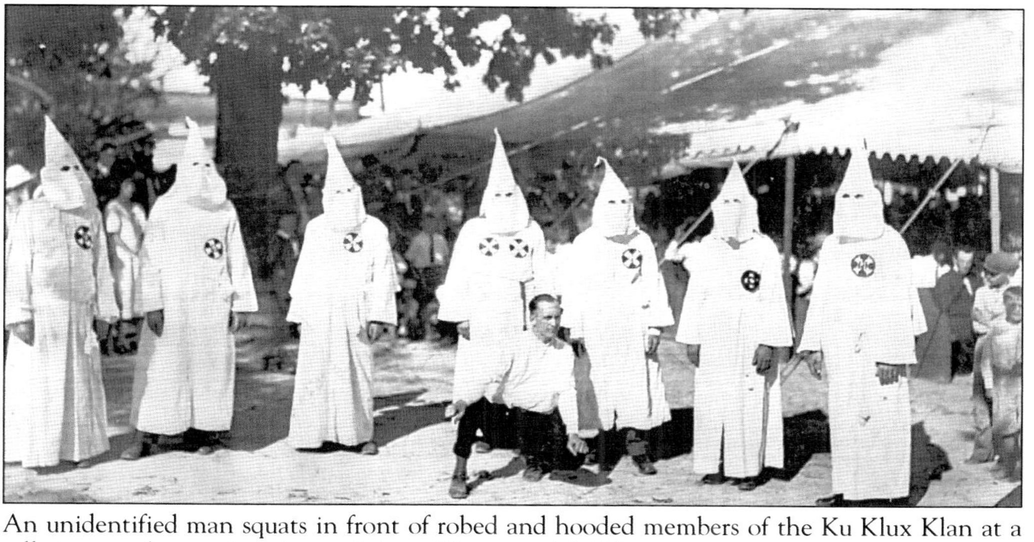

An unidentified man squats in front of robed and hooded members of the Ku Klux Klan at a rally in an unknown location and time. (Courtesy A&H.)

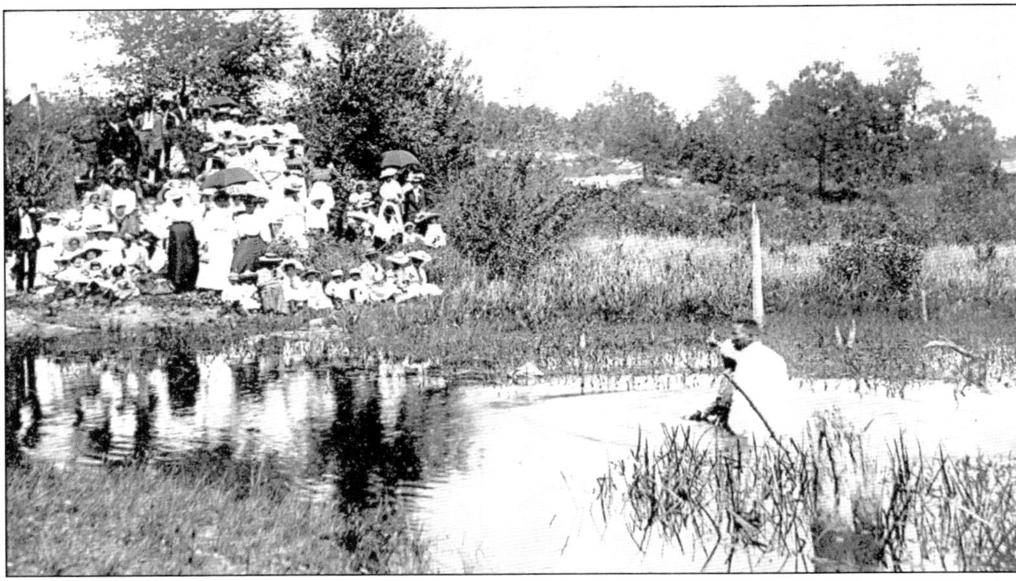

A crowd on the banks of this body of water witnesses an African-American "Baptizing in the Branch." The place and date of this event are not recorded. (Courtesy Wayne Chapman.)

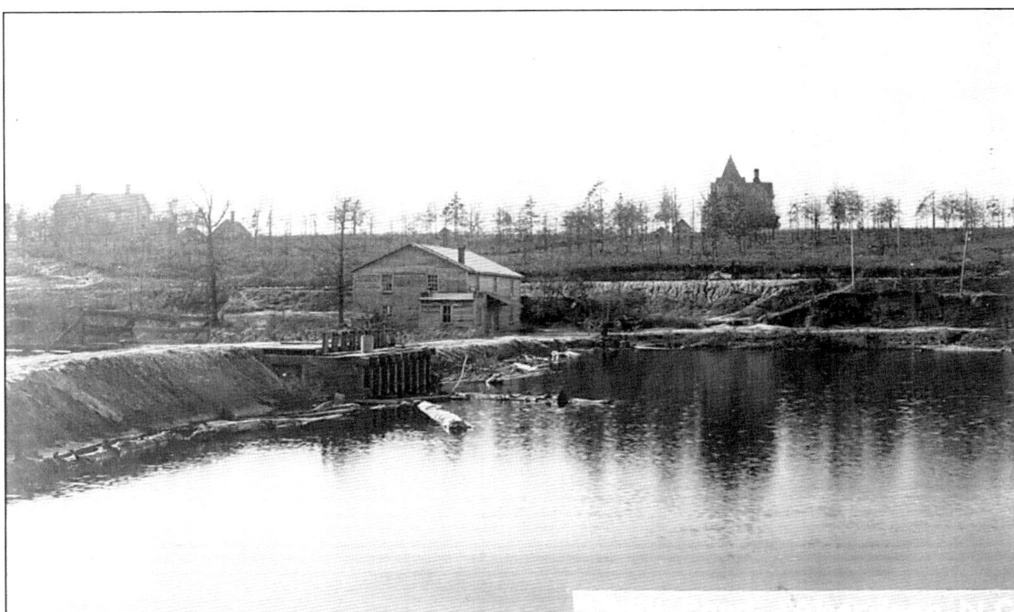

Marchant rode the train a few miles northeast from Hamlet to Moore County to make this exposure of a millpond in Aberdeen. The date was not recorded. (Courtesy C. Vernon Vallance.)

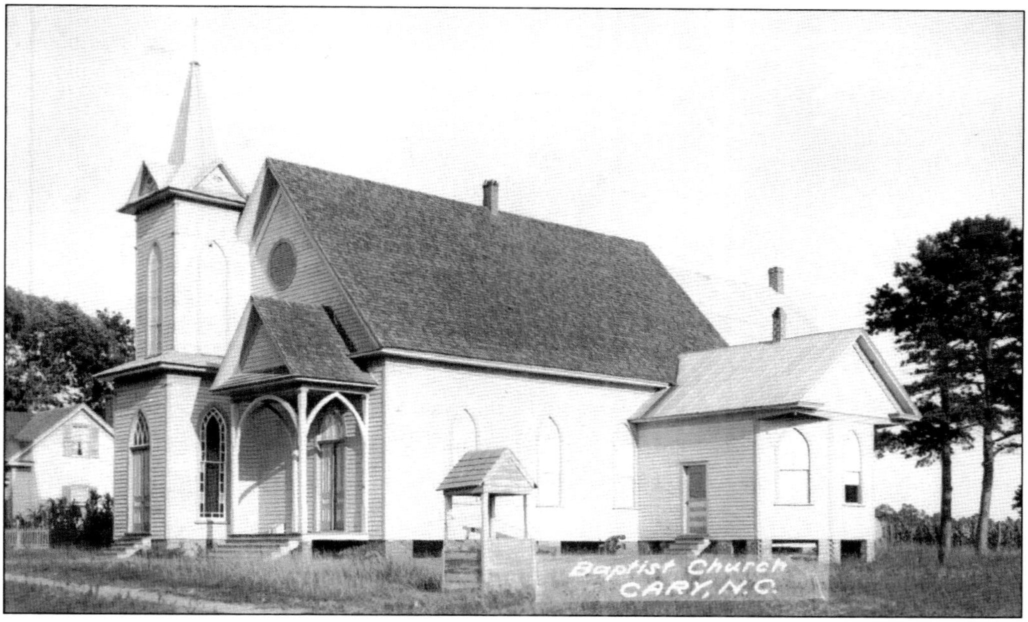

During trips to Wake County, the Richmond County photographer took pictures of these two buildings in Cary. The Baptist church was photographed about 1911, while the high school was pictured about 1914. (Courtesy Durwood Barbour.)

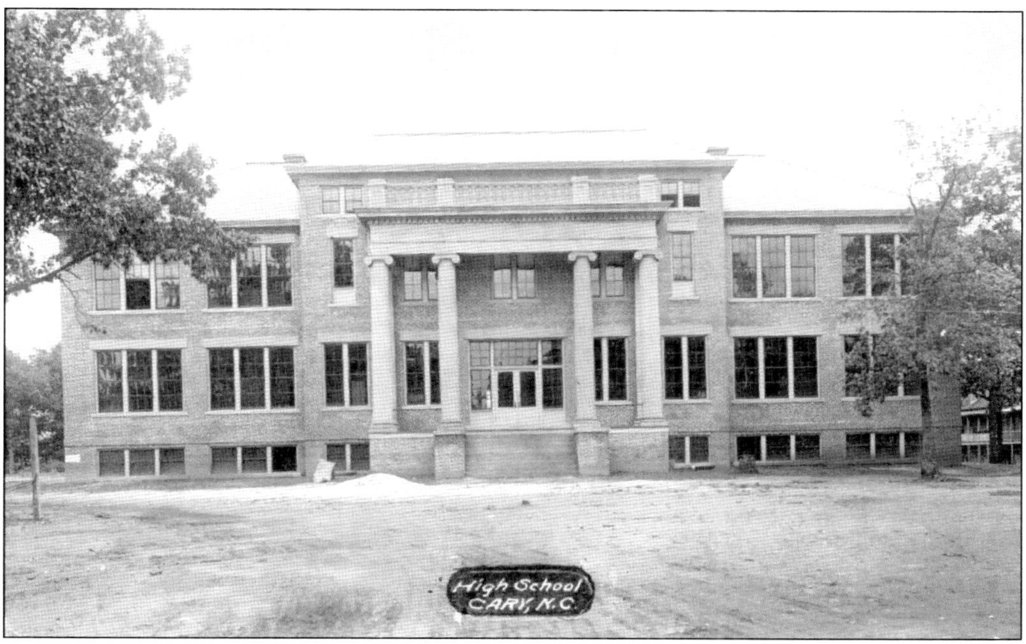

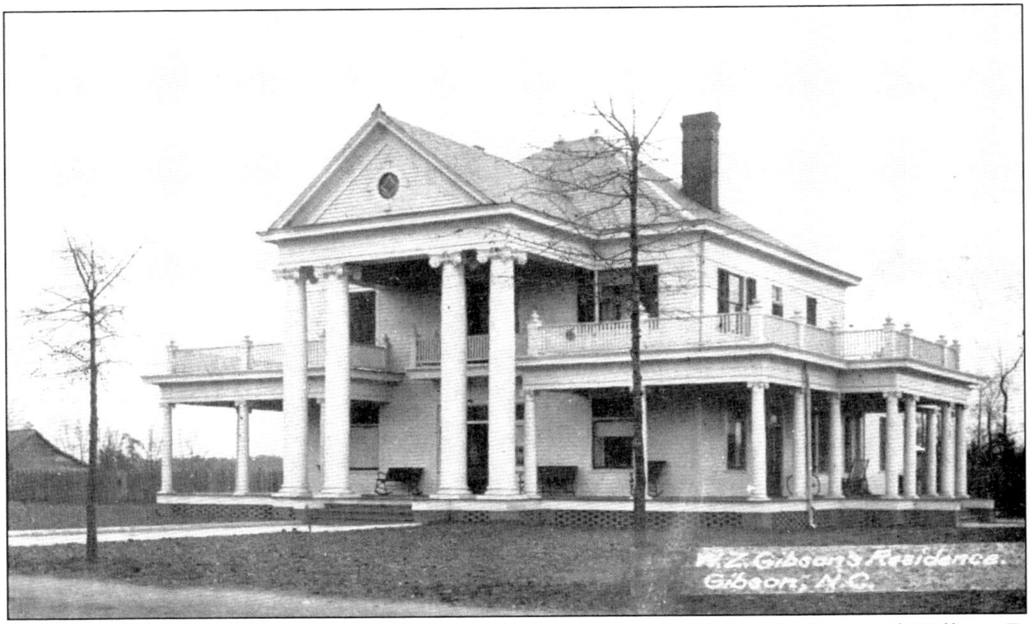

One of the largest residences in the town of Gibson about 1913 was the home of William Z. Gibson. He was born in North Carolina about 1871 and operated a drugstore in that Scotland County town located near the South Carolina border. (Courtesy Durwood Barbour.)

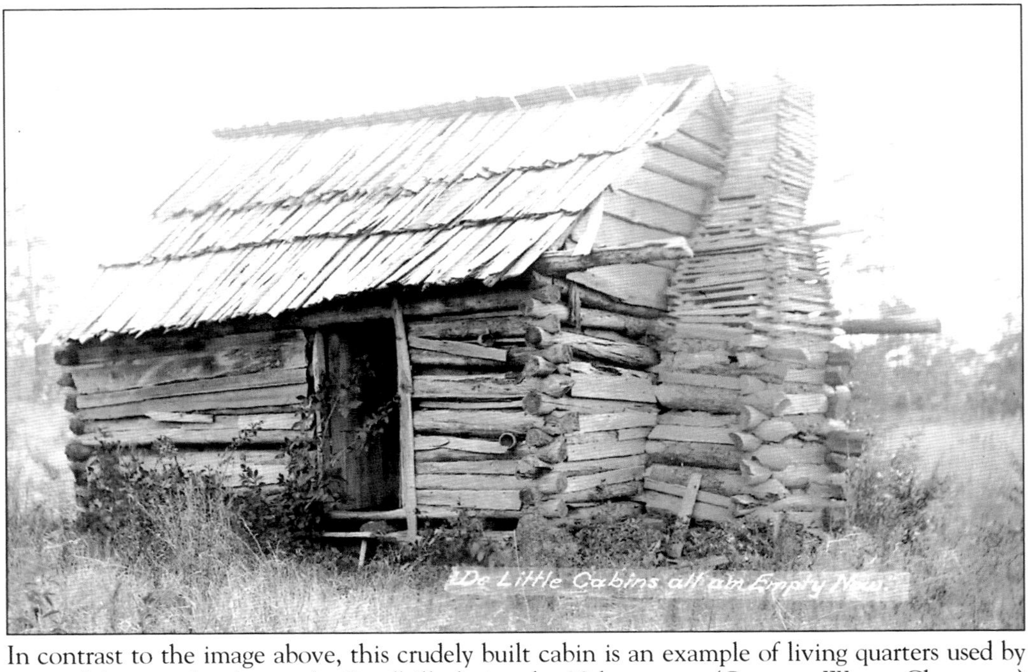

In contrast to the image above, this crudely built cabin is an example of living quarters used by some of the poor families in the Sandhills during the 19th century. (Courtesy Wayne Chapman.)

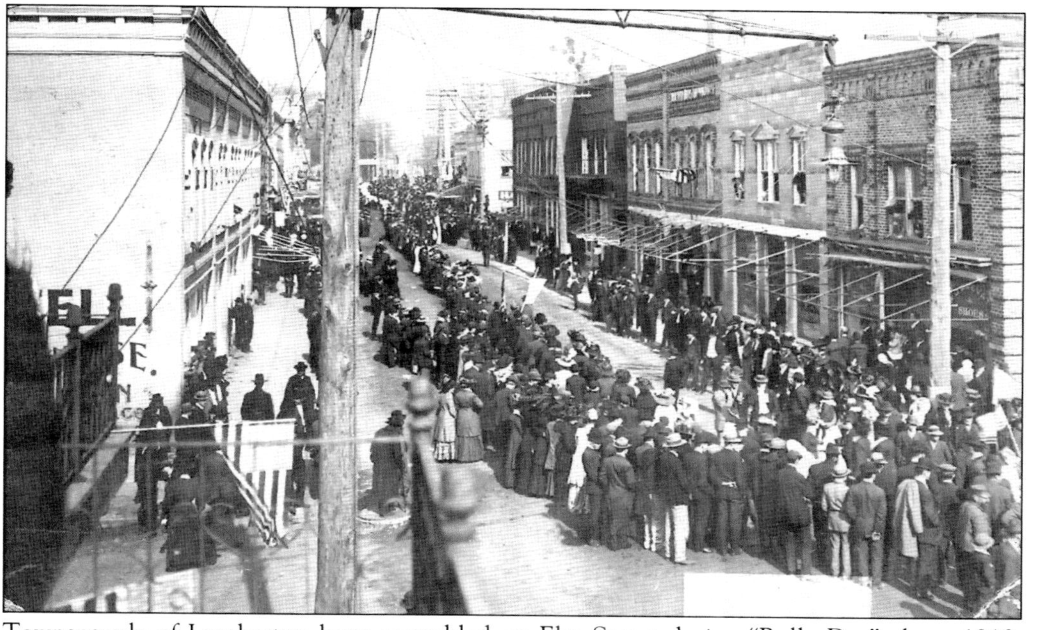

Townspeople of Lumberton have assembled on Elm Street during "Rally Day" about 1910. The special day was likely a commercial, civic, political, or religious occasion. (Courtesy Wayne Chapman.)

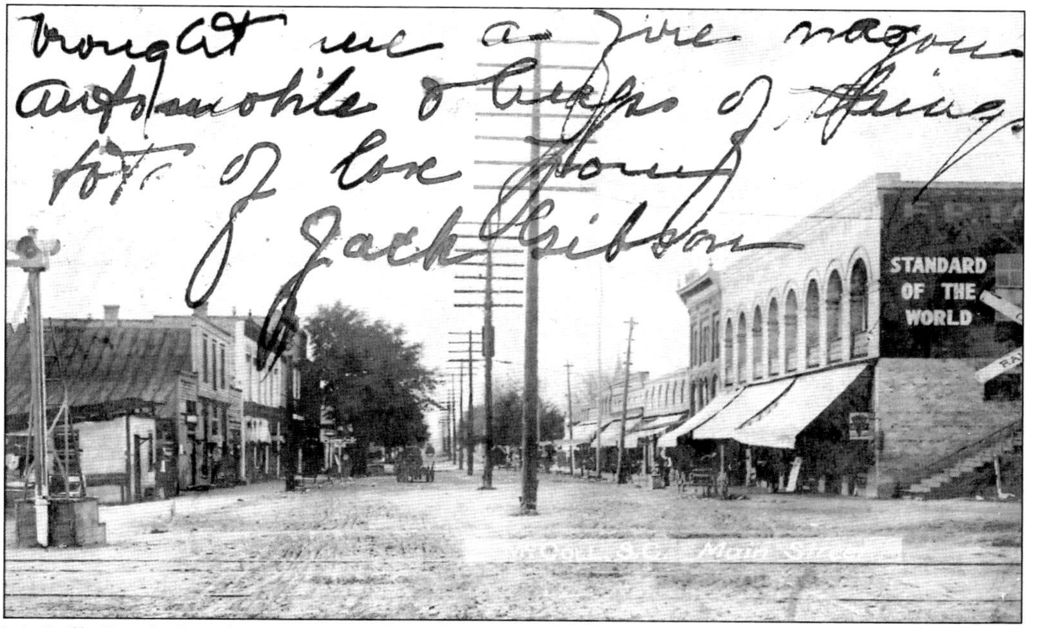

McColl, South Carolina, is situated just across the border and only about 17 miles southeast of Hamlet. Here, Marchant has photographed Main Street from the railroad crossing about 1908. (Courtesy Wayne Chapman.)

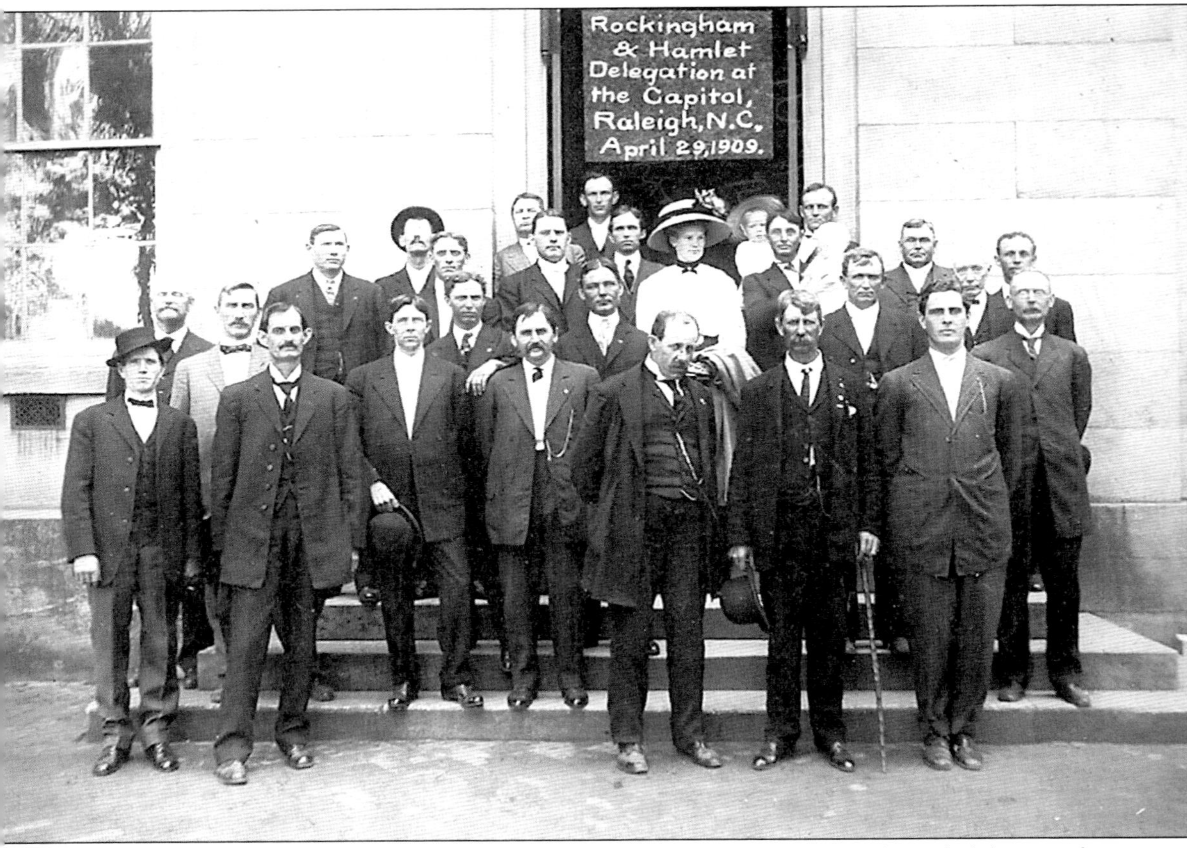

A woman and two young children are among this group of well-dressed delegates from Rockingham and Hamlet who visited the North Carolina State Capitol in Raleigh on April 29, 1909. In the front row, second from left, is Erwin N. Rhodes, a well-known merchant in Hamlet. (Courtesy Hamlet Public Library.)

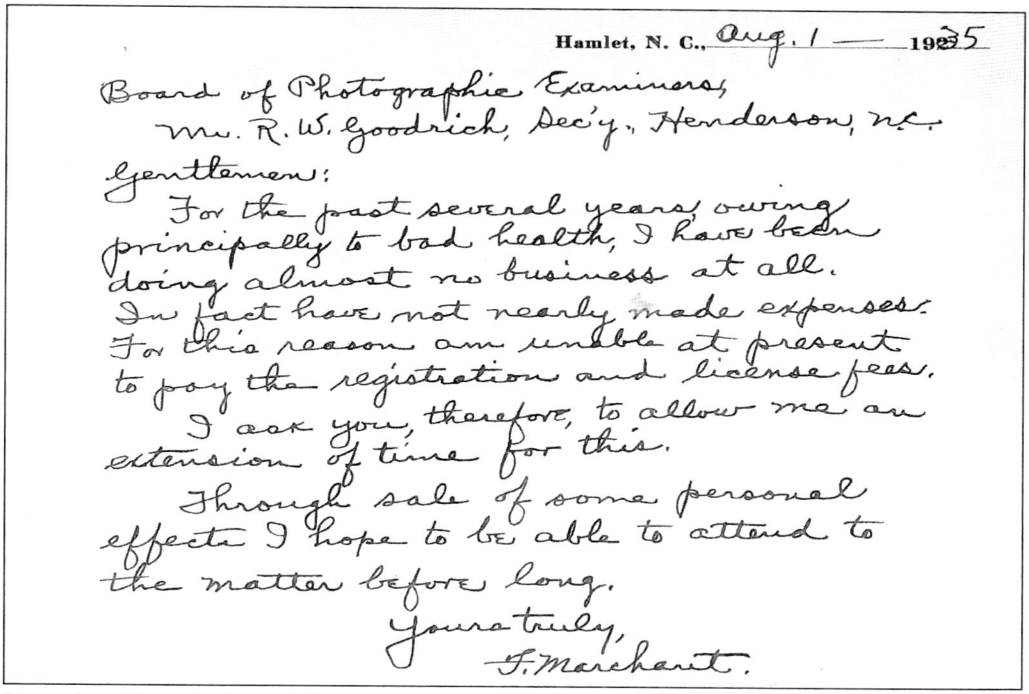

Hamlet, N. C., Aug. 1 — 1935

Board of Photographic Examiners,
Mr. R. W. Goodrich, Sec'y., Henderson, N.C.

Gentlemen:

For the past several years, owing principally to bad health, I have been doing almost no business at all. In fact have not nearly made expenses. For this reason am unable at present to pay the registration and license fees.

I ask you, therefore, to allow me an extension of time for this.

Through sale of some personal effects I hope to be able to attend to the matter before long.

Yours truly,
F. Marchant.

Reproduced here is the only known correspondence of Frederick Marchant. The photographer penned the note to the State Board of Photographic Examiners on August 1, 1935. Marchant writes that he is unable to pay $10 for the registration and license to practice his profession because of poor health and slow business conditions, undoubtedly brought on by the Great Depression. (Courtesy A&H.)

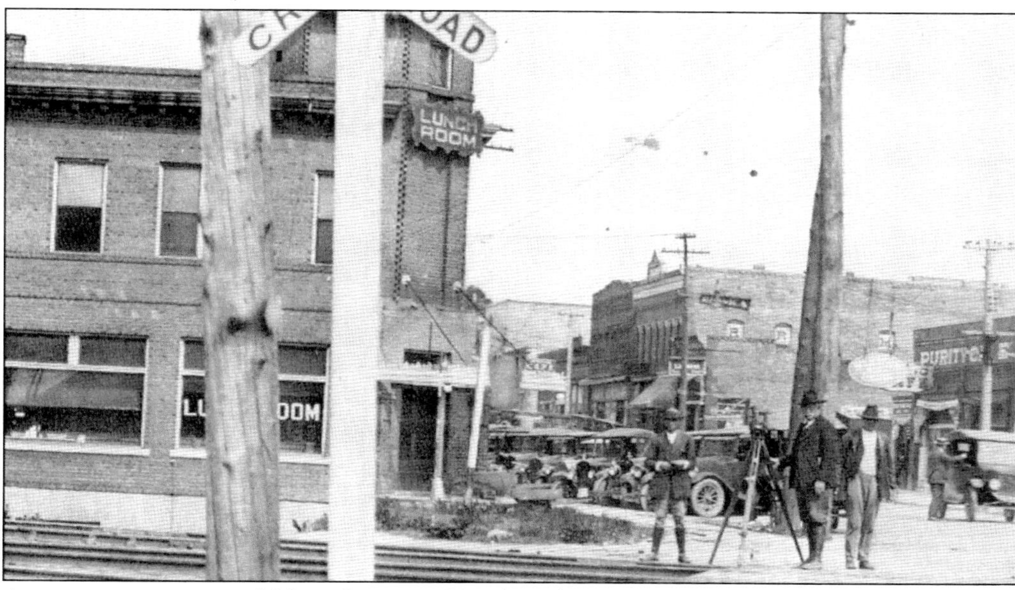

A panoramic picture of Main Street in Hamlet taken in 1925 by Sargeant Photo Company includes a photographer standing beside his tripod camera stand. Perhaps this is Frederick Marchant. (Courtesy Edward "Tug" Jones.)

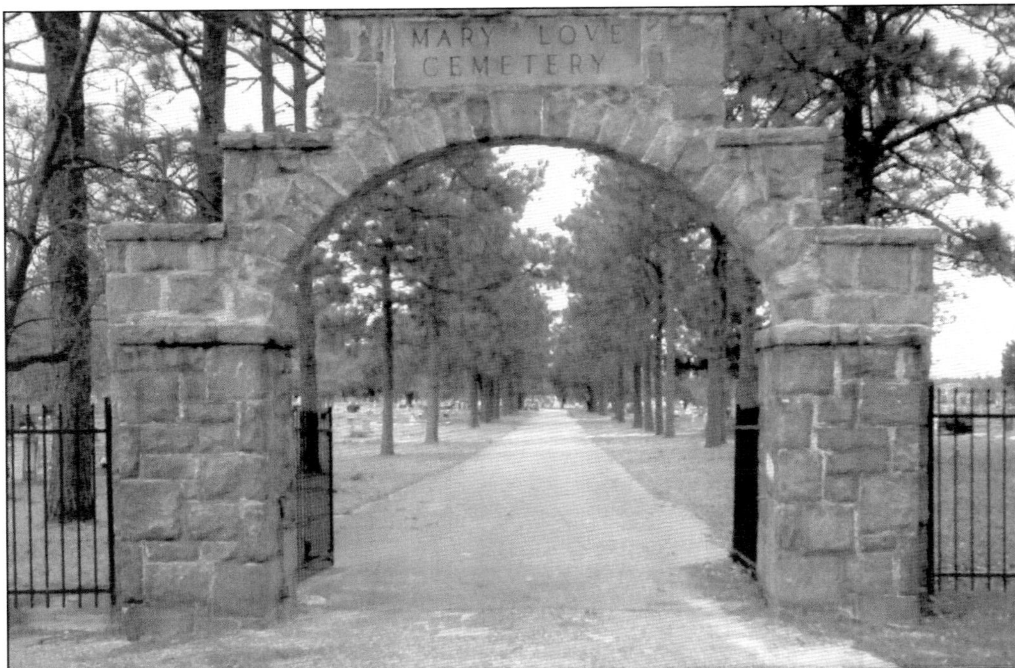

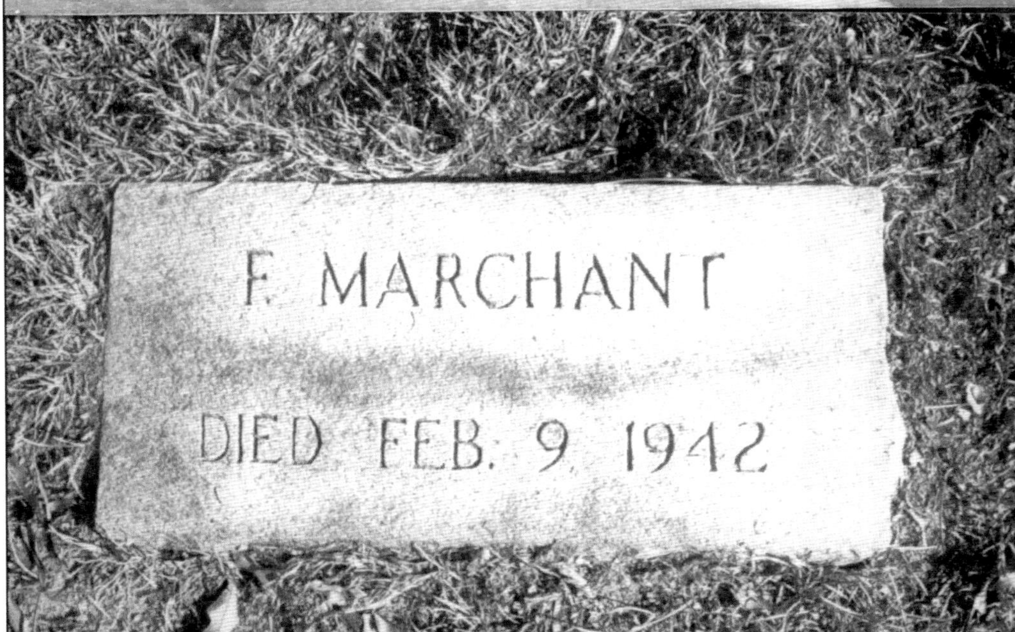

This simple headstone marks the final resting place of Frederick Marchant in Mary Love Cemetery in Hamlet. (Courtesy Charlene Gilmore.)

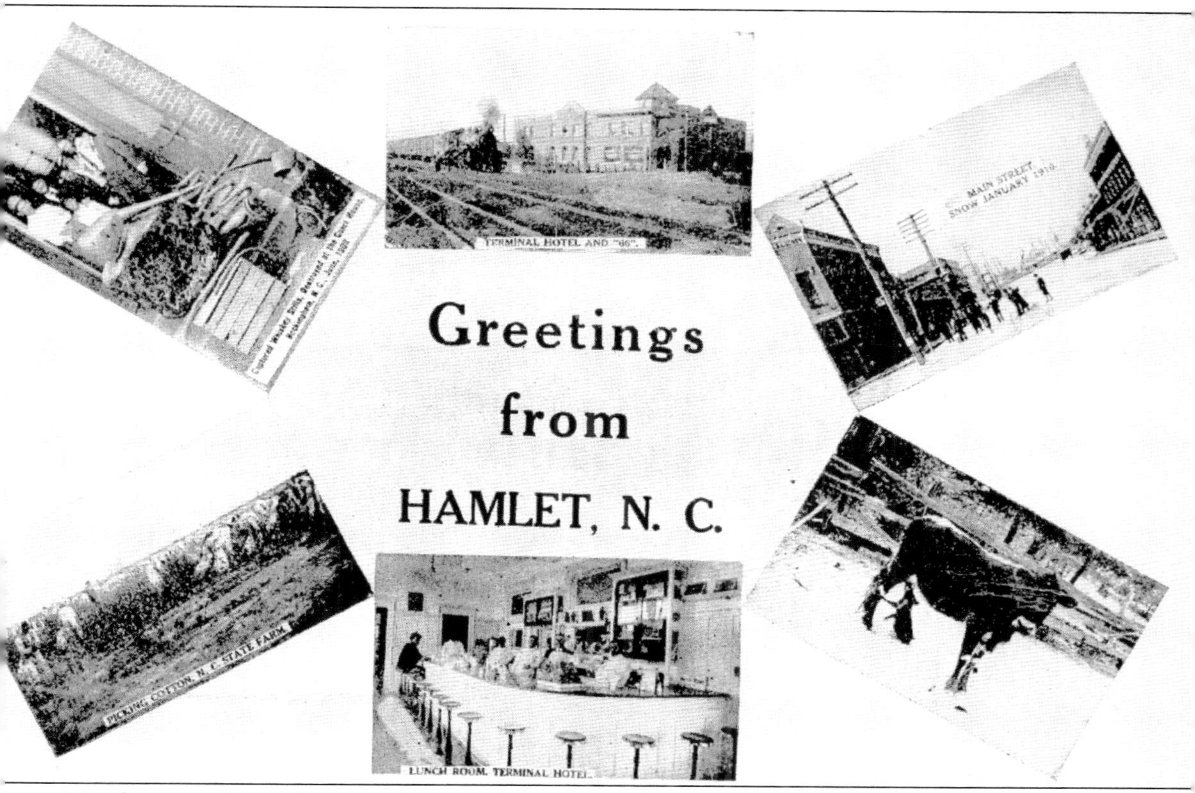

Marchant combined these six photographs into a single postcard that travelers could mail back home as a pictorial reminder of their visit to the Rockingham County town. (Courtesy A&H.)

Index